14 DAY BOOK

This book is due on or before
the latest date stamped below

REMAKING THE WORLD

DR FRANK N. D. BUCHMAN

From the mural painting 'Remakers of the World'
by Erling Roberts, at Mackinac Island

REMAKING THE WORLD

The Speeches of

FRANK N. D. BUCHMAN

LONDON

BLANDFORD PRESS

1961

FIRST PUBLISHED IN GREAT BRITAIN
BY BLANDFORD PRESS LTD
16 WEST CENTRAL STREET
LONDON, W.C.1
IN DECEMBER 1947
NEW AND REVISED EDITION
FEBRUARY, 1953
REPRINTED JANUARY, 1955
REPRINTED JANUARY, 1956
NEW AND REVISED EDITION
JUNE, 1958
REPRINTED JUNE, 1961
POCKET EDITION JUNE 1961
107TH THOUSAND

ALSO PUBLISHED IN
CHINESE, DANISH, DUTCH, FINNISH,
FRENCH, GERMAN, ITALIAN, JAPANESE,
NORWEGIAN, SWEDISH

PRINTED IN GREAT BRITAIN BY TONBRIDGE PRINTERS LTD,
PEACH HALL WORKS, TONBRIDGE, KENT

CONTENTS

CONTENTS

III THE OUTBREAK OF WAR

IV DEMOCRACY'S INSPIRED IDEOLOGY

CONTENTS

V AN IDEA TO WIN THE WORLD

CONTENTS

SUPPLEMENT

FRANK BUCHMAN

BY ALAN THORNHILL[1]

FRANK BUCHMAN stood amid the green, gently rolling hills of Pennsylvania. It is the countryside in which he was born and brought up, and it was the spot where his parents lie buried and where he himself hopes one day to rest. Gripped by deep emotion he stood for many minutes in silence. Then quietly he repeated to himself several times the words 'I have been wonderfully led.'

Many have set themselves to characterise the life and work of this man. Between them they have all but exhausted the vocabulary of love and loyalty and of hatred and prejudice as well. His own verdict on his life is strangely unaffected by either. It is always the same, 'I have been wonderfully led.'

The man who uses these words so simply and so naturally lives in the full midstream of the twentieth century. He loves humanity, not in the abstract but in the railway carriage. He can take up his abode in any one of thirty different capitals, and live and move among friends as though he had been there half his days. In countless homes, great and small, he is at home. He loves life because to him life is always people. He enjoys pleasures and he turns pain to rich account. To him every occasion from the simplest meal to the history-making event is something to be savoured and experienced and used to the very full, something to be woven into the texture of a great over-arching plan.

He is a man of his age; yet no man has more vigorously countered the prevailing trends of his age. In an age of mass

[1] Formerly Fellow of Hertford College, Oxford, and author of the industrial play and film *The Forgotten Factor* (see footnote, page 158).

materialism he has fought to put people before things. In an age of self-seeking individualism he has demonstrated the effectiveness of selfless teamwork. In an age of godless dictatorships he has re-kindled the militant heart of democracy.

For the full understanding of his work it is above all necessary to bear in mind two things. First: the key to it is to be found not in theory but in experience. How that experience first came to him is told, partly in his own words, at the end of this book.[1] How that experience has blossomed and borne fruit through the years the reader of this book will be able to judge for himself. The second point is this: for Frank Buchman a personal knowledge of Christ is not a thing to be folded away and secretly treasured; it is to be put to work for others. 'The best way to keep an experience of Christ is to pass it on,' he says; and he sees no limit to its effectiveness in a world where millions in every nation are athirst for spiritual reality.

Among the gifts bestowed on Frank Buchman is the rare ability to give his full heart to the individuals who surround him and at the same time always to maintain the perspective of national and world-wide needs. And the answer for one is the answer for both. Saint Augustine once said that he never had any difficulty in believing in miracles since he had experienced the miracle of change in his own heart. For Frank Buchman there had never been the shadow of a doubt that the Power which changed him was able to change the world.

And so it is that in an age of revolutions he has fostered the greater revolution, which anticipates and answers all other revolutions by dealing radically and constructively with the hearts of men. In an age of ideologies he has given compelling expression to the one ideology which, because it answers the deepest needs in human nature, is as universal as human nature and so offers the one hope of unity to a torn and divided world.

[1] See Supplement, I, 2.

x

The originator of the Oxford Group and of the programme of Moral Re-Armament was born on 4 June, 1878, in Pennsburg, Pennsylvania. His family was cradled and nurtured in a love of liberty. Two hundred years ago his Swiss ancestors left their home in St Gallen and sought freedom and opportunity in the youthful State of Pennsylvania. Today these thriving, thrifty 'Pennsylvania Dutch' communities, with their trim farmhouses and their gaily-painted barns, their spotless kitchens, and their lovingly tended churches and churchyards, still speak of generations brought up with democracy in their blood. Here are folk who reverence God and love life.

Frank Buchman still likes to take his friends to the simple, dignified streets of Allentown and to show them his old home where as a boy he loved to paint pictures, plan fishing trips and above all entertain his friends. The Buchman home was always full of people, and even now, after so many years, if Frank returns on a visit, he will not be there more than an hour or two before old school friends and neighbours begin to drop in and call. Once, as a boy, Frank escorted twelve girls to a dance, not wanting any of them to miss the fun. Mary the cook used to say you never could tell how many there would be for dinner, because you never knew how many people Frank would meet in the street on his way home.

Shortly after graduating from Muhlenberg College, he went to live in the poorest part of Philadelphia and there founded a hospice for orphans and destitute boys. When, later on, he was appointed leader of religious work in Pennsylvania State College, one of his best friends was Bill Pickle, the hard-drinking boot-legger, who not only changed his own ways but powerfully affected generations of students long after Buchman himself had left.

Everything he is and does springs out of an all-consuming care for people. 'Have an intense preoccupation with the individual person,' he would say to his early followers in Oxford. He has no use for the kind of Christian work that deals with crowds and masses, but neglects the individual. 'It's no good throwing eye-medicine out of a second storey window,' he says.

I have never met anyone who knows so quickly and so surely what is going on inside another person. In a room full of people he has an unerring eye for the one who specially needs help or encouragement, a stimulating challenge or maybe a drastic warning. Frank Buchman seldom gives a man what he expects, but nearly always what he needs. I have gone to him expecting a rebuke for some serious mistake, only to get the warmth and welcome of a father and the complete understanding of a fellow-offender. I have equally gone to him expecting a pat on the back and received a well-merited dig in the ribs. His understanding of men is a priceless gift and a costly one. 'I asked God,' he told me, 'to make me super-sensitive to people. And there have been times when I have been tempted to wish I had never prayed that prayer.' For to know men and women as they are, and yet to know what they can be, is to be committed to a life-long human battle that demands endless sacrifice. He burns with impatience at the miserable picture that most of us have of the lives of our fellows, and the equally meagre vision we have for our own. And that applies to the clerk at the desk, to the cook in the kitchen and to the Cabinet Minister in the council chambers of State.

Once in Edinburgh he found himself at a dinner party next to an elderly lady who told him that after a life devoted to good works she was now 'getting ready to die'. 'Ready to die!' said Buchman. 'Why not start to live?' And it was that lady whose vision opened up the way for the work of the Oxford Group in Geneva and the League of Nations in the years between the wars.

In 1921 Frank Buchman was invited to Washington by a military member of the British delegation to meet delegates to the Disarmament Conference. Hopes were high that Pacts and Leagues would outlaw war. He was convinced that nothing would succeed unless the transforming power which he had seen at work in individuals be brought to nations. As he travelled on the night train to Washington, the conviction came to him to resign the comfortable University post which he held. Since then he has never drawn a salary nor had the security of a human position.

Three months later he returned to England, where he had previously been invited by two Anglican bishops. He had come to Oxford unheralded and unknown. One by one he had met people and made friends. He loved and understood that sceptical, rest-less, war-scarred generation. He listened to their theories about life and told them true stories about people. He answered argu-ments with experience. Some of the leading undergraduates of the University gathered around him. Many who had been problems to the authorities became pioneers in a new spirit. Prayer was publicly offered from a University pulpit giving thanks for the illumination that had come to Oxford.

In these early years his task was mainly that of choosing and training leadership. Men came to him for help, and stayed with him for life. His conception of Christian living was not measured by his own achievements but by the growth and quality of those around him. Where other men founded organisations he tended the growth of an organism. Others were exhorting the world with pronouncements. He encircled the world with a family. Then, as now, he bound no one to him by vows or commitments or by financial or other ties. Thousands were bound to him and to each other by unbreakable bonds of caring and loyalty. He issued no orders. Every man has the privilege of being personally guided by God.

Each year his work grew and spread from country to country. In 1928 several South African Rhodes Scholars and other Oxford students travelled to South Africa. They had something to say to the nation that came with the fire of personal conviction. Their visit was news. They were christened 'The Oxford Group', the name which has since gone with them around the world. A larger group led by Dr Buchman himself returned the next year. Twelve years later, in 1941, though war had stirred the racial tensions in the country, the Hon. Jan H. Hofmeyr, Minister of Finance and right-hand man to General Smuts, and other prominent South Africans, wrote of that visit that it was 'of national significance and started a major and continuing influence for racial reconciliation throughout the whole country, white and black, Dutch and British.'

As the years passed his work took on new scope and even greater urgency. I remember walking with him on a golden English summer day in the early 'thirties. I remarked on the beauty of some ancient buildings that we were passing. He broke in suddenly, 'Yes, but in a few years, they will be gone—unless we change.' At that time I thought he was merely trying to startle me with a figure of speech. The tragedy is so many others thought so too.

Back and forth across the Atlantic, in America and Canada, in Holland, Switzerland, Scandinavia and many other parts of the world, he travelled, working unceasingly. But he never travelled alone. Where he had once gone quietly with a handful of friends, now he was setting hundreds, even thousands of vital, propagating men of faith on the move. He showed a general's genius for massing spiritual forces at the right place at the right time to make the greatest possible impact. With him the ordinary man found himself doing extraordinary things. Statesmen began acting like Christians. Christians like statesmen. To many a church leader he gave an entirely new conception of the familiar words 'Like a mighty army moves the Church of God.'

Few of his followers in those crowded years before the war realised the full significance of what, under Frank Buchman's leadership, they were being inspired to build. They hurriedly packed their bags and moved to and fro across the world. They lived in crowded streets and spacious homes. They addressed huge assemblies and their words were translated into many languages. Among them, as they worked and journeyed together, there might be an ex-agitator from East London or a lady-in-waiting to the Queen, a group of Army officers or Trade Union leaders, a courtly oriental philosopher or a raw, rumbunctious American 'teenager'. It made no difference. They were all part of a world-wide family. They were a classless society. They were true democracy in action. They learnt the difference between the little things they could do alone and the magnificent things they might do together. With some pain as well as much joy they discovered the fascination and power of a team. 'He is a big frog in a little pond,' Frank Buchman would say of some worthy but inflated individualist. And, in a whimsical afterthought, he added once, 'The Oxford Group is a big lake where a lamb can wade and an elephant can swim.'

And all the time, while totalitarian forces were rising to conquer the earth, men of every colour and creed, under Frank Buchman's leadership, were actually learning and living and creating a great answering ideology. While harassed statesmen talked democracy, Buchman went around the world building it. While other nations were being enslaved he worked and fought that whole nations be inspired. While the world piled up arms, he called and planned for moral and spiritual re-armament on as grand a scale.

War came, involving thousands of the men of Moral Re-Armament. While like millions of others they gave their sweat and blood on battlefield and lonely outpost, they could also give a further thing, the fruit of their unique training.

Meanwhile others fought steadily on the home front. Passions run high in wartime, often obscuring the true nature of world trends. Those who spent the war years with Frank Buchman can witness to the unerring penetration with which time and again he saw through the immediate crisis to the greater issues lying beyond. Evidence of this is in his speeches of the period. They reveal a deep conviction that, far beyond the outcome of the armed struggle, the fate of democracy depended on the full mobilisation of the moral and spiritual strength which is hers by right. Only so could democracy outstrip the ideologies of materialism (whether of Berlin or of Moscow) and, purified and inspired, give peace and longed-for security to the people of the world.

Moral Re-Armament emerged from the war stronger than ever. Not that adverse criticism had at this or at any other time been lacking. How could it be otherwise? Frank Buchman's work had not only made complacent people uncomfortable, it had also flung a challenge to the forces of revolutionary materialism with their conscious and unconscious allies. No informed observer was surprised when the counter-attacks came. A senior Army officer once analysed the type of opposition encountered by Moral Re-Armament. He noted that it drew fire equally from Nazis and Communists, from the extreme right and extreme left in politics, from aggressive atheists and narrow ecclesiastics. It had been charged with being both militaristic and pacifist. Certain elements in labour denounced it as anti-union; certain elements in management as pro-union. 'Nothing,' this officer concluded, 'but a potentially vast moral and spiritual reformation of global proportions could possibly be honoured by antagonisms so venomous and contradictory in character, and so world-wide in scope.'

Frank Buchman, while he had never courted criticism, has never feared it. His answer has been that of Abraham Lincoln: 'With firmness in the right as God gives us to see the right, let us strive on to finish the work we are in.' He has believed that the only conclusive reply to criticism is the quality of his life's work; and that since at the bar of history both he and his critics will be judged by their fruits, he has no reason to fear. Being Spirit-led his work cannot be cut off from its sources of power. Being vitally Christian it has been everywhere irrepressible. Its past record can be left to speak for itself. What is more important now is to understand its strategic role in the vast struggle that lies ahead.

One of the interesting aspects of Frank Buchman's work is the way in which he has been inspired to create and use ever new forms and patterns in which to express his message. In the more leisured, spacious days of twenty to thirty years ago, there was the 'House Party'—an informal gathering of friends in a hotel or college or large country house, where countless people who would never have darkened the door of a church found a practical, work- ing faith in surroundings where they felt at home. Later there were the great national and world gatherings where many of the speeches in this book were delivered. In the crucial early war years there were round-table conferences, where men of manage- ment and labour met in a new atmosphere and often found a new approach to old, embittered problems. These led to the great world assemblies and ideological training centres at Mackinac Island in the State of Michigan and at Caux in Switzerland.

Most men tend inevitably to develop their work along the lines of the things they themselves can do well. Buchman's work develops along the lines of the things which he can inspire others to do better. He does not now make many speeches. He does not need to. All over the world through books, plays, films and other instruments, teams he has trained are winning men and nations to a superior ideology.

In one night the same play may be given in five different languages, before the critical public of London's West End, in an industrial neighbourhood of a great Italian city, before an audience of diplomats in the Imperial Theatre in Tokyo, in a Scandinavian university and for German miners in the heart of the Ruhr. From one end of the world to the other millions are attracted by the dramatic quality of these plays; they find there more than good theatre: they find hope, an answer for themselves and their nations and the chance of becoming part of a world force on the march.

This spirit finds expression in many varied forms. It may be a meeting in the vast hangar of an American airport, an international chorus singing for Buddhist monks in Burma or, on the borders of the Sahara, a Nigerian audience watching a film under the starry vault of the African night. Everywhere the same fight goes on for the thinking and living of the world.

Task forces of men and women trained in the many phases of MRA, sometimes several hundred strong, are constantly at work in different parts of the globe. Wherever they go, often as guests of governments, always working without pay, their task is the same: to understand men and answer their deepest needs and aspirations. Here, the result may be the solving of industrial conflict and a rise in wages and production; there, age-old barriers of racial and national enmity crumble and vanish. Unity comes as bitterness gives place to the mighty positive of an all-out commitment, in Frank Buchman's words, 'to remake men and nations'.

From every side come proofs of the gratitude inspired by the initiator of Moral Re-Armament. The highest decorations have been bestowed upon him by the governments of Greece, Japan, China, Thailand, the Philippines. In token of all that he had done for better relations between France and Germany he has been given the Legion of Honour from the French Government on the one hand, and on the other, at a time when he was in New Delhi with a force of two hundred, Frank Buchman received from the German Government the Grand Cross of Merit of the German Order of Merit 'in recognition of his significant work for peace and understanding between the nations'.

Such official gestures reflect the gratitude of thousands upon thousands, capitalists and communists, white, yellow and black, who have received from Frank Buchman not only the vision of a changed and united world, but the means of bringing it to pass.

These varied developments of Frank Buchman's work reveal a mind free from the trammels of convention and precedent and a rare quality of self-effacing leadership. But there is something more—one constant element on which it all rests—a real, infectious and growing knowledge of the power of God. This is the essential equipment for anyone, be he teen-ager or octogenarian, who takes his place beside Frank Buchman on the world-wide battlefront.

Countless lives have been lit on their way by occasional flashes of divine illumination. Many have followed a star. But for Frank Buchman it would be more truthful to say that the detailed, constant, accurate leading of God is as natural and powerful as daylight. It comes to him fresh every morning, like the sunrise— as welcome and as inevitable. No man would more readily admit that he is fallible, that he like other men can miss the way. He would claim nothing for himself that is not available to everyone. Yet no man, perhaps, in our generation has accepted so completely the guidance of God as the be-all and end-all of living, as the golden thread running through every day.

The speeches in this volume were made within the span of the last thirty years. Written for widely-differing occasions, and delivered against the fast-changing background of some of the most dramatic years in the world's history, they none the less make up a coherent whole.

It might be claimed that by virtue of his personal achievement Frank Buchman had earned the right to speak to the men and women of today. But it is less by virtue of what he has done that he commands attention than by the burning relevance of what he has to say. For in these days powerful ideologies, many of them as seductive as they are false, are fighting a determined battle for the hearts and minds of men. They begin by affirming their belief in man and man alone. They end by despising and betraying him. They promise him liberty and give him regimentation. 'Man is so great,' they say, 'that he can do without God.' Soon man is so helpless that he cannot do without dictators. 'Dispense with the ten commandments of God,' they tell him. Soon he is saddled with the ten thousand commandments of men.

Into this confusion of half-truths Frank Buchman comes with a message of trenchant simplicity, a message backed by a sensitive understanding of human nature and by an ever-relevant experience of the transforming power of Christ. The words he uses are for the most part simple words; it is the language of every day. The truths he utters, too, are simple; but they are the truths by virtue of which the world may come to salvation and sanity in our lifetime or for lack of which our civilisation may perish for ever from the earth.

I

THE RISING TIDE

The cause of the world's state is not economic; the cause is moral. It is there where the evil lies. It is the want of religion which we ought to possess. If I may use a phrase which is common in a great movement which is taking place at this moment in this country and elsewhere, what you want are God-guided personalities, which make God-guided nationalities, to make a new world. All other ideas of economic adjustment are too small really to touch the centre of the evil.

THE MARQUESS OF SALISBURY

Speaking in the House of Lords
20 March, 1936

OUR PRIMARY NEED

At the end of the First World War, Frank Buchman saw, beyond the prevailing optimism, the dimension of the crisis facing the civilised world. Vast revolutions were taking place in Russia and in Asia. It would take more than leagues and disarmament conferences to keep the peace and create the new social order for which so many longed. In 1921 Frank Buchman had already defined his aim as 'a programme of life issuing in personal, social, racial, national and supernational change.' In Europe and the Americas, in Africa and Asia, men rallied to fight with him for a world remade through a revolutionary change in men. In January, 1932, Frank Buchman issued the following statement in Geneva:

HUMAN WISDOM has failed.

The modern world—disillusioned, chaotic, bewildered—demands a solution adequate to its disorder.

The international problems of today are, at bottom personal problems of selfishness and fear.

Lives must be changed if problems are to be solved. Peace in the world can only spring from peace in the hearts of men.

A dynamic experience of God's free Spirit is the answer to regional antagonism, economic depression, racial conflict, and international strife.

God-control is our primary need.

A NEW ILLUMINATION

During the decade following the First World War, the leadership of the Oxford Group was drawn from universities on both sides of the Atlantic, and especially from Oxford. In Oxford, each year from 1930 onwards, was held a series of Assemblies which grew in numbers to many thousands. In 1934, forty-five countries were represented from all the continents, including a strong delegation from Canada where Mr R. B. Bennett, the Prime Minister, had said, 'The work you are doing has made the task of government easier. Your influence has been felt in every village and city, even in the remotest outposts of the Dominion.' At this Assembly, July, 1934, Dr Buchman outlined the aims of the Oxford Group.[1]

THE OXFORD GROUP is a Christian revolution, whose concern is vital Christianity. Its aim is a new social order under the dictatorship of the Spirit of God, making for better human relationships, for unselfish co-operation, for cleaner business, cleaner politics for the elimination of political, industrial and racial antagomisms.

A new spirit is abroad in the world today. A new illumination can come to everyone and bring men and women of every creed and social stratum back to the basic principles of the Christian faith, enhancing all their primary loyalties. The solution of our difficulties must come from such a spirit rising from within people.

[1] See also the statement made by Dr B. H. Streeter, Provost of The Queen's College, Oxford, during this Assembly, Supplement IV, 1.

Leaders in all walks of life are now convinced that our hope rests in a change of heart. One sees abundant evidence of this throughout the Empire. World-changing will come through life-changing.

To bring about this new world order the Oxford Group believes that a world-wide spiritual awakening is the only hope.

Upon a foundation of changed lives permanent reconstruction is assured. Apart from changed lives no civilisation can endure.

NORWAY ABLAZE

At a meeting in the British House of Commons, in December, 1933, the Hon. C. J. Hambro, President of the Norwegian Parliament, invited Dr Buchman to visit Norway. In November, 1934, he invited 120 Norwegian leaders to meet Dr Buchman and thirty of his workers at Hösbjör, near Oslo. Over 1,200 came. Among them were Bishop Berggrav, later Primate of Norway; Mr Johan Mellbye, leader of the Farmers' Party; Ronald Fangen, novelist and playwright, President of the Norwegian Authors' Association; Professor Mowinckel, and others outstanding in industry, education and politics. In March, 1935, Dr Buchman spoke to a crowded meeting in Oslo City Hall.

FIVE MONTHS AGO we started in this hall. Think of the wonderworking power of God in those five months. You have seen some of it tonight. Doctors have spoken, businessmen, students. Think what it would mean to you if some of these young people had been your own sons and daughters. Now multiply that throughout a country like this.

Before I landed in Norway it came to me constantly in my quiet times, 'Norway ablaze for Christ.' Illumination has come to Norway.

In the earlier days some of you who are sitting here now thought of this as a revival. I believe in the necessity of revival. But in these days we need more than revival. The present age needs revolution. Many who have travelled with us in this country say that they have seen a movement that has gone beyond revival; it has been revolution.

I believe a third stage is coming in Norway—renaissance.

Turn your minds back to the things which followed the re-awakening at the close of the Middle Ages. That can happen again in Norway today.

I have just been three days' journey away from Norway. I found Norwegians there. The message had reached them. Putting it their own way, they said, 'We must go "Oxford".' I have heard of Norwegian sailors changing English sailors in Liverpool. Today I was reading one of the leading papers of Latvia. It had long accounts of miracles in Norway. I have just travelled twice through Europe. In many papers there is news of what is happening here. A light has started in Norway, and they are reading about it in the nations.[1]

You have heard the truth tonight. The time has come for action. Here is the challenge—a challenge to the will: 'Give me twelve men who are wholly surrendered to God and I will convert the world.' The man who wrote that was a Christian statesman; and the qualifications he asked for were these:

> To give and not to count the cost;
> To fight and not to heed the wounds;
> To toil and not to seek for rest;
> To labour and not to ask for any reward
> Save that of knowing that we do Thy Will.

[1] The Oslo daily newspaper *Tidens Tegn* wrote, 'A handful of foreigners, who neither knew our language nor understood our ways and customs, came to this country . . . A few days later the whole country was talking about God, and two months after the thirty foreigners arrived, the mental outlook of the whole country had definitely changed.'

In London, *The Spectator* stated, 'A national awakening has sprung to life . . . It has abundantly revealed that social regeneration comes as a fruit of changed lives. Four professors of the University of Oslo have sum-marised their conviction in the following words: "Your visit will be a deciding factor for the history of Norway. You have come at a strategic moment with the right answer." '

That challenge is clear. It was a call to twelve men. There are twelve hundred here tonight. What will twelve hundred do?

What could twelve hundred do in Trondheim? Think what forty men, surrendered to the living God, have just done in that city! The Dean said he would never have dreamt that what happened in Trondheim was possible. Some who were sitting at that first Oslo meeting will be saying that they would never have dreamt that what has happened in Norway was possible. Norway has been illuminated. The living Christ has been at work in many lives. You feel the influence in Denmark. You feel the influence in your neighbour Sweden. You feel it in England. You feel it on the Continent.

But you have only begun. Five months! . . . Five years?

Every person changed? Every business? Whole cities getting direction? Politics? And Parliament? A nation listening to God? International relationships?

May I ask you as you go home tonight to begin to read the seventh chapter of Jeremiah, starting at the twenty-third verse. He is a prophet with a message for modern people. Begin with the seventh chapter, and then study the whole, because you have to have in your minds a framework for the rebuilding of a nation.

> Hearken unto my voice, and I will be your God, and
> ye shall be my people; and walk ye in the way that I
> command you, that it may be well with you.

Jeremiah's nation 'hearkened not' and so 'they went backward and not forward'. That was a tragedy. But it is not true of Norway. I believe that we shall say of Norway, 'This is the nation that *hath* hearkened to the voice of the Lord their God.'

8

I believe that Norway *will* be ablaze for Christ. I believe that Norway *will* take this message to other countries. I believe the Revolution *will* be a Renaissance.

Note: Ten years later, in April, 1945, Bishop Arne Fjellbu of Trondheim said in an address in St Martin-in-the-Fields, London: 'I wish to state publicly that the foundations of united resistance of Norwegian Churchmen to Nazism were laid by the Oxford Group's work.' Later, in a press interview, Bishop Fjellbu, who took a leading part in Norway's resistance throughout the war, added: 'The first coming of the Oxford Group to Norway was an intervention of Providence in history, like Dunkirk and the Battle of Britain . . . They helped to bridge the gap between religion and the people and make it real every day. We have been fighting more than an armed enemy. We have been fighting godless materialism. The Oxford Group gave us men who helped us to fight for a Christian ideology.'

GOD CALLING THE WORLD

In March, 1935, Copenhagen opened its doors wide to the Oxford Group, and 35,000 people attended meetings in the first eight days. At the culmination of a three months' campaign, Dr Buchman addressed a national demonstration, 10,000 strong, in Kronborg, Hamlet's Castle of Elsinore, on Whit Sunday.[1]

IN COPENHAGEN on Jubilee Day I heard London calling the British Empire. People in far corners of the world heard the same message. In Singapore, Ottawa, Cape Town, Melbourne, Hong Kong and hundreds of other cities and villages, millions were listening in. Today all Scandinavia is listening in to the broadcast of a Whitsun demonstration in the Castle of Kronborg, where the waters of Sweden and Denmark meet. Newspapers the world over are featuring it. From Riga to San Francisco and from Iceland to South Africa there are eager listeners.

By a miracle of science millions can think and feel as one. Barriers of time and space are swept away. A commonwealth of many nations and languages becomes a family.

Radio listeners understand that miracle. And they will also understand the Oxford Group, which is showing people how to listen in to God.

'God calling the world' is becoming a daily experience in the lives of hundreds and thousands of people in the more than fifty countries where the Oxford Group is at work.

[1] See Carl Henrik Clemmensen's vivid description in *Dagens Nyheder*, 'History was written at Kronborg', Supplement IV, 2.

We accept as a commonplace a man's voice carried by radio to the uttermost parts of the earth. Why not the voice of the living God as an active, creative force in every home, every business, every parliament? Men listen to a king when he speaks to his people over the air. Why not to the King of Kings? He is alive, and constantly broadcasting.

Norway listened in, and in the words of one of her leading editors, 'The whole mental outlook of the country changed.'[1] Canada listened in, and the Prime Minister said that the message had made his task of government easier, and that its influence has been felt in every town and village in the Dominion. South Africa listened in, and racial unity began to come in a country torn by decades of racial strife.

What might not happen if Denmark also listened to the perfect programme of the King of Kings?

At the first Whitsun God spoke to a group of ordinary men. They changed the course of history. May He not today have a plan which can solve the problems of a troubled world?

---

[1] Among the first Norwegians to accept the challenge of the Oxford Group was Fredrik Ramm, who represented the Press of the world as the only journalist to accompany Amundsen on his flight over the North Pole. The decision of the International Court of Justice in favour of Denmark in the dispute over the Greenland fisheries had left in Ramm's mind intense bitterness against Denmark. He became notorious for the violence of his writing on the question.

Ramm took an active part with Frank Buchman in the campaign in Denmark. *Dagens Nyheder*, 15 January, 1935, described his new attitude in a Press interview, and quoted Ramm, who said, 'The main thing I am here to tell you is that my greatest fault was the hatred of the Danes. My mind was poisoned with that hatred. I used my pen as well as I could in the service of my hatred and justified myself as an idealist. Then I met the Oxford Group with its challenging quality of life . . . Now I am here to put things right with my old enemies.' (See also Supplement I, 5.)

The Holy Spirit is the most intelligent source of information in the world today. He has the answer to every problem. Everywhere when men will let Him, He is teaching them how to live.

The world needs a miracle. Miracles of science have been the wonder of the age. But they have not brought peace and happiness to the nations. A miracle of the Spirit is what we need.

Divine guidance must become the normal experience of ordinary men and women. Any man can pick up divine messages if he will put his receiving set in order. Definite, accurate, adequate information can come from the Mind of God to the minds of men. This is normal prayer.

There must come a spiritual dynamic which will change human nature and remake men and nations. There must come a spiritual authority which will be accepted everywhere by everyone. Only so will order come out of chaos in national and international affairs.

If this miracle is to come into the world some nation must give a lead. Some nation must find God's Will as her destiny and God-guided men as her representatives at home and abroad. Some nation must produce a new leadership, free from the bondage of fear, rising above ambition, and flexible to the direction of God's Holy Spirit.

Such a nation will be at peace within itself, and a peacemaker in the international family. Will it be your nation?

SPEARHEAD
OF A WORLD ANSWER

In July, 1935, a large delegation came from Scandinavia to the Assembly at Oxford, which was attended by 10,000 people from many nations. They returned to Denmark with an international force, and moved, 600 strong, into Jutland. Before their departure, on 28 July, Dr Buchman addressed the Assembly.

BRIEFLY AND SIMPLY at the close of this marvellous month of fellowship with this family of many nations, I want to try and show the secret that lies back of this miracle-working power of the living God. It seemed to me, as these hundreds came up together to offer themselves for national service, that they were like a spearhead, an arrow, pointing to the solution for a world in chaos.

If I could sum it up in a sentence—the simple secret is this: individual lives, wholly surrendered to the living God.

There is a bishop at my side who in 1921 was the human instrument that brought this work to Oxford, and the man who presided today was the man in whose rooms at Christ Church this work began. In many countries a stream of life has begun.

I want to speak now to the ordinary person. I have in mind a woman of seventy. She thought her life's work was ended —but I hope that you will catch the vision that came to her. She saw that, in fact, she was only beginning. She went to

Geneva. She arranged for one hundred of us to come, and a mighty work began.

Two years ago at a luncheon given in Geneva for the Oxford Group, the President of the Norwegian Parliament made a statement. The guests were leaving when he did a most unusual thing. He called them back and said, 'I feel today we have heard something more important than most things on the agenda of the League in Geneva.'

He took courageous action. Later he spoke in Westminster, in the Parliament buildings, to one hundred and twenty-five members of Parliament, and there invited the Oxford Group to come to Norway.

In October last year thirty men crossed over into Norway. Humanly it seemed absolutely absurd that thirty foreigners who knew nothing of the customs or the language, and had only a few friends there, should be the instrument of the living God so that today Norway is ablaze for Christ.

A bishop came to the house party in those early days. His two sons looked to Communism for an answer. Those two sons came into a living experience of Christ. They became flaming apostles.

The newspapers are alive with the news of the new world order. The leading paper in Oslo, when there was news of many lives changed, gave more space to that kind of news than had ever been given before. It was good news, the news that Norway wanted.

The movement went to Denmark. Now, again, more than 300 of you in addition to 300 Danes are moving into Jutland.[1] We are accustomed to read about the Battle of Jutland. We

---

[1] Emil Blytgen-Petersen, then London correspondent of *Dagens Nyheder*, wrote in his book *Oxford i Danmark:* 'In the month of August the Oxford

are going to hear of a new battle, and the guidance that comes is that Denmark will be shaken.

What is the philosophy back of all this? Are we beginning to see that not only individuals, but cities and nations may be different? Illumination has come to Norway; illumination has come to Denmark, to Latvia, to Estonia, to Sweden, to Finland.

Think of the significance of God-controlled, spiritually-illumined nations. Suppose that God-control becomes the policy of all these Nordic countries—what will that mean for Europe?

These are not simply my own words. Bishops are speaking of it, statesmen, the editors of newspapers. They see, pervading the whole, a new spirit among nations and people.

Now, frankly, let us be honest with ourselves. How many of us really believe that Jesus Christ is the answer? How many of us really believe that if there was a mighty awakening of the living Spirit of God, that would be the answer? Statesmen sometimes take the risk and say it. One statesman said it to a group of newspapermen: 'We need a moral and spiritual renaissance.' It was flashed across the country, but I see no demonstration in that country of a moral or a spiritual renaissance.

Now we turn to the ordinary people. Could a quiet army of ordinary people, God-controlled, God-directed and God-

Group swept over the peninsula like a sandstorm. They say the Jutlanders are sober and hard to move, yet they came in thousands to Aalborg, Sonderborg and Aarhus . . . .

'At Aarhus the great tennis hall was filled by 7,000 people a night for four nights. The meetings ended with a mighty demonstration in the cathedral, overflowing into and filling the cathedral square.' (See also, comment by the Primate of Denmark, Supplement IV, 3.)

illumined, be a force in a country, changing that community so that political leaders would live in harmony and peace, so that parliaments would be God-guided and governments God-controlled?

Is that your vision for the future? If that is your vision, then I think we can indeed begin to sing:

>Like a mighty army
>>Moves the Church of God;
>Brothers, we are treading
>>Where the saints have trod.

Can that come in England? Can this group answer the needs of people in the depressed areas? Is God the answer? Can a group of people move up and down this land, as they moved up and down Norway and Denmark, with the living Spirit of God as the answer?

ONE HEART, ONE WILL,
ONE GOAL

*In September, 1935, the President of the Swiss Confederation, M.
Rudolf Minger, officially welcomed the Oxford Group to Switzerland.
In Geneva the President of the Assembly of the League of Nations, Dr
Edouard Benes, gave a luncheon for delegates to meet them. A few
days later in Zürich, on 6 October, Dr Buchman made this speech.*

TWO DAYS AGO in Zürich, as I read the news of the war
in Abyssinia, I thought, 'Has Christianity after all the
answer? Is the answer a Dictatorship of the Holy Spirit? Is
the answer a spiritual mobilisation for Europe?'

Your President says it is. I quote from his recent statement: 'Is there any release to be found from this dilemma?
The answer is a courageous "Yes". What is needed is the
changing of lives through new spiritual power so strong that
it reconciles dangerous conflicting forces and produces
brotherhood and solidarity. It is in attaining this goal that
the Oxford Group sees its task. Their next advance will take
place on Swiss soil and will make a real contribution in
reconciling the nations. The initial work of the movement
has been great with promise and we wish it every success and
triumph.'

Switzerland has welcomed the Oxford Group. She did
more than welcome it. Thousands of her people have made
its life their own.

But Switzerland, I believe, will do more than this.

God is calling Switzerland to conquering Christianity. God is speaking to her in the spirit of the New Testament: 'You are the consecrated nation, the people who belong to Him, that you may proclaim the wondrous deeds of Him who has called you.'

I can see Switzerland a prophet among the nations, and a peacemaker in the international family. I can see vital Christianity becoming the controlling force of the State through individual responsibility to God. I can see the Church in Switzerland in such power that she sends out a mission to Christians in many lands. I can see Swiss businessmen showing the leaders of the world's commerce how faith in God is the only security. I can see Swiss statesmen demonstrating that divine guidance is the only practical politics. And I can see the Swiss Press as a powerful example of what a Press should be—the herald of a new world order.

One man changed. A million changed. A nation changed. That is the programme of the Oxford Group.

A statesman has said that the Oxford Group is supernational. Nationalism can unite a country. Supernationalism can unite a world. God-controlled supernationalism is the only sure foundation for world peace.

There are four million people in your country. Four million people listening to God? Four million people—one heart, one will, one goal. A spiritual mobilisation for Switzerland? A spiritual mobilisation for Europe?

The world is waiting to see what the Prince of Peace can do in, for, and by one nation entirely given to Him.

Will Switzerland be that nation?

MIRACLES IN THE NORTH

On 20 November, 1935, Dr Buchman spoke in the Metropolitan Opera House, New York, on the new spirit arising in the Scandinavian countries. He was preceded by the President of the Norwegian Parliament, who had recently said, 'The work has been spreading in Norway, and hundreds and thousands of lives have been changed. The Oxford Group has also conquered Denmark in a way that none of us would have thought possible.'

THERE IS A BOOK in the store windows in London and New York. The title is *It Can't Happen Here*.

Some of you who read the very important word of the Secretary of State, 'Our own country urgently needs a moral and spiritual awakening,' may have said the same thing, 'It can't happen here.'

Before I sailed from London, I saw headlined in the great London newspapers another important word from Mr Hull, that the instant need of America is for flaming apostles. It seems an extravagant word. But is it an impossible thing that this country needs flaming apostles?

To be quite frank, people today are afraid of the word 'spiritual'. Just plainly nervous. You can imagine what our friend Mr Hambro felt like when he invited thirty Oxford Group workers to cross the sea to Norway—and what I felt like! [1]

Think of it. Thirty ordinary men and women who did not know the language or the customs of the country. Every

---

[1] See Supplement I, 5, for the Hon. C. J. Hambro's account.

word we spoke in public meetings in Norway had to be interpreted sentence by sentence. But, even with that handicap of language, the great thought broke through. As our friend has told you—a reality in a little more than a year—Norway is ablaze for Christ.

Now let us find out how. There was high courage there. I think if you would attempt it, too, you would realise how high that courage was. Mr Hambro invited 125 of his friends to live with us for ten days. It was a daring thing to do.

Miracles of change began to happen. The first of the two men he referred to—the author—was a widely-known agnostic. He came with two bottles of Scotch and a novel. As he said, he never had time to read his novel and he forgot the Scotch. He lived with us for ten days and was changed. Now he has written the most important book of his life, *A World Christian Revolution*. See how highly productive, how creative a time like that can be!

There is great truth in that title. I believe it is what every country needs—a world Christian revolution. That man has become a Christian revolutionary. That is miracle number one.

The second miracle is a newspaper editor. He had flown with Amundsen over the North Pole. He hated the Danes because of the dispute over Greenland, and through his position as a newspaper editor he unhesitatingly told Norway and the Danes what his feelings were. As he said, he was a Dane-hater. But he was soundly changed. I heard him in Denmark make open apology over the radio to the Danish people. Think what it means for one man to go to another country and not only admit his hates and his defeats, but share his victories. See the whole new understanding which comes between nations.

People usually said to us in Norway, 'It will never reach the farmers.' (And anyone today who thinks of national awakening for America must think of the farmers of Iowa.) But at that gathering the leader of the Farmers' Party was actually present. He became a national spokesman for a new spirit to the farmers of Norway.

Now, the Danes have a pleasant land and are a pleasant people. If there are any Danes here tonight, I want to say I know of no country where one feels so instantly at home— such charming hospitality. And the Danes have a keen sense of humour. But for years they have been living under the influence of an atheistic philosophy. Everyone said they would make fun of the Oxford Group. They said we might succeed for a week. But even the leading comedian couldn't get a laugh at our expense in the theatre.

Somebody asked me about the workers. Well some people tried to put on an anti-Oxford Group meeting. The changed workers of Copenhagen took over the meeting. They simply described the change that had taken place in their lives. The newspapers came out with big headlines: 'ANTI-OXFORD GROUP MEETING A COLOSSAL FIASCO'—and this in the country where we were told *we* might be laughed out of court.

My guidance for those days was this, 'Denmark shaken, Denmark shaken!' And that old country has certainly been shaken. You feel it in every department of life—not only the butcher, the baker, the candlestick-maker, but the intellec- tuals of the country. Tonight in Viborg, the judges, the bar- risters and the lawyers, the intelligentsia, are witnessing to the positive power of Jesus Christ. People who were confirmed atheists six months ago are intelligent life-changers today.

Do you wonder that in that country of Denmark twenty-five thousand people gathered together a few weeks ago in a single Oxford Group meeting?

The man who led that meeting was the Dean of Copenhagen Cathedral. He interpreted for me the first night. Today the Dean is a flaming apostle. He recently spoke at the Cathedral ceremony which opens the sessions of the Danish Parliament. Have you ever thought of a sermon having three columns on the front page of any newspaper in New York? Well, the Danish press has much the same sense of news values, yet there were three columns on the front pages of the newspapers, three columns on the sermon preached by the Dean.

I heard today from Copenhagen that the Primate had spoken to a conference in Paris with a prophet note. Is that not what our Secretary of State said America needed—the prophet note? The Primate had been present at our first public meeting in Denmark. Now the nation hears a prophet note from a Primate, a Dean, a saddler, a butcher, workers, businessmen.

A country gripped, a country shaken. Let's think of the philosophy of it—one man changed; a million changed; a nation changed.[1]

This is a challenge to every one of you tonight—not merely coming to a meeting. Meetings are not going to change the

[1] Dr B. H. Streeter took part in the Danish campaigns. He wrote (see Supplement IV, 1): 'What I saw there convinced me that the movement was not merely an instrument of moral rebirth and psychological liberation for individuals; but was capable of moving nations as such by initiating a new mental attitude in economic and political conflicts . . . Evidence accumulated of the effect on the conduct of everyday life . . . Thus in one country in Europe, in the space of one year, there has been born a new spirit in facing the conflicts which threatened the collapse of civilisation.'

world. Tonight is only the beginning, and I trust that every one of you will respond to its high challenge. Thirty men, ordinary men, cross the sea a year ago to Norway and illumination comes to that country. A thousand people go to Denmark and an awakening comes to that country.

Think of Switzerland. Tonight I read in the newspaper of a distinguished Swiss. He is perhaps the most cautious man I know. He is like the Scot who always looked both ways when crossing a one-way street. I am of Swiss descent and I know how cautious these Swiss are, but this man says that in Switzerland today there is not only a new movement, but there is a mobilisation, a world Christian front. That is what this Swiss leader says—a Swiss Christian front and then a world Christian front. Is that our answer?

Leaders today in the thought of Europe are all thinking of that word 'Renaissance'. It is rebirth—the rebirth of the individual; the rebirth of the nation; the rebirth of the nations.

Wherever I go people say one thing: 'If only so-and-so could be changed!' You probably thought of the very person. Or you probably thought of five persons. Well, think of five persons changed. Think of nations changed. Is that the answer? The world today is looking for an answer, and, by the Grace of God, there is an answer. But be clear on this point, the answer is not in any man or any group of men. The answer rests in the living God. It rests in a God-controlled person. It rests in a God-controlled nation. It rests in God-controlled supernationalism.

THE PLACE TO START

A year after the Oxford Group first came to Denmark, 15,000 gathered over Easter, 1936, for a national demonstration at Ollerup.[1] *On Easter Sunday, Frank Buchman addressed the Assembly.*

EVERYBODY WANTS to see the other fellow changed. Every nation wants to see the other nation changed. But everybody is waiting for the other fellow to begin.

The Oxford Group is convinced that if you want an answer for the world today, the best place to start is with yourself. This is the first and fundamental need.

Everybody admits the necessity of a moral and spiritual awakening. You find selfishness and fear everywhere—in men and in nations. One person really different. A million people different. A nation changed.

Look what Denmark has done—in one year. The secret is God-control. The only sane people in an insane world are those controlled by God. God-controlled personalities make God-controlled nationalities. This is the aim of the Oxford Group.

[1] *Berlingske Tidende*, Copenhagen, wrote on 13 April, 1936: 'We stood at a window watching the crowd going in this morning. The folk on the highroad were typically Danish, the ordinary Danish people whose names never get into the newspapers. There was something unforgettable about the picture of that massed stream of people moving forward with set purpose towards a single goal, as they worked their way against the wind to where the white-crossed flags of Denmark waved. This was no haphazard concourse of people. It was an army on the march . . . Last Easter a few Danes spoke of their decision to change; this Easter thousands were here who had carried decisions into their daily lives and occupations . . .'

The true patriot gives his life to bring his nation under God's control. Those who oppose that control are public enemies. The God-controlled nation will add to her armament an army of life-changers, to her national defence the respect and gratitude of all her neighbours. Such a nation will demonstrate that spiritual power is the greatest force in the world.

World peace will only come through nations which have achieved God-control. And everybody can listen to God. You can. I can. Everybody can have a part.

Will it be you? Will it be your nation?

AMERICA AWAKE!

In June, 1936, a National Assembly at Stockbridge, Massachusetts, was attended by 5,000 delegates from every part of the United States and Canada. This occasion gathered up the work of many years, which had included two visits from coast to coast by Dr Buchman and a large group from twenty-five nations in 1932 and 1934. On 4 June, Dr Buchman gave the following transatlantic broadcast.

I AM DEEPLY MOVED by the thoughtfulness and vision of you, my friends in England, in making possible this transatlantic broadcast as my birthday present. By next year I may be able to share with you my birthday cake by radio!

I am speaking to you this afternoon from the village green of quiet Stockbridge, in the heart of the wooded Berkshire hills of liberty-loving New England. Down the principal street, bordered by rows of stately elms and rich lawns rolling unbroken from the footpath to the doorsteps of the white and red Colonial houses, came a few days ago an historic pageant. At the head of this cavalcade rode in his colourful garb Uhm-Pa-Tuth, Chief of the Stockbridge Indians, Prince of the Indian royal blood, last of the Mohicans, whose ancestors roamed these hills for centuries before the white men came. Behind him you could see Jonathan Edwards, famous preacher and first President of what is now Princeton University, riding in the old stage coach, with John Sargeant, the first missionary to the Stockbridge Indians. Then followed the returning pioneers from the West, with their covered wagons representing the hundreds who have come from the Pacific Coast across three thousand miles of country. British and American generals walked side by side, followed by servicemen of many countries. Then followed a large body of businessmen and workers from city and farm; while the youth carried the standards of the forty-eight United States and the flags of those many nations whose citizens have been working with us in America.

Stockbridge has links with Britain. Here you can still see the green-shuttered white cottage at the cross-roads opposite the old inn, where Cyrus Field received the first message sent by cable from England to America. The words of that message sent from Queen Victoria were, 'What wonders God hath wrought!' The miracles of science have this week carried the message of the Oxford Group, the message of Christian recovery, to the American people. Today, in 1936, the message flashed to the ends of the earth is 'America, Awake!'

Through the towns and villages of Massachusetts on an April night in 1775, Paul Revere rode to arouse the countryside. The Minute Men, volunteers of their day, instant for action, responded. Over these same villages and towns last week a modern Paul Revere rode the skies trailing the message from his aeroplane 'America Awake—Oxford Group, Stockbridge.' That first Paul Revere was the forerunner of a revolution that roused a people. The modern Paul Revere is calling for a spiritual revolution to unite a world.

From Alaska to New Mexico, from Copenhagen to Shanghai, by land, sea and air, has come this modern cavalcade as the answer to delusion, chaos and confusion. Bartender and banker, pick-pocket and peer, employed and unemployed are all to be found gathered here in the eight house parties of the Oxford Group National Assembly, in Stockbridge and the neighbouring towns and villages. One of these takes the form of a tent city. Four hundred Canadians have crossed the undefended boundary on the north and are leading this meeting here today at which I am speaking.

Why are they here?

The Oxford Group is a Christian revolution for remaking the world. The root problems in the world today are dishonesty, selfishness and fear—in men and, consequently, in nations. These evils multiplied result in divorce, crime, unemployment, recurrent depression and war. How can we hope for peace within a nation, or between nations, when we have conflict in countless homes? Spiritual recovery must precede economic recovery. Political or social solutions that do not deal with these root problems are inadequate. Man-made laws are no substitute for individual character. Our instant need is a moral and spiritual awakening. Human wisdom alone has failed to bring this about. It is only possible when God has control of individuals.

Through this control men find true freedom in a world haunted by insecurity and fear. They discover creative purpose in an age of bewilderment. They find new moral power amid moral decay. They learn to work together, in a world of conflicting interests, through common obedience to God. They weave the threads of understanding that make possible a new diplomacy in which statesmen can achieve enduring results. They create a new confidence as nations work together in common action for the freedom of mankind.

The true patriot gives his life to bring his country under God's control. When God has control, a nation finds her true destiny. Only a God-controlled nation can lead the world into sanity and peace.

But everyone is waiting for the other person and the other nation to begin. The answer lies in an awakening which starts in ourselves and, consequently, in our nation.

Thousands of ordinary people across the world are learning obedience to God's control. They are forming a new public opinion which demands a new quality of leadership. Such leadership can only come from men and women who speak with authority—an authority based on daily experience of the guidance of God.

The problems of the world reflect the people who live in it. Remake people and nations are remade.

We must not delay. The forces of evil threaten even the sanctity of marriage and the security of the home; and when the home collapses, the nation collapses with it. The responsibility is personal to you and to me. The challenge of the Oxford Group is a challenge to decision—a challenge to listen, to listen and to act. When man listens, God speaks. Everyone can listen to God. Everyone can begin just where he is.

WILL GOD CONTROL AMERICA?

1936 was election year in the United States. A newspaper columnist, Walter Locke (Dayton News, 13 June, 1936), wrote: 'Frank Buchman wants the country governed by men under instructions from God as definitely given and understood as if they came by wire, men who listen and hear, and then speak with the inspiration of "Thus saith the Lord" . . . Here is the answer, Dr Buchman says, to the war problem, the race problem, the problem of clashing classes, the problem of a happy individual life—Thy Will be done.' The following address was broadcast from Philadelphia, 19 June, 1936.

HAVE YOU EVER THOUGHT where America's real safety lies? America's safety lies in God-control.

God-controlled individuals, God-controlled homes, God-controlled schools, God-controlled industry, God-controlled politics, God-controlled nations. This means that everybody takes his orders from God.

A dishwasher recently said to his employer, 'I'm hungry.' 'What's wrong?' said his employer. 'Don't you get enough food to eat around here?' 'Yes, plenty; but I'm hungry for God. I can't get enough.' 'Perhaps I need it too,' said his employer.

The common denominator of our national need is the human need for God. Our greatest national need is moral recovery. The barriers that separate men from God and from other men must be destroyed.

Most of us have the conviction that the other fellow ought to be honest. At least we have that basis of union, that we

30

want the other fellow to be honest. And if you want it badly enough for the other fellow you may catch some of it yourself. We may even wake up some morning and find *ourselves* getting honest, because we want the other fellow to be honest. Everybody believes in honesty, purity, unselfishness and love—for the other fellow. And some might even go so far as to wish it for the other party! But the Oxford Group goes one better, and believes that you might even start with yourself—and your own party.

The other day I was talking with a coloured fellow about the Oxford Group. He said, 'It's a great idea, if they all does it.' He is right. Our friend has the philosophy. Everybody has got to do it.

Few people today seem to have any definite plan, or any idea of what the cost will be of moral and spiritual recovery. They don't seem to have thought through the united, disciplined action, under God-control, that is necessary to bring it about. And there are even those who hope to reap where others have sown, without paying the price themselves.

Fortunately, a growing number over a period of years have been paying the price, and today their influence is felt in fifty countries. Fortunately, too, there are statesmen who not only state the need, but point the answer. Such a statesman is the Marquess of Salisbury who, speaking of the Oxford Group, said recently in the British House of Lords:

'The cause of the world's state is not economic; the cause is moral. It is there where the evil lies. It is the want of religion which we ought to possess. If I may use a phrase which is common in a great movement which is taking place at this moment in this country and elsewhere, what you want are God-guided personalities, which make God-guided nationalities, to make a new world. All other ideas of economic adjustment are too small really to touch the centre of the evil.'

Such a statesman is the President of the Norwegian Parliament. Broadcasting recently from New York, in a radio interview with Mr Lowell Thomas, the well-known commentator, he said:

'There is a growing conviction among European statesmen today that any solution on the usual diplomatic basis can at best be only temporary. Many of us European statesmen have come into touch during the past year with the work of the Oxford Group, and have felt that here is a new hope for a more permanent solution to international crises.'

Such statesmen, again, are the Premier of New Zealand and the Finance Minister of China. Premier Savage says that he sees 'in the Oxford Group the only true policy'. Dr Kung, Chinese Minister of Finance, sent a cable which was quoted last week by Lord Addington in the House of Lords. It read as follows:

'The world today is in a state of chaos, degeneracy and disintegration, because men are dominated by selfishness, jealousy and materialism. The Oxford Group advocates the four principles of "absolute love, honesty, purity and unselfishness". It is a movement which transcends geographical divisions, racial distinctions, party differences and class conflict. I believe the principles and the discipline of the movement will help to bind men and women of the world together in a common moral and spiritual awakening which is urgently needed to evolve a new and better social order. Only the inspiration and guidance of a Higher Will can change human nature and conciliate men and nations so that there may be "peace on earth and goodwill among men".'

There is an election on. Let's not confuse issues. The greatest election issue is whether we will elect God as the guide of our individual lives, and so of our national life. In the words of a well-known editor, 'Get God in the delegates and the plat-form, the candidate; all the rest will be added unto them.'

God is the Person that the American voter has got to reckon with in the coming election. The real question is, 'Will God control America?'

The country must be 'governed by men under instructions from God, as definitely given and understood as if they came by wire'. This is the true dictatorship of the living God, and the answer to all dictators. This is the true patriotism, for the true patriot gives his life for his country's resurrection.

Here you begin to see the meaning of the phrase of the well-known political leader who said: 'The Oxford Group has nothing to do with politics. Still, it has everything to do with politics. For it is a revolution in all politics, because God directs not only the platforms, but the politicians.'

Back to God, and on to a new world order. The only hope for world relief is to begin instantly on a colossal scale.

God needs every American as a partner in the working out of His plan. National recovery and resurrection will come when we accept our full responsibility to work with Him. America must get ready to do her part in the creation of a new world order under God's control.

America's safety lies in God-control. Her destiny as a great nation depends directly on what you and I are like. What does God want me to do? That is the issue at this time or any time. The place to begin is with yourself. The time to begin is now.

HOW TO LISTEN

On 26 July, 1936, Dr Buchman addressed 25,000 people gathered for a national demonstration in the British Industries Fair building, Birmingham. With him spoke a cross-section of the British people—'the type who are the backbone of Britain', wrote the Sunday Graphic: *'The great gathering recognised the simple philosophy of changing the world. They saw themselves mirrored in what these plain men said.'*

LEADERS EVERYWHERE now say that the world needs a moral and spiritual awakening. They say it in the universities, in politics, in business and in chancelleries throughout the world. A lot of people say it—some in striking phrases. But it is still just *words*.

The problem is *how*. It is one thing to talk about it. It is another thing to demonstrate it. It seems to me that most people who feel the need for awakening are confronted with the difficulty that faced me twenty years ago: how to bring it about—how to get the disciplined action on the part of the many to make it national.

Now I find when we don't know how, God will show us if we are willing. When man listens, God speaks. When man obeys, God acts. The secret is God-control. We are not out to tell God. We are out to let God tell us. And He will tell us.

The lesson the world most needs is the art of listening to God. A general once sent me a postcard, during an international conference, with the picture of a man on it. The thought below was this, 'God gave a man two ears and one mouth. Why don't you listen twice as much as you talk?'

This is a daily possibility for everyone—to listen to God and get His programme for the day.

It is thoughts from God which have inspired the prophets all through history. And it is the prophet note that the American Secretary of State said was our instant need. He said that what the world needed was a modern Amos. You remember Amos, speaking of a famine abroad in the land, declared it was not a famine of water or of bread, but a famine of hearing the words of the Lord. I believe Mr Hull was right when he said it was this same famine which was afflicting the world today.

Anyone can hear the words of the Lord. It is only necessary to obey the rules. The first rule is that we listen honestly for everything that may come—and if we are wise we write it down. The second rule is that we test the thoughts that come, to see which are from God.

One test is the Bible. It is steeped in the experience through the centuries of men who have dared, under Divine revelation, to live experimentally with God. There, culminating in the life of Jesus Christ, we find the highest moral and spiritual challenge—complete honesty, purity, unselfishness and love.

Another excellent test is, 'What do others say who also listen to God?' This is an unwritten law of fellowship. It is also an acid test of one's commitment to God's plan. No one can be wholly God-controlled who works alone.

It is to a group of willing men and women that God speaks most clearly. And it is through God-controlled people that God must one day govern the world.

A REVOLUTION TO CURE
A REVOLUTION

A transatlantic broadcast from London, 9 August, 1936

I AM SPEAKING to you all from Europe where, hourly, news of revolution is coming in. During the next fifteen minutes you can, if you like, learn how to take part in a revolution yourself. It takes a passion to cure a passion. It takes a revolution to cure a revolution. And the Oxford Group's answer to revolution is more revolution—the revolution in human nature, which is our only hope.

What is this Oxford Group? Well, a newspaper man puts it this way:

> It's not an institution,
> It's not a point of view;
> It starts a revolution
> By starting one in you.

Now, let me give you a picture of the Oxford Group demonstration in the buildings of the British Industries Fair, Birmingham—largest covered hall in Europe, and industrial show-room of the British Empire. Something happened that week-end. You saw Britain on the move. Thousands came from every part of the Empire. There were contingents from thirty-five different countries—five hundred from Holland alone. Europe today echoes to the tramp of marching feet. Picture the response of that vast audience at Birmingham to more than a thousand youth of many nations marching together in a new enlistment.

What is this enlistment of the Oxford Group? Where are they marching? And why are they marching? In an age of material revolution they have enlisted in a spiritual revolution. They are enlisting in the moral equivalent of war.

The world today presents the spectacle of nations losing their way—of nations losing their traditions, their character, their nationhood. Many of us are blind to the haste with which events are hurrying on.

What is our real problem? You all know what a drought is. Well, we are suffering today from a spiritual drought. Fear and greed are like a dust storm. They spread over nations. They blind and choke people. They set man against man, class against class, nation against nation.

Take the war in Spain. Whichever side wins, the human factor will remain. War is no answer to suspicion, jealousy, lust and fear. No, the answer does not lie in a winning side— even in an election campaign—once we have got away from the things that really matter. National and world problems remain the same because the root problem—human nature —remains unsolved. Until we deal with human nature thoroughly and drastically on a national scale, nations must still follow their historic road to violence and destruction.

Three thousand miles of ocean do not change this fundamental problem—and will not save us if we fail to solve it. The symptoms may differ in Europe and America. The disease is the same.

What is the disease? Isn't it fear, dishonesty, resentment, selfishness? We talk about freedom and liberty, but we are slaves to ourselves.

The only possible alternatives today are collapse or God-control. And collapse is simply the selfishness of all of us together. Collapse or God-control. You and I, if we are selfish, are part of the disease; just as you and I, if we are God-controlled, can be part of the cure.

The Oxford Group is a revolution of God-control where God really guides you and your nation. Everyone is guided by something. What are you guided by? Is it your own desires? Is it your pocket-book? Your fears? Your wife? Your husband? Or what the neighbours think? If it is your own selfish plan, you are an enemy of the nation.

God made the world, and man has been trying to run it ever since. That must stop. You remember what Will Rogers used to say: 'God made man a little lower than the angels, and man has been getting a little lower ever since!' But now a new age has begun, where God is going to have right of way.

What we must have is a world-wide Christian front against the oncoming forces of materialism. We read of burning churches. The only answer to burning churches is a Church aflame.

The god of efficiency is not enough. Goodwill and good works do not reach the heart of the trouble. Idealism has not succeeded. The truth is that any lasting social and economic recovery can only be built on the foundation of a moral and spiritual recovery.

When you and I are not one hundred per cent God-guided and God-controlled, we are really helping chaos. All lukewarm people are really helping chaos. The fate of nations depends upon whether you and I are God-controlled.

A new illumination must come to the world. I knew the

man who gave us electric light. You can still see his first bulb, which Mr Henry Ford treasures in his laboratory at Dearborn. Everyone can get light today provided he makes contact with the power station. And it is just as practical to make contact with God. Steinmetz, the great scientist, foresaw this when he said that the next great discoveries would be in the realm of the spiritual. God has illumination for us, if our contact is good.

What we need is a supernational network of live wires across the world to every last man, in every last place, in every last situation. Many have been waiting for a great leader to emerge. The Oxford Group believes that it must be done not through one person, but through groups of people who have learned to work together under the guidance of God.

The Oxford Group believes that the ordinary person can do the extraordinary thing if he is in touch with God.

God can put thoughts into your mind. Have you ever listened for them? Have you ever tried taking pencil and paper, and writing down the thoughts that come to you? They may look like ordinary thoughts. But be honest about them. You might get a new picture of yourself. Absolute honesty, absolute purity, absolute unselfishness, absolute love. Those are Christ's standards. Are they yours? You may have to put things straight. I had to. I began by writing to six people, admitting that ill-will between us was my fault, and not theirs. Then I could really help people. Remember—if you want the world to get straight, get straight yourself.

God-control is the answer not only *to* revolution, but *in* revolution. In a revolution I went through not long ago, God gave me direct orders to stay in a place which the authorities had said was the most dangerous of all. I stayed. Others, who fled in search of safety, nearly lost their lives. My friend and I were perfectly safe.

The world's safety, America's safety, your safety, the safety of your home, lies in God-control.

Brains alone are not enough. It is obedience that counts—obedience to God. America, Canada, must learn to obey.

God spoke to the prophets of old. He may speak to you. God speaks to those who listen. God acts through those who obey.

Suppose tomorrow morning you get up a bit earlier and try listening to God. Why not get the family to listen too? Why not a spiritual radiophone in every home?

We can listen in every day. If we do, and if we obey what we hear, it is conceivable that together we will usher in the greatest revolution of all time, whereby the Cross of Christ will transform the world.

THE DESTINY OF NATIONS

A manifesto in RISING TIDE,[1] *November,* 1937

BY A MIRACLE of science, men can speak by radio to millions. By a miracle of the Spirit, God can speak to every man. His voice can be heard in every home, every business, every government.

> When man listens, God speaks.
> When man obeys, God acts.

It does not matter who you are or where you are. Accurate, adequate information can come from the Mind of God to the minds of men who are willing to take their orders from Him.

This is the revolution which will end revolution by changing human nature and remaking men and nations.

People believe that their leaders should be guided by God. But the rank and file must be guided too. A God-guided public opinion is the strength of the leaders. This is the dictatorship of the living Spirit of God, which gives every man the inner discipline he needs, and the inner liberty he desires.

Your security, the world's security, lies in God-control. No other social, political or economic programme goes to the root of the disease in human nature.

Only God-controlled men will make God-controlled nations to make a new world. In this adventure every man can find his vocation, every nation its destiny.

[1] *Rising Tide,* a pictorial review of the Oxford Group, appeared in eight languages, with a circulation of 1,500,000.

II

WORLD IN CRISIS

May the answer not be found in a reawakening to the fundamental values on which democracy was built; in a rededication of our people to those elementary virtues of honesty, unselfishness and love which so many of us have allowed to take a secondary place? In an age when lowered moral standards have become a breeding-ground for destructive forces, is it not time for democracy to seek again the sources of her strength, and to demonstrate to the world the power of moral principles?

Thirty-three Members of Parliament of all parties, in a letter to The Times *on Moral Re-Armament,* 1 *September,* 1938

MORAL RE-ARMAMENT

In the spring of 1938 Europe was undergoing a war of nerves. Hitler's march into Austria had speeded the defence measures of the democracies, but their need for a united spirit to meet the challenge of militant ideologies was increasingly clear.

On 29 May, at a reception in his honour in East Ham Town Hall, cradle of the British Labour Movement, Frank Buchman launched Moral Re-Armament. His aim was a world-wide mobilisation of the moral and spiritual forces, which urgently needed a rallying point and a philosophy. Over 3,000 overflowed the Town Hall. With him on the platform were more than sixty East London Mayors, Aldermen and Councillors. Within a few days, press and radio had carried Frank Buchman's concept of Moral Re-Armament around the world.

THE WORLD'S CONDITION cannot but cause disquiet and anxiety. Hostility piles up between nation and nation, labour and capital, class and class. The cost of bitterness and fear mounts daily. Friction and frustration are undermining our homes.

Is there a remedy that will cure the individual and the nation and give the hope of a speedy and satisfactory recovery?

The remedy may lie in a return to those simple home truths that some of us learned at our mother's knee, and which many of us have forgotten and neglected—honesty, purity, unselfishness and love.

The crisis is fundamentally a moral one. The nations must re-arm morally. Moral recovery is essentially the forerunner

E

of economic recovery. Imagine a rising tide of absolute honesty and absolute unselfishness sweeping across every country! What would be the effect? What about taxes? Debts? Savings? A wave of absolute unselfishness throughout the nations would be the end of war.

Moral recovery creates not crisis but confidence and unity in every phase of life. How can we precipitate this moral recovery throughout the nations? We need a power strong enough to change human nature and build bridges between man and man, faction and faction. This starts when everyone admits his own faults instead of spot-lighting the other fellow's.

God alone can change human nature.

The secret lies in that great forgotten truth that when man listens, God speaks; when man obeys, God acts; when men change, nations change. That power active in a minority can be the solvent of a whole country's problems. Leaders changed, a nation's thinking changed, a world at peace with itself.

'We, the Remakers of the World'—is that not the thinking and willing of the ordinary man? The average man wants to see the other fellow honest, the other nation at peace with his own. We all want to *get*, but with such changed leaders we might all want to *give*. We might find in this new spirit an answer to the problems which are paralysing economic recovery.

Suppose everybody cared enough, everybody shared enough, wouldn't everybody have enough? There is enough in the world for everyone's need, but not enough for everyone's greed.

Think of the unemployed thus released for a programme

46

of Moral Re-Armament; everyone in the nation magnetised and mobilised to restore the nations to security, safety and sanity.

Every man, woman and child must be enlisted, every home become a fort. Our aim should be that everyone has not only enough of the necessities of life, but that he has a legitimate part in bringing about this Moral Re-Armament, and so safeguards the peace of his nation and the peace of the world.

God has a nation-wide programme that provides inspiration and liberty for all and anticipates all political programmes.

Every employed and unemployed man employed in Moral Re-Armament; this is the greatest programme of national service—putting everybody to work remaking people, homes and businesses. A Swedish steelworker told me: 'Only a spiritual revolution goes far enough to meet the needs of men and industry.'

A Labour leader said: 'I have seen the Labour Movement triumph and felt in the midst of triumph an emptiness. The Oxford Group gave my life new content. I see in its message the only key to the future of the Labour Movement and of industry the world over.'

Only a new spirit in men can bring a new spirit in industry. Industry can be the pioneer of a new order, where national service replaces selfishness, and where industrial planning is based upon the guidance of God. When Labour, Management and Capital become partners under God's guidance, then industry takes its true place in national life.

New men, new homes, new industry, new nations, a new world.

We have not yet tapped the great creative sources in the Mind of God. God has a plan, and the combined moral and spiritual forces of the nation can find that plan.

We can, we must, and we will generate a moral and spiritual force that is powerful enough to remake the world.

Note: This speech was widely reported and reproduced in newspapers in every part of the world. In Washington it was reproduced as a full-page editorial in the *United States News*, 6 September, 1938, and was linked by the editor, David Lawrence, with Woodrow Wilson's last published article, 'The Road Away from Revolution' (*Atlantic Monthly*, August, 1923). Mr Lawrence wrote: 'With Europe in the midst of a crisis which could conceivably bring on another World War . . . I have placed the two addresses alongside of each other because the note struck in 1923 by Mr Wilson is paralleled in 1938 in such eloquent fashion by this eminent American leader, Dr Frank Buchman, who has begun to awaken in fifty countries of the world a realistic conception of human brotherhood.'

A BIRTHDAY TALK
TO EAST LONDON FAMILIES

East Ham Town Hall, 29 May, 1938

I THOUGHT I would begin this evening by thanking our younger friends who brought me flowers this afternoon. One of them gave me this poem. He is ten years old.

> We go on marching, we are going to win.
> With God as our Leader we will surely beat sin.
> Our army travels—north, east, south and west,
> Knowing in our hearts we are doing our best.
> We just have a quiet time and see what God has to say,
> As things go wrong, we just kneel and pray.
> We are very happy, we are very gay.
> When the world is like this, things will be O.K.

Now, there is real philosophy in that. I wish we could all say, 'Everything's O.K.' Well, are we going to make it like that? Somebody's got to begin. That somebody may have to be you. I had to begin. I came to England seventeen years ago alone, unknown, simply because two very good people wanted to see two of their family different, and that is how this work began. I still remember walking the streets of a certain town in England and feeling I wanted to pinch myself because the things that came in my quiet time were so amazing. God used to tell me in 1921 that there would be a mighty awakening of God's Almighty Spirit in this land.

One man changed, a city changed, a whole nation changed. Every man, every woman, every child mobilised in this mobile army. If Ken, aged ten, can do it, every one of you ought to do it—a part of that mobile army for bringing Britain under God-control. Begin to see a moving army, something on the march.

Every home a fortress; every home a life-changing centre, where people just naturally learn how to change others. Suppose we begin to magnetise and mobilise people in different cells throughout the country; we will soon begin to change the moral climate of Britain.

'Britain and the world must re-arm morally.' God gave me this as a key thought for this year specially.

God will begin to be in charge of these Isles. Somebody has got to start. Will you be that person? Forget all about Frank Buchman, and that one day he had a quiet time and now you have a movement in fifty-two countries. Otherwise, you will miss the point of all this.

This is my birthday message to you. Why have we been so long learning this? The only sane people in an insane world are those guided by God. Is East London going to bring the world back to sanity and security?

A MESSAGE TO GREECE

On Dr Buchman's sixtieth birthday, 4 June, 1938, messages of affection and respect poured in from all parts of the world. Friends in different countries also asked him to send them some special word on this occasion. Typical of these is the following message sent at the request of friends in Greece.[1]

I TAKE SPECIAL PLEASURE in responding to the request of my Greek friends for a message on my sixtieth birthday, because for thirty years of those sixty I have had the privilege of personal acquaintance with many foremost citizens of your great country. And perhaps the observations of half a lifetime give one a certain perspective.

All the world knows how, in the past, Greece thwarted the enemies of civilisation. Other enemies are on the march today. But they can no longer be overthrown on a single battlefield, and even those cultural forces which once saved Europe are in many countries in danger of turning traitor to the cause.

The enemies today are selfish materialism and moral apathy. They are the source of all national ills. Only one power is strong enough to oppose them—the power of God-inspired men. Against these moral and spiritual foes we must launch a moral and spiritual offensive. The soul of the nations is at stake.

[1] In November, 1949, HM King Paul of the Hellenes conferred the Order of Commander of the Royal Order of King George I of Greece on Dr Buchman.

In this fateful struggle, where the fullest measure of courage, discipline and sacrifice is required, there are many who look to the Hellenic people with confidence and hope. They believe that the glory of Greece lies not only in the past, but also in the present and the future. They believe that she will be faithful to her great traditions.

Note: Political leaders from many countries sent greetings to a dinner given for Frank Buchman in the House of Commons by Members of all parties. Other tributes came from Church leaders, industrialists and representatives of Labour.

But the majority of the greetings were from the thousands of homes and individuals who had found new life through the Oxford Group—Yorkshire mill girls, Clydeside shipyard workers, Danish farmers, Swedish steel-workers, South African gold-miners, former head-hunters in Papua, all sorts and conditions, from Hammerfest in Norway, northernmost town in the world, to Buenos Aires and New Zealand.

Minorities in Burma 'deeply grateful for you—century-old barriers disappearing'; a thousand Swiss at a national assembly, sending thanks for 'new hope and new destiny that you gave to this country'—these are some of the living messages of thousands which accompanied the greetings of statesmen. Among them was the following, from the Archbishop of Canterbury: 'I would like to send a message of congratulation to Dr Buchman on the great work which he has been able to achieve in bringing multitudes of human lives in all parts of the world under the transforming power of Christ. COSMO CANTUAR.'

REVIVAL, REVOLUTION, RENAISSANCE

In August, 1938, following a far-reaching response in Sweden, especially amongst the intellectual leaders of social democracy and the industrial workers, a Scandinavian Assembly for Moral Re-Armament was held in the old Hanseatic city of Visby, on the Island of Gottland. Here, on this Swedish 'island of ruins and roses', hundreds gathered in the ruined cathedral, the only building large enough to hold them. In this speech, 16 August, 1938, Frank Buchman addressed those who had been drawn to Moral Re-Armament but had not, as yet, fully comprehended its aims and accepted from God the task of saving nations in a time of world danger.

TODAY WE WANT to forge a united battlefront. The clear issue is whether we are guided by God or not. It is not whether we are clever. It is not what nation we belong to. We meet here today as Christians and we meet as guided people, and our final source of authority is God's plan.

I hope that by the time I finish speaking some of you will have made a decision. We have come here with different objectives. First, some of the people have come here hoping to be changed. That is very good, very necessary. Some of you come here with the hope that you will learn to change others. That, too, is very necessary.

But the danger is that some of you want to stop there. I am tremendously interested in a third point—how to save a crumbling civilisation. That is the thing that interests me.

53

But then I want a fourth thing. I want to reach the millions of the world.

All these things ought naturally to follow each other. If you are changed, you naturally want to change other people. The next thing is you want to save civilisation. Then you want to reach the millions out there. It is a natural programme.

But sin comes along. I don't know if you believe in it or not, but it is here. Don't spend the rest of the day arguing if it exists or not. That is what some of you would like to do. You would miss the whole point. We are not here to argue; we are here for constructive planning and action.

I know what some of you would like out of the Oxford Group—a nice comfortable awakening; you would call it a revival. A nice armchair religion. That is the thinking of some people. But if we stopped there, I should be sorry. If you stop there, I am your enemy unless I warn you. A person who has that conception today is not adequately thinking and planning to save the millions.

I am not interested, not do I think it adequate, if we are going to begin just to start another revival. Whatever thoughtful statesman you talk to will tell you that every country needs a moral and spiritual awakening. That is the absolutely fundamental essential. But revival is only one level of thought. To stop there is inferior thinking. Unless we call for something bigger than that we are done for.

The next step is revolution. It is uncomfortable. A lot of Christians don't like the word. It scares them. It makes them goose-fleshy. That's where some of your critics come from— goose-fleshy Christians with armchair Christianity.

Begin to work out how many still go to church and ask

why the church today is not reaching one hundred per cent of the people. I know revolution makes people uncomfortable. I am not here to make you comfortable, and I am not here to make you like me. What the Oxford Group will give this and every nation is a spiritual revolution.

But some of you are not thinking this way. Some of the cleverest people in the world are thinking along the line of destructive revolution, and they are already at work. May I say a very strong word to you this morning? I find here the same sort of inflammable matter that made Spain possible. Unless we and others see the bigger vision of spiritual revolution, the other may be possible.

Think of the uncomfortableness of that kind of revolution. We are met in a ruined church. How many churches are in ruins in Spain today? That is revolution—very uncomfortable. The point is this. Are the Christians going to build a Christian philosophy that will move Europe? Are you the kind of Christians that can build that revolution? Is that the New Testament? Is that Christian? Is that the sort of thing you are going to do? Is that your programme? Is that your policy?

If you are not going on that battlefront, I wish you well. I am not going to quarrel with you or criticise you. You do exactly what you like in the way you like. That's your idea of democracy.

I don't say it's true democracy, but it's the popular practice of democracy. For an increasing number of citizens in democratic states are now unwilling to acknowledge in speech and action those inner authorities on which the life of democracy depends. Each man has his own plan. It's so wonderful each to have his own plan. It's such freedom, such liberty! Everyone does as he pleases. But not in the Oxford Group. There you have true democracy. You don't do as you please, you do as God guides. You do God's plan.

I cannot go into all the qualities necessary for a revolutionary this morning. There were some people in the Acts and the Gospels who gave everything. There were others who did not give everything. Even in a revolution some people want an amount of padding around them. I want to ask you this morning whether you want to be that kind of a revolutionary. If so, there may be a comfortable place for you behind the lines. But somewhere on the battlefront we will have the real revolutionaries.

There is a third stage—renaissance. The rebirth of a people, individuals and the rebirth of a nation. I know what you may say. Illusion. Illusion. Illusion. Insanity. What is the insanity? Where is it?

Can we have this rebirth of a man and nation? Some people do not like the idea of nations reborn, or of reaching the millions. They deride such a programme by calling it 'publicity'. Read the Old Testament. Look at Isaiah 52. You can begin at the sixth verse. Let me read the seventh to you: 'How beautiful upon the mountains are the feet of him that bringeth good tidings, that publisheth peace; that bringeth good tidings of good, that publisheth salvation.' Does it say 'publish' there? There is publicity. It is amazing how many Christian people and otherwise clever people are put off by a thing like this. You mustn't get publicity when you want to build something! All the publicity must be for destruction—or must it?

Take the word 'Gospel'. Gospel means 'good news', front-page news. But people object if it gets on the front page. One critic objected. He started a clever phrase. His criticism got wide publicity. Do you know why he started this clever phrase? Why do people do these things? Why might I do such a thing? If I don't want someone to meet my needs, I put up a nice barricade, a nice smoke-screen. Now that man's clever phrase has gone over this country like a poison gas and the average man hasn't had on his gas mask.

Do you see it? The man who started that clever phrase is defeated in his own life. That's the enemy. It may be a very amiable enemy, but it is all the more dangerous. He is going to keep thousands of people from getting the real thing. People are going to sit back in their cells of defeat and you will never get at them. You will never heal their lives.

People are shy and hesitant and fear criticism. Criticism is uncomfortable. I know that. It was like a dagger through my heart when I was first attacked. I suffered. I know what it means. But if you are a real revolutionary, you always maintain perspective, no matter what people say about you. No matter how stones come, you go straight ahead. Stones of criticism are so bracing—they just set you up for the day.

I thank God tremendously for what has been done in this place, for all the preparations you have made, for all the difficulties you have overcome. Grateful for all that, but let's remember there is still sin in the camp. And that sin may be inferior thinking.

You will do well today to read the fifty-first psalm. It is a tremendous human experience. And then read in the New Testament about the Cross of Christ. You will never, never, never come into this experience until you know the Cross of Christ. Some of you have heard about it, Sunday by Sunday, but it's not an experience. If it were experience, you would not shrink from anything.

I am going to promise you one thing. I am not turning back. I am not turning back, no matter who does, no matter what it is going to cost. I do not want you to come along just because I am here—that isn't it. That would be a poor revolution. That would be a poor fellowship. Let us for a moment see a picture of the Cross of Christ, and let me say, if you join in this great crusade, you will get the way of the Cross. I am not going to lure you by hopes of material success. I am not going to lure you by saying you are going to be heroes. I am not going to lure you, although I believe that these lands can give a pattern on how to live. It is a personal experience of the Cross. It is not I, but Christ. It is not I at the head, but Christ who leads.

There are meetings this afternoon—the lawyers, the educationalists. These are important, but there is another more important. Cancel all others if you must for this one—the meeting between God and yourself. The biggest thing this afternoon for you may be to go off alone and decide whether you are going to be one of these fellow-revolutionaries, where you are going to stand on this battlefront. I am not going to ask you to make a decision right now. The thing you have got to decide is between you and God. Do it alone. Write it down if you want to. It is a deed, like the transfer of property—so you turn over your life to God, for full and complete direction as a fellow-revolutionary.

Then you are going to be free. Then you are going to have true democracy because you are free. That's my challenge to you.

PATTERN FOR STATESMANSHIP

In September, 1938, the first World Assembly for Moral Re-Armament was held at Interlaken, in Switzerland, at a time when the nations seemed on the verge of war. In London, gas masks were issued to all civilians, and in Hyde Park, by the light of flares at night, people were digging air raid shelters. Armed forces were being mobilised, and young men of many European countries were recalled from Interlaken to join their units.

For Frank Buchman the Assembly was pre-eminently an occasion for proclaiming a message of sanity to those men in whose hands the destiny of an entire generation seemed to rest. His opening address, on 2 September, 1938, follows.

NOW WE MUST DEVELOP the framers of the just and lasting peace that is to be. The actual conditions prescribed for world peace have proved to be without peace and have even worked against peace.

We must create such a spirit that the nations even in times of decisive decisions have those qualities at hand and operative that are over and above the human wisdom which has so often failed us in the past.

We must bridge seemingly impossible and humanly hopeless situations. We must have justice, whereby each sees not only his difficulties, but the difficulties of others also. We must find that answer which will give satisfaction and security to all—an answer that is above party, that is above class, that is above faction, that is above nations.

What is the answer to this negative cloud that hangs over

the whole of Europe? What will drive away the clouds that have been hanging over the Jungfrau during these ominous days? The very mountains seem to reflect the mood of a disturbed Europe.

We need to reach a whole new level of thinking, willing and living. It is only sheer blindness that leads us to any other conclusion. Anxiously the people are awaiting from the statesmen and leaders those pronouncements that will give them a maximum security for all, the freedom, peace and justice which the common mind of all should always supply, but which in times of crisis is delegated to the few.

The Oxford Group's aim ever since the last war has been to give a whole new pattern for statesmanship and a whole new level of responsible thinking—faculties only given to men who are living under God's guidance, who are changed through daily contact with God and through daily obedience to God. Its aim is to remake the world and provide those principles of living that cumulative experience has proved to be practical and demonstrable everywhere.

What is the particular genius of presenting truth that has made the Oxford Group so effective in so many countries? It goes to the root of the problem—a change of heart.

We have set ourselves the difficult task of trying to liquidate the cost of bitterness and fear, which mounts daily. The odds are seemingly against us, but just as individuals are delivered from their prison cells of doubt and defeat, so it is possible for nations to be delivered from their prison cells of fear, resentment, jealousy and depression, and oftentimes through one illumined man, one masterful prophet. How often this has been true in history! If this is true of one man, what can happen if a group of people in every nation carry through the illumination and give a whole new public opinion?

When Moral Re-Armament is a reality, then the maintaining of prestige need no longer be a factor in national policy. Every nation then finds its prestige in its new mission, in taking new responsibility.

The world lives today in the climate of suspicion, fear and greed. The world awaits an inspired answer from statesmen as well as the ordinary man. Yes, inspired statesmen, guided not alone by human wisdom, but by that added help which sees and recognises the Supreme Plan. There must be an adequate plan for the world's ills, and if God has a plan, He also has God-prepared instruments.

GUIDANCE OR GUNS?

Interlaken, 6 September, 1938

THE WORLD is at the crossroads. The choice is guidance or guns. We must listen to guidance or we shall listen to guns.

Every statesman admits that the world needs a new moral climate. It is one thing to articulate a great truth like spiritual leadership. It is another thing to live it and make it the constant of a nation's life. That is really the crux of the matter. It is there we need the daily willing of every man under God's control. Though the lack of that sort of living we have starved the nation's life and the lives of the nations.

Spiritual leadership must have a content of positive action far greater than what the world now associates with the term. A great many people when they hear someone speak about spiritual leadership say, 'Thank God, someone is articulating the need. I need do nothing about it. All's well.' People agree and do exactly as they please. The Oxford Group is a phalanx of God-controlled people from all lands who are constantly waging a world war against selfishness. It has been in action since the last war training men for the moral re-armament of the nations.

Everybody knows of somebody else they would like to see different. Every nation immediately thinks of some other nation that should be different. What if they were? That would be the answer to all our problems, if people were different and had the power to change the men and the nations. And that is what the Oxford Group believes. It is just as simple and natural and normal as that, and it is just what everybody is waiting for. It is a national necessity. Why don't we reach the age of sanity and do it? On the lowest basis it is the best insurance for everyone, and it means security if nothing else, for God has a sufficient answer.

Every man in every land should listen to guidance. For every home, in every land, the natural and normal thing should be to get their programme from God. In industry, in the workshop, in the nation's life, in Parliament, the normal thing is to listen to God. Each nation expresses it in its own way—one nation in one way, and another in another, but all God-controlled and God-led. Thus, with God leading, all will understand each other.

Here in this philosophy is lasting peace, and only here. You will not find it in any other quarter. It is the peace that is born of God-control. I need not remind you that God-control means asking for guidance.

It is a forgotten factor in world politics today—listening to guidance. Yet in certain countries all the laws of the land are still made—at least according to the Statute Book—'under Divine Guidance'. But suppose every individual had the moral re-armament of God-control. Think what a strength that would be throughout the world!

It would bring into action those latent powers which we oftentimes hide under a cover of false reserve—and call it national character. If those latent powers were released and mobilised under God they would generate enough power to change the thinking and living of the world.

There is a tremendous power, too, in a minority guided by God. Think of a person like Joan of Arc. She saved her nation.

The voice of God for her became the voice of reason for her nation. This is what our age needs. The voice of God must once again become the will of the people.

Think what God can do through the influence of the millions who are being reached through this message of God-control. Spiritual power is still the greatest force in the world.

HUMANITY
AT THE CROSSROADS

Interlaken, 10 September, 1938

I LOOKED OUT on the fire of sunrise on the Jungfrau this morning, as the Alps became illumined with the start of a new day. Is it to be God's light of a new day for Europe and the world; or is it to be the fading light of a doomed civilisation? The world faces this historic choice.

Immediate decisions lie with the few who hold the reins of history in their hands. Yet each of us must make the crucial decision that, come what may, our lives and our nations are to be controlled absolutely by the living God, and that we accept His plan for the world.

The Oxford Group builds the strong fabric in the nation's life that holds it firm. It makes the nation conscious of the living God. It holds before the nation its primary national policy—obedience to guidance.

Then family life ensures the nation's health and prepares God-governed children who are fit to be citizens. Then education finds its inspiration as teachers and students, morally sane, are taught by God.

Then industry takes hope. For confidence brings expansion and God-control brings harmony and efficiency. Capital and labour work together, like the fingers on the hand. Each man has a share in labour. Each man builds up the nation's capital.

Government, as one Prime Minister said, is then made easier. For the more men, under God, govern themselves, the less they need government from outside. Taxation goes down as honesty goes up. And the people naturally choose as leaders those who are most clearly led by God.

Moral Re-Armament creates white and red corpuscles, energy and protection, in the national blood-stream. The poisons of decadence and division are thrown off, as a healthy organism throws off disease.

The Oxford Group is building a world organism that takes the needs of nations and answers them with men. It is a challenge to every man and every woman to enlist under God's control in that colossal task. What is your part in remaking the world? He who refuses to enlist under God's orders thereby enlists in the cause of world destruction.

In time of war, a nation mobilises every energy for national defence. If nations see a common enemy, they will unite in common action, sinking their national differences. Suppose the world were invaded by a vast army from Mars, threatening our existence, would not the whole world join forces in self-defence?

Is there no common enemy against which all the nations must fight shoulder to shoulder? There is. The common foes of fear, greed and resentment have worked with deadly accuracy to bring the nations to the brink of catastrophe.

Why should the methods which have failed to influence individuals influence nations? Do you respond to lectures, to pious pronouncements from those who lightly skip over their own mistakes? Then why should we expect nations to respond?

Only Moral Re-Armament can bind the nations together.

It arouses not fear, but confidence and gratitude. It unites all in the world organism of God-directed men and women, the responsible family of mankind.

Humanity is at the crossroads. We must reach a final decision for ourselves and for our nations. Do we choose the road of selfishness that leads to uncontrollable violence and darkness? Or will it be the road of the Cross to a sound world, where we learn how to live together, where the ancient virtues of justice, understanding and peace rule under God over a sane humanity?

The choice rests with every man. For every man can under God be a remaker of men, and every God-controlled man becomes a force for Moral Re-Armament.

Is this conviction a passion in your heart? Then it will spread like fire through your nation.

Where are the men in every land who will rise and accept the sovereignty of the living God, who will fight for their nations now by enlisting under the King of Kings, and who will answer the aching hunger of mankind for peace and a new world?

ONE THING
CAN SWING THE BALANCE

Following the World Assembly at Interlaken, Dr Buchman was invited to Geneva where a luncheon was given, on 15 September, 1938 attended by diplomats and delegates to the League of Nations from fifty-three countries. He was introduced by the Hon. C. J. Hambro of Norway.[1]

AT TIMES OF CRISIS we must re-examine all our values. Our commonly accepted standards fail to be adequate. We need a new quality of life for all. We must possess some superior quality—a quality of living that rises above resentment, jealousy, greed and points of view, because all these may keep us from a maximum message.

People and nations for a long time have been thinking abnormally. Men and nations suffer from the numbing

[1] In his introduction, the Hon. C. J. Hambro said: 'Some of us delegates to the League Assembly have asked you to come here today to meet and to hear Dr Buchman and some of his fellow workers in the Oxford Group. We have done so because we have felt that in this hour of grave apprehension and fear it is of vital importance to meet hope and faith and strength.

'We have the impression that these people have succeeded in fundamental things where we have failed. They have created a fellowship of men and women irrespective of nationality and political doctrine. They have created that constructive peace which we have been seeking in vain for years. So we have asked them to come to give us the right mind for preparing that Moral Re-Armament which they have already prepared among so many nations.

'Where we have failed in changing politics, they have succeeded in changing lives, and giving men and women a new way of living.'

disease of auto-intoxication. The world is drugged with its own sin and blinded with its own selfishness. People have accepted standards lower than they know they ought to accept.

Some superhuman power is needed to change the thinking of the ordinary man and of those who lead. We need to call into being a whole new philosophy of living—that quality of life that is above party, above class, above faction, above nations—God-control.

It is one thing to say that God-control is the only true policy. It is another thing to make it a reality in the life of a nation. A whole new fabric needs to be woven. Any of us can recall a succession of conferences which started with high hopes but ended with failure. Yet conferences, God-controlled, would surprise everyone, because they would be successful and accomplish what they set out to do.

It is the super-statesmen who make God-control their programme, who will solve the ills of mankind and usher in lasting peace. The great men of history are the men who can articulate and translate into action the answer to war, the men who will confess their own shortcomings instead of spot-lighting those of others.

Individuals and nations need to have a sense of repentance. Awaken the individual and you awaken the nation. Then we shall have a new moral climate and an answer to present crisis and recurrent crises. This colossal task requires the combined wisdom of God and man.

Statesmen everywhere are becoming convinced that this is the only lasting programme, but we still need to develop men who will put it into action in their different countries. It is like the early days of the Bell telephone. Installation is still defective and reception is still limited.

The only thing that can swing the balance between defeat and victory is the decisive voice of God—statesmen and their people unitedly under God's control. Statesmen of the world must have the courage to inaugurate a new day and a new way—to be the peacemakers of the new world.

Note: A few days later the editor of the *Journal de Genève*, M. Jean Martin, sent to editors all over the world a special supplement of his paper reporting the news of Moral Re-Armament. In an accompanying letter he wrote, 'Whatever happens in Europe, Moral Re-Armament remains the only answer to recurrent crisis and the one foundation for reconciliation and permanent peace . . . In these critical days the Press of every nation can play a decisive part in the moral re-armament of world public opinion. I am anxious that my paper shall contribute to this programme.'

FRAMEWORK OF
A MIGHTY ANSWER

Through the period of the Munich crisis, in the autumn of 1938, *Europe faced the threat of war. In this Armistice Day message, given in London,* 11 *November,* 1938, *Frank Buchman sought to recall to reality those who blindly hoped that peace could be preserved while they themselves remained undisturbed, without facing either the extent of the danger or the need of radical change in personal and national life.*

My loved brother rests in a grave in France. Armistice Day brings back treasured memories. There is a spot in France that is for ever mine. It is marked in perpetuity. Many, very many, share a similar fate. We are comrades in a great sacrifice. How can we make this Armistice Day serve so that the day may come when such a loss can never happen again?

The secret lies in those two minutes of silence—if we, as a nation, could catch the reality of God's guidance in those precious moments.

For many, those two minutes are a great experience but do not serve the fullest purpose. To many it is an awkward time. So much might happen; so little actually does. We are not certain what to do. We try to remember the faces of those loved long since and lost awhile. We want something, but it seems to elude us. We come away with only a vague sense of uplift.

Grief may be selfish and keep us from contact with God. Grief may cloud the presence of God and so make us fail in giving an adequate answer. The people who wallow in selfish grief are in the grip of self-pity and become traitors to the cause for which their loved ones died. They go from crisis to crisis and from problem to problem. Their very selfishness makes another generation of graves possible and even necessary. They see the other man and other nations as their problem, and have no constructive answer for themselves or their nation.

They fail their generation because they do not wish to be involved. They are too preoccupied ever to articulate the great truths that God has a plan for their generation, and that a whole new philosophy of living is possible.

Shall I tell you what happens when I listen? I give my mind to disciplined direction. I find that God's thoughts can become my thoughts. Direct messages come from the Mind of God to the mind of man—definite, direct, decisive. God speaks.

Radio has given us a counterpart. Whenever we see that instrument, we know that if we tune in, we shall find a response. But many who ought to know better still fail to listen. They must follow their egocentric way still further, continue to talk, talk, talk, rather than learn the great compelling truth, the great symphony that comes to us when we listen. God has a plan for the nations. Nations are searching for a whole new experience of truth.

Shall we at last as a nation, during our silence, make a high resolve that we shall at all costs discover in that silence the answer for enduring peace? Armistice Day can become the framework of a mighty answer. If we give those two minutes on Armistice Day, we may form a daily habit. We may find those two minutes so satisfying that guidance becomes the daily source of all our creative thinking and living. In this way silence can be the regulator of men and nations. For guidance comes in silence.

Note: On Armistice Day, 1938, *The Times* published a letter from the Earl of Athlone and other national leaders which read, in part, 'The strength of a nation is shown in the courage to admit her own faults. The glory of a nation is to have a creative message for the world. For this we need not only inspired statesmanship but daily inspiration in every business, every workshop, every home. We must teach ourselves to apply practically to conduct the Christian standards of honesty, purity, and love, and to make fulfilment of the will of God the touchstone of public and private life . . .

'Moral re-armament must be the foundation of national life, as it must be of any world settlement. The miracle of God's Living Spirit can break the power of pride and selfishness, of lust and fear and hatred; for spiritual power is the greatest force in the world . . .

'Throughout her long history this country never failed, and has not failed now, to meet recurrent crises with the courage which each demanded. But the spiritual crisis remains, and calls for action. Nation and Empire must stand or fall by our response to that call. The choice is moral re-armament or national decay. That choice will decide whether ours is ultimately to go the way of other dead kingdoms and empires, or whether our Commonwealth, led by God, may become a leader of the world towards sanity and peace.'

CHAOS AGAINST GOD

In this broadcast, arranged by the British Broadcasting Corporation, 27 November, 1938,[1] Dr Buchman gives content to the revolutionary change required personally, socially and nationally, to bring a permanent answer to world conflict.

THE WORLD TODAY is waiting for guidance. We are now fighting a greater war than any war since the world began. It is not nation against nation, but Chaos against God.

The world today is waiting for the answer.

New men, new nations, a new world—God-controlled. There you have a programme valid for a world crisis.

Valid religious experience has power to change a person, a home, an industry, a nation. Some expression of religious experience greater than ever before must be called into being, something unlimited by our prejudices, far above our personal points of view, something instinctively recognised by everyone as the long hoped for solvent of every problem.

We must rethink and relive our whole conception of religious experience. Much, admittedly, has not been valid experience. Oftentimes it has been religious invalidism—a crass, insipid, dull, tepid, unimaginative maladaptation of what ought to be great life-giving, nation-forming experiences. It has been a warped conception, marred by moral twists. Due to our spiritually poverty-stricken lives, we even glibly admit that business and politics do not mix with religion.

[1] In a series of talks entitled *The Validity of Religious Experience*.

74

We have been so long on the low levels of religious experience that we cannot readily grasp what an Alpine range of experience could be ours if all our thinking, acting and planning were God-controlled and not man-controlled. We need a whole new creative force let loose in the world—a religious experience so dynamic, so wholly adequate that, in the words of Isaiah, 'Nations shall run unto thee because of the Lord thy God.'

President Roosevelt has said, 'I doubt if there is any problem—social, political or economic—that will not melt before the fire of a spiritual awakening.'

Today we drift with the tide instead of creating the experience that will turn the tide. In the recent crisis many people again turned to God. Man's extremity may be God's opportunity. But as an Edinburgh landlady told me, 'It is one thing to pray during the crisis, as hundreds have done. It is another thing so to live that it does not happen again.'

Now, how can we find this new quality of living? How can we capture that spirit that can change the world? It can only come from a genuine religious experience—that is valid for a change of heart, for changed social conditions, for true national security, for international understanding. It is valid because it originates in God, and issues in actual changes in human nature.

To bring such an experience to every citizen is the highest form of national service, and must be our supreme national objective.

Here is work for everyone, everywhere. Our great need today is not to vouch for that validity by argument or explanation, but to demonstrate it by creating new men, new nations, a new world.

We must recapture the power of personal religious experience. Children are born every day. It ought to be just as natural for people to be reborn every day.

Let me quote from the diary of an East London woman, unemployed, but fully employed because she is bringing a religious experience to others. She says:

'For me every day in East London is full. It is wonderful to see the fighting spirit of the people in spite of all the difficulties. I have just been to stay with my mother, who is eighty-six, and my family. When I arrived they were just as curious as they could be to hear about people being reborn every day in East London. My brother, who was a pagan and used to ridicule all I did, said, "After all you have told me I begin to see you are right. I need to be different." His wife was changed the day before I left, and I heard them talking it over before five o'clock in the morning. Now my sister and niece are well on the way to being changed, and also a younger brother and his wife and two sons. The crisis has made many of us women think. Tomorrow night we older women of East London meet, and our guidance is that we talk on how to make every home a centre for Moral Re-Armament.'

That is the work of an unemployed woman. Now listen to her son's diary:

'A barge-builder got changed last week. And last night a fellow from the gas-works. At one meeting there was a milkman, three grocers, two laundry workers, a telephone operator. We have just succeeded in getting a strike settled, and some two hundred men went back to work.'

The work of that mother and son can be a pattern for the nation. It is a pattern which, if multiplied by the thousand, would be an answer to unemployment, for in the divine scheme of things there is no such thing as unemployment. It would make for true equality and brotherhood. If everybody cared enough, if everybody shared enough, wouldn't everybody have enough?

Daily the work of making new men out of old goes on apace. How quickly real spiritual experience can multiply and reach a whole community. Brother speaks to brother and neighbour to neighbour. So the new spirit spreads. Out of one new home can come a hundred new homes.

Changed lives are the true foundation of a new world order. An eminent editor has said that life-changing on a colossal scale is the only hope left for the world today. We know that everything else has failed. Disarmament has failed. The League of Nations has not fulfilled the plan of its designers. Human plans fail in human character. Why not try God's plan? For those of you who are still unconvinced, the thing to do is to try it.

And remember, to be valid, a religious experience must have a moral backbone.

A few weeks ago at Geneva a Foreign Minister[1] told his fellow delegates his experience in difficult political decisions:

'I was recently diplomatic Minister in a country which had a dispute with my own. We lost the case. I was annoyed at the way certain papers reported the affair. The attitude of my country was made to look ridiculous.

'At that time I had been invited to speak at an important dinner in the capital city to which I was accredited. It was suggested that I should speak about this case. At first I resolutely refused. But just before I was about to respond

[1] Dr J. A. N. Patijn, Foreign Minister of the Netherlands.

to the toast, the conviction came to me that I had to refer to the dispute. I complimented my hosts on their success and said that in the future we should be better friends.

'From that day all bitter comments against my country ceased. The fact that I was able to make such a speech was only because of my deep conviction that it was much more in accord with God's Will than the speech which I had previously wished to make.'

Later this Foreign Minister, in presenting his foreign policy to his Parliament, stated:

'We can perceive a new spiritual life in the world, which promises hope for the future. It finds expression in the efforts for Moral and Spiritual Re-Armament.

'The Government shares the wish expressed by several Members of Parliament that these efforts may powerfully penetrate every country without exception. They deserve all support our country can give them.'

He said that of his country. What of ours?

The world is slow to realise that the spiritual is more powerful than the material; that God's plan for the world is infinitely greater and more perfect than any imposed by a government on its people; that what we need is the dictatorship of the Holy Spirit.

Only a great spiritual experience on the part of national leaders of every party, class and creed will ever make any world conference or any League of Nations a workable basis for bringing peace. Such efforts must be God-directed. Mark you, there is no alternative.

We must let the Prince of Peace Himself dictate the programme of peace to men who have learned that the secret of peace lies first in their own hearts, then in their homes. Then they can hope to bring peace in the family of nations.

A peace conference or a League of Nations can only succeed with new men. First we must have new men. New nations will follow naturally and logically. Then we shall have a new world where war shall be no more, where faction shall not rise against faction, class against class, interest against interest, or nation against nation.

Children, too, understand these great truths. A boy of ten in East London says, 'If you want to stop war in the world, stop war in the home.' Ask yourself how many really happy homes you know—and the home is the basis of the nation's life.

Ask youself, 'Is your home governed by a democracy or a dictatorship?' I fear that many, all too many, ardent advocates of democracy reserve for themselves the right to be dictators in their own home. Selfish in the home, they have no constructive programme for a selfish world.

Disunity in the home makes disunity in the nation. Compromise and conflict sap the power of national life. Countless families everywhere, who want peace in the world, are waging a private war of their own, and so are robbing their country of a united effort. Thus democracy, too, misses in practice the experience of a God-led nation.

In industry, oftentimes, the forgotten factor is that God has a plan. And that forgotten factor is the key to every problem that industry faces. Only a new spirit in men can bring a new spirit in industry and create the fair play and efficiency that industry needs. Industry can be the pioneer of a new order.

A Canadian farmer whose crops have failed for eight years —last year through drought, this year through grasshoppers

—says, 'The greatest hardship we can have on our farm would be to get out of touch with God.'

Today one hears too much the voice of man. One is sated with it. One longs again for the Voice of God. Yes, longs for the Voice of God to become the voice of the people, the Will of God the will of the people.

Then a new spirit would sweep all countries, overcome all difficulties, bridge all points of view, conquer all prejudices, enhance all primary loyalties, and give unity to national life. A whole nation can respond to the great essentials. An Oxford shop-girl says, 'What England needs is a Magna Carta inspired by God and signed by everybody'. A valid religious experience would be the foundation stone of the State.

To be valid in these decisive days, our religious experience must once again become a marching, fighting, conquering world force. A mighty change on a colossal scale is the only hope left. This change begins with a change in human nature through Jesus Christ.

New men—new homes—new industry—new nations—a new world.

The world is anxiously waiting to see what Jesus Christ can do in, by, for and through one man wholly given to Him—God-led. You can be that man.

The world is anxiously waiting to see what Jesus Christ can do in, by, for and through one nation wholly given to Him—a nation God-led. It can be your nation.

A nation led by God will lead the world.

LABOUR'S SPIRITUAL HERITAGE

At a luncheon given in honour of Dr Buchman by the National Trade Union Club, London, November, 1938.

I WANT TO SAY at the outset how happy I am to be here today. I am glad I can have the luncheon in this upper room, in these surroundings hallowed by many an hour of the fellowship of those who have the cause of the worker nearest their hearts. You must have hatched out many a plot here! I feel at home with old revolutionaries, like those sitting here, Ben Tillett[1] and Tom Mann. What I like about you men is that you are hard-hitters and square-shooters. You and others here know what it is to face persecution. I am a revolutionary, too, and I know what persecution means. It was during a time of great persecution that God gave this thought to me—'Persecution is the fire that forges prophets'.

The Oxford Group is a revolutionary movement. That is the reason Labour understands it. That is why the Oxford Group understands Labour. They are both out for revolution.

I am talking to men who are authorities in their special subjects, men with vast experience. We can't hope to cover in twenty minutes all the important questions involved. The

---

[1] Ben Tillett, the veteran dockers' leader, became a warm friend. 'I like Frank Buchman,' he said. 'He talks simply. He is a great man because he is a great lover of his fellow men.' When he lay dying, he sent a message to Frank Buchman: 'Tell him to go on fighting. Give him my love and wish him the best of luck. Tell him: You have a great international movement. Use it. It is the hope of tomorrow. It will bring back sanity to the world.'

main point I want to make is that the background we need for solving all these important questions is a new spirit, new men with a new spirit.

Think of the new spirit that Keir Hardie brought into the world of Labour. Think of the debt England and the world owe socially and economically to Keir Hardie.

British Labour was cradled in a spiritual awakening. Who can measure the far-reaching effects in social and economic policy of such an awakening?

We believe in trade revival, in business revival. But there is an even more important factor—and this is the aim of Moral Re-Armament—moral and spiritual revival that leads into a spiritual revolution and a social economic renaissance. As President Roosevelt has said, 'I doubt if there is any problem—social, political or economic—that would not melt before the fire of a spiritual awakening.'

British Labour and Moral Re-Armament have the same birthplace—East Ham. And the same spirit that cradled British Labour has cradled Moral Re-Armament, and it, too, has caught the imagination of the world.

Leaders of British Labour recently wrote in the *Daily Herald:*

'Basically, the world unrest is to be found in the root disease of materialism showing itself in widespread selfishness, fear and greed—not in this nation or that, but in all. We are all guilty. Labour in all countries, if true to its traditions of placing human and spiritual values before material things, can build bridges over national barriers and play a decisive part in the reconciliation of nations.

'It can make such a contribution to world conditions that the voice of faction and self-interest can be effectively dealt with, fear will go and God's great plan for mankind will be revealed and find expression. Such was the dynamic spirit of the early Labour leaders, and it must again be re-created. This is what Moral Re-Armament means for Labour.'

I have known and shared the lot of the working man. My first venture was a home for working boys in an industrial city. I wanted them to have sufficient food and the right surroundings. I began by taking care of a family who had only had one poor room to live in. The father died in the almshouse. The mother was a dipsomaniac. The children were little wild men. School to them was a penalty, and oftentime when I had them safely in school in the morning, by noon they were off again for another three days' holiday. Getting them started in a job didn't interest them, because that meant regular hours at work. For them it was a hardship even to sit down for three meals a day.

In addition I had difficulties with my Board. They did not understand the problems of nutrition and training. We got up against each other and it was then that I learnt that I too, like those children, wanted to have my own way and that the solution of our social problems lay in the human heart. When I changed, I found the spirit of those around me changed. We learnt to pull together. We learnt to unite.

That is the great lesson that Labour can teach the world. After a recent conference with Labour a leader said to me, 'You have given us a new fellowship. It must become the spirit of a world fellowship'.

'What we need is a new unity,' says a friend who is sitting here with the other Labour women today. They as good housewives know what happens when they make jelly. It is the 'jell' that makes the jelly, and every housekeeper knows that the secret is that the jelly must 'jell' to give it consistency and unity. And that is what we need in Britain today. We need to 'jell'. We need the secret of unity.

I have a message today from the President of a CIO union in the steel industry in America. He came over to this country recently to study British Labour. He got a new vision for Labour in America. We have unusual conditions over there. We have a split, a schism. Not all the Labour leaders there see eye to eye! This man's message was that the rival Labour leaders could see eye to eye. They all ought to be different and then they all could get together.

My friend can say things like that, because everyone knows he is doing a good job and not looking for anything for himself. Think of the overhead of such a split in American Labour. Think how it saps our productive energy.

In one country we visited, two political parties openly called each other pickpockets. After our visit the leaders of these two parties got together. A new unity was born and out of it came new policies. The Conservatives became so constructive that the Labour Party passed a vote of confidence in them. The Labour leaders said ,'On this basis we shall have to rethink the philosophy of Labour and build unity.'

The world needs a new moral and spiritual climate. The Oxford Group is a national necessity because it is creating that moral and spiritual climate where people in every party, class and creed can live and work together.

Labour united can unite the nation. Labour led by God can lead the world.

MRA—A NATIONAL NECESSITY

During the winter following the Munich crisis, Britain was awakening to the need for immediate re-armament. In addition, national leaders, concerned with the moral total preparedness of the country, took up the call for Moral Re-Armament. Through a series of statements in the correspondence columns of The Times *and other newspapers, they placed the issue before the country. This call was answered by the Press and by the national leaders in many European countries, in the Dominions and the United States, in the Middle East and in Asia. In a few months the hope contained in the two words 'Moral Re-Armament' caught the imagination of nations and, gathering momentum, circled the world. The following New Year message was given at the request of the British Press Association, January,* 1939.

MRA MEANS personal and national Moral Re-Armament.

MRA is the answer to the dark forebodings and fears for 1939. It is the minimum necessary equipment for the New Year.

MRA is as essential as ARP, and takes away the fear. MRA is a commodity for every householder.

MRA stands for a prejudice-free level of living. It stands for a common denominator of immediate constructive action for everyone, above party, race, class, creed, point of view or personal advantage. It is God's property—the new thinking, the new leadership that everyone wants. It means God in control personally and nationally. It means the knowledge and exact information that God's guidance brings. It is God's gift to bring an insane world to sanity.

MRA means honesty, purity, unselfishness and love—absolutely, personally and nationally. MRA means power to change people—our enemies as well as our friends—the other fellow and the other nation.

MRA is good for everyone, but necessary for us. It will help other nations, but most of all our own and ourselves. It will rearm people and nations against selfish and divisive points of view.

The aim of MRA is twofold: first, to restore God to leadership as the directing force in the life of nations; and then to work for the strengthening of morale within a country and so build a healthful national life.

MRA must go to every heart and home throughout the world.

MRA is a race with time to remake men and nations. It is the ordinary man's opportunity to remake the world.

Note: To the leaders of Nazi Germany Moral Re-Armament appeared as 'the Christian garment for world democratic aims'. The official Gestapo report on the Oxford Group (see Supplement IV, 9) denounces Dr Buchman and the Oxford Group for 'uncompromisingly taking up a frontal position against National Socialism', and states, 'The Group breathes the spirit of western democracy . . . they encourage their members to place themselves fully beneath the Christian Cross, and to oppose the cross of the swastika with the Cross of Christ, as the former seeks to destroy the Cross of Christ.'

REPORT TO
THE NATIONAL PRESS CLUB

In the spring of 1939, Frank Buchman returned to the United States with a force of 130 trained workers from many nations. His aim was to make known the idea of Moral Re-Armament across the whole American continent. Through great assemblies in New York, Washington and Los Angeles, they spoke to the nation, and MRA was carried from coast to coast by press and radio. On the eve of this campaign, Dr Buchman was invited to address the country's leading newspapermen at the National Press Club, Washington, 8 May, 1939.

THREE GREAT TASKS confront this generation. To keep the peace and make it permanent. To make the wealth and work of the world available to all and for the exploitation of none. And with peace and prosperity as our servants and not our masters, to build a new world, create a new culture and change the age of gold into the Golden Age.

Often men have believed they could achieve the Golden Age by their own efforts. But man's wisdom has proved wanting. Today we are at our wit's end. The new world we all long for will not come by our own wisdom, but by obedient co-operation with God in the task of Moral Re-Armament. MRA points the way. It is God's answer to this generation.

What this age needs is a new pattern of democracy, designed by God and worked by everyone.

Let me report to you something of the wide response to

Moral Re-Armament across the Atlantic. A recent remarkable series of letters in the London *Times* and other papers brought it to the attention of Europe. Its urgent need as the strength of national life was stressed in a statement signed by a group of Members of Parliament from different parties:

'Democracy without high character disintegrates. Nor is it enough to be the self-appointed judge of other systems. In an age when lowered moral standards have become a breeding-ground for destructive forces, is it not time for democracy to seek again the sources of her strength, and to demonstrate to the world the power of moral principles? ... A crusade for Moral Re-Armament appears to be spreading rapidly and providing a common meeting-ground in many of the chief storm centres of the world. We believe there would be general agreement among thinking men that something of this kind is generally required ...'

A history-making letter which stirred Europe and which included in its signatories, as an expression from the fighting forces, a Marshal of the Royal Air Force, an Admiral of the Fleet and two Field-Marshals, as well as senior statesmen like Lord Salisbury and Lord Baldwin, contained these words:

'The real need of the day is therefore moral and spiritual re-armament ... A growing body of people in this and other countries are making it their aim ... Were we, together with our fellow men everywhere, to put the energy and resourcefulness into this task that we now find ourselves obliged to spend on national defence, the peace of the world would be assured.

'God's living Spirit calls each nation, like each individual, to its highest destiny, and breaks down the barriers of fear and greed, of suspicion and hatred. This same Spirit can transcend conflicting political systems, can reconcile order and freedom, can rekindle true patriotism, can unite all citizens in the service of the nation and all nations in the service of mankind.'[1]

No world movement can succeed which does not have the support of Labour. Fortunately Moral Re-Armament has this support. The present chairman of the Trades Union Congress, representing five million workers, and three former chairmen, are wholeheartedly back of it. It is the new thinking and the new philosophy that everybody wants. Moral Re-Armament was cradled in East London, birthplace of the British Labour Movement. This is what Tod Sloan says—one of Keir Hardie's old collaborators in the Labour Movement. He describes himself as a 'watchmaker by trade and agitator by nature':

'Here in East London the people are really hungry for a new leadership. They want this new thinking and since Moral Re-Armament came to West Ham it has reached out in all directions, and today there are many homes where whole families are living this quality of life. This to me is the only revolution that matters—the change in human nature—and it does happen.'

My final word comes from a group of your colleagues in Britain—newspaper publishers and editors. Writing in their trade journal the *Newspaper World* they stated their con-

---

[1] The signatories of this letter which appeared in *The Times*, 10 September, 1938, were: Earl Baldwin of Bewdley, the Marquess of Salisbury, Lord Amulree, Field-Marshal Lord Birdwood, Sir William Bragg, the Earl of Clarendon, Admiral-of-the-Fleet the Earl of Cork and Orrery, Lord Desborough, Lord Kennet, the Earl of Lytton, Professor J. W. Mackail, Field-Marshal Lord Milne, Sir David Ross, Viscount Sankey, Lord Stamp, Lord Stanmore, Marshal of the Royal Air Force the Viscount Trenchard.

viction that the programme of Moral Re-Armament is the 'primary condition of national service':

'In this we in the Press, who set so high a store by our traditions of responsible freedom, have a special part to play. This requires of us . . . that we deliberately set ourselves to create and inspire through our newspapers the will to unity and active reconstruction in the nation. This is a practical contribution which we can all make at this time, as well as the best defence of our professional freedom.'

A week later the following response from a group of newspapermen appeared in the same columns:

'We, the undersigned working journalists, all members of the Parliamentary Press Gallery, welcome the letter published by you last week from the representatives of the proprietors' and journalists' organisations, emphasising the decisive part which the Press can play in the moral and spiritual re-armament of the nation.

'We pledge ourselves to work unceasingly for this ideal, and thus build

> 'Bridges from man to man,
> The whole round earth to span.'

BACKBONE OF
THE REAL AMERICA

Moral Re-Armament was launched in Washington at a National Meeting in Constitution Hall, 4 June, 1939.

MRA IS THE TRIUMPH of a God-given thought. It came as the answer to a crisis that threatened civilisation. A re-emphasis of old truths was let loose in the world—simple home-spun truths that have been the backbone of the real America—the guidance of God and a change of heart.

Everyone agreed that these great truths had to be re-captured, relived and restored to authority—truths which, were they practised, would bring the answer. The phrase that riveted itself upon the attention of men and women everywhere was 'Moral and Spiritual Re-Armament.'

Leadership of the future goes to the men of moral courage; the men who ask and give three feet to the yard, sixteen ounces to the pound. As Americans, as patriots, we find that MRA is the common denominator on which everyone can unite. In an age of material perfection we must usher in the age of spiritual force. The Voice of God must become the voice of the people; the Will of God the will of the people. This is the true democracy.

America is not without her problems in business, the home, in industry, in civic and in government life. We need a re-dedication of our people to the elementary virtues of honesty, unselfishness and love; and we must have the will again to find what unites people rather than what divides them. It must become the dawn of a new era, a new age, a new civilisation.

The future depends not only on what a few men may decide to do in Europe, but upon what a million men decide to be in America.

Note: On this occasion, when Moral Re-Armament was launched in Washington, Senator Truman read a message of support from President Roosevelt. Other messages of support to this meeting were also received from 240 Members of the British House of Commons, from a distinguished group of Members of the House of Lords, from British industrial and trade union leaders, and from representatives of Governments and Parliaments in all parts of the world, as well as from many leaders of American life.

Senator Truman's report to Congress on this meeting is given in Supplement IV, 4. In concluding he said, 'It is rare in these days to find something which will unite men and nations on a plane above conflict of party, class or political philosophy. I am sure that I voice the sentiment of all of us here today in expressing gratification at a response so remarkable to a need so urgent, and confidence that America will play her full part in this cause on whose fortunes the future of civilisation must largely depend.'

AN ILLUMINED AMERICA

From a talk to students and faculty at Oglethorpe University, Georgia, June, 1939. On the previous day the University had conferred on Dr Buchman the honorary degree of Doctor of Laws.

AMERICA may not have been moving from war crisis to war crisis, but we have had plenty of economic crises. It seems to many people that we have been moving from depression to depression and from strike to strike. What will happen to America if war comes to Europe?

If, as Emerson suggests, America is God's last chance to make a world, then we have to have a different America. That means different people—new men with a new spirit. An age of speed does not easily lend itself to the creation of great new productive ideas. America today demands everything in tabloid form. It is one of the major products of our bald materialism. Heaven help the man who tries to outline in twenty minutes the new thinking and the new philosophy that everyone needs!

A great new revolution came into my life when I began to listen to God each morning. The danger of our age is that we fail to listen. We talk, talk, talk. The answer is listening— that is the secret. It is open to all.

Everyone wants to illumine America, but so many want to do it without installing an electric light plant. We must get the new spirit through men. Universities hold a key position in bringing this about. The function of universities in a world crisis is to create new men who can fashion the new civilisation.

America needs a challenge to a new national quality of life which will empower her to speak with authority to the world because she has an answer at home. She needs Moral Re-Armament on a large enough scale to bring a new factor into her own life and then to every other nation. We need a new solidarity—national unity with one aim, one mind, one goal. The battle must be won over here, if we are to win the battle 'over there'.

America can give a whole new pattern to civilisation. The time is over-ripe. We must change and give a world-wide message with a national voice.

PREVIEW OF A NEW WORLD

Over 30,000 people crowded the Hollywood Bowl for the Moral Re-Armament 'Call to the Nations' Assembly on 19 July, 1939, and 15,000 had to be turned away.[1]

TONIGHT IS A PREVIEW of a new world—the world of which we have dreamed, and Hollywood is a matchless setting for this preview.

Moral Re-Armament is the ordinary man's opportunity to remake the world. It is a world necessity. It is finding a world response.

The clouds of fear and insecurity hang heavy over the nations. Hate and fear are at work everywhere, undermining confidence, destroying hopes. Leaders and citizens alike, every one of us, are longing for permanent peace.

But longing for peace is not enough. There must be a new spirit. There must be a fight against the causes of conflict, against selfishness, greed and hate. In this battle everyone has a part.

Moral Re-Armament is the scenario of a Golden Age—a God-directed production—a preview of a new world. Holly-

---

[1] The *Los Angeles Times* reported (20 July, 1939), 'They came in limousines. They arrived in jalopies that barely chugged along the traffic-jammed roads leading to the Hollywood Bowl. They came afoot, in wheel-chairs, in buses, taxicabs. One and all, they came marvelling. The Bowl rally brought together all the strength of the vast movement—leaders from Burma, London, East Africa, Australia, China and Japan—and showed 30,000 persons how it might work.'

wood, that goes to every home, can become the sounding board for Moral Re-Armament to the nations.

Look at those four standards. See how they reach up strong, unbroken to the stars. They are the four standards of Moral Re-Armament—absolute honesty, absolute unselfishness, absolute love and absolute purity—personally and nationally. They are the four standards of personal, national and international life.

The Moral Re-Armament of America begins when you and I face them honestly and obey courageously.

MRA will win, because it advances with the strength of a united mind, because it awakens the fire of true patriotism, because it holds the secret of lasting peace.

III

THE OUTBREAK OF WAR

Moral Re-Armament shares equally in importance with material re-armament in these critical days.

THE HON. CHARLES A. EDISON

Secretary of the Navy, Washington, 1940

WE MUST FORGE
NEW WEAPONS

The second World Assembly for Moral Re-Armament met on the eve of war on the Monterey peninsula in California. The failure of human wisdom to find the answer to crisis had been all too clearly demonstrated by the preceding months. There was still time for a solution to be found, but the terms of that solution were inflexible and the causes of war had roots deeply sunk in the lives of nations. Nevertheless there is a certainty which reaches far beyond the immediate crisis, because it is based on eternal values.

Dr Buchman's opening address, 22 July, 1939, follows.

ONE YEAR AGO we met at Interlaken, Switzerland, under the threat of war. The thought that riveted the attention of the world at that time was 'Guidance or Guns'. The intervening months have only served to emphasise the truth of that alternative. It is clearer now than ever before that Moral Re-Armament is the essential foundation for any world settlement.

The next step is for men and women in every nation to enlist in MRA for the duration.

At times of great crisis people just naturally look to God, and they expect their leaders to give them the lead. In a fateful hour when pronouncements are made, men hope against hope that there will be some force at work that will put off what we all deserve.

We are waging the greatest battle of history in this world

99

war against selfishness. We must forge new weapons of warfare. We cannot live on the past. Our weapons of statesmanship seem like relics from the armoury of some illustrious ancestor, which in their day were useful, but now, outmoded, leave us defeated and defenceless. We must have superior forces of spiritual armour. We need for reconstruction the same characteristics that distinguish a great general—the plus of character, the plus that will change the world.

Events are focusing us on the only programme of sane control—God-control. I was called into conference with one of the great world statesmen. He simply said that he was living in an insane world. He began to realise the great truth that the only sane people in an insane world are those guided by God.

We all agree on one thing—that we ought to be different, and that the world ought to be different. If people were different and had the power to change men and nations, that would be the answer to all our problems.

We will find our national security only in Moral Re-Armament. Moral Re-Armament will become the keynote of world reconstruction. The choice is 'Guidance or Guns'. We must listen to guidance or we will listen to guns. The choice is between a vortex of fear and a pageant of triumph.

THE ONE SURE HOPE

The final sessions of the Assembly were held in San Francisco at the World's Fair, and representatives of many nations spoke by radio to the world. On 28 August, 1939, Dr Buchman broadcast to Asia and South America.

THE PERMANENT CURE for crisis can only be found in the fearless application of Moral Re-Armament by the statesmen and the people of all nations. The spirit dominating the counsels of nations provides the one sure hope of a just and lasting settlement.

We need to think not of man's plan, not of this or that nation's plan, but of God's plan. Again we face a time of crisis—crisis that teaches men that man's extremity is God's opportunity.

The Oxford Group is accustomed to crisis, because MRA was born in crisis in the dark days of last year. MRA was born in East London, the cradle of the workers' movement. In twelve months, Moral Re-Armament has girdled the globe and brought the message of constructive answer. It has spread with speed, because it is the fundamental cure for a fundamental disease.

We all look at the headlines. But we can do more than that. Moral Re-Armament is everybody's chance to do something about them. We can look at ourselves and our own nation, and see where we need to be different. For when men change, nations change.

Moral Re-Armament is a world network of hate-free,

fear-free, greed-free people. MRA speaks across frontiers and across barriers of class, race and conflicting political systems. These men and women have sworn an enduring pact with God and with each other to bring their nations into the master pattern of a new world.

Note: Messages to the Assembly were received from political leaders in many countries. Lord Halifax, the British Foreign Secretary, cabled: 'I am glad to add my greetings to those of so many thousands of my countrymen who have joined in the National Message to the World Assembly for Moral Re-Armament. Fresh insistence in thought and action on those principles of morality and faith which are fundamental, will not only build national well-being, but is the only source from which we may draw sure hope for peace and prosperity for a disturbed world.'

THE FORGOTTEN FACTOR

As armed conflict drew inexorably nearer, Frank Buchman clarified in a world broadcast from Boston, on 27 August, 1939, the basic moral issues facing mankind and the one hope of re-creating a new world beyond the oncoming war.

I SPEAK ON BEHALF of those millions, known and unknown, in every country who have found in Moral Re-Armament a common life transcending all the barriers that separate man from man and nation from nation, and who are convinced that Moral Re-Armament is the only permanent cure for crisis.

There is an answer to crisis and it must be made known.

Crisis shows our failure. Before crisis ends in catastrophe, have we the courage to face its real cause? We ourselves are the cause. It is the way every nation and every one of us has been living that has brought us where we are.

Every nation and every individual is responsible for the existing situation.

The failure lies not with one nation, but with all. We are all to blame. For in every nation those forces are at work which create bitterness, disunity and destruction. Nations, like individuals, have turned a blind eye to their own faults while pointing the finger at each other. Selfish men and selfish women make front-line trenches necessary. A wave of unselfishness sweeping through our nation and every other nation would be the permanent answer to war.

We have all wanted peace. We have sought it in pacts, in

leagues, in alliances, in changes of systems, in economic and disarmament conferences, and we have sought in vain. We have wanted peace, but we have never yet paid the price of peace—the price of facing with God where we and our nations have been wrong, and how we and our nation, as God directs, can put wrong right.

A new spirit comes when we make an honest apology for our own mistakes instead of spot-lighting the mistakes of the other nation. There is a common meeting ground in the fact that we all need to change—nations as well as men. In a crisis of this kind, if leaders change, they can change their people. If people change, they can change their leaders.

The crisis is moral and can only be met in the spirit of Moral Re-Armament—the spirit of honesty, justice, and love. Moral Re-Armament means the power to change people—your enemies as well as your friends, the other nations as well as your own. We must be prepared for un-expected paradoxes.

Every man is responsible for his nation. Nations will make honest apologies and rectify past mistakes when the peoples of those nations demand that kind of national policy.

Each man has an immediate part to play. He can accept for himself a change of heart. He can decide to listen to God daily. He can start to build a hate-free, fear-free, greed-free world.

The sacrifice necessary for lasting peace is nothing com-pared with the sacrifice of war.

There is still time for a selfish, fear-driven world to listen to the living God. The forgotten factor in diplomacy is that God has an inspired plan for peace, and the means to carry it out through men and women who are willing to obey.

Above every other loyalty is loyalty to God. In obedience to the God of all peoples every nation will find its true destiny. This is the truest patriotism. It requires the highest courage. It gives the greatest strength.

A nation's surest defence is the love and gratitude of her neighbours. The people of the nations will support to the utmost those statesmen who shall seek in this spirit to avert catastrophe and build that peace without bitterness which all men desire. Will the statesmen and leaders of every nation unite in this programme which puts right the past and reconstructs the future?

The millions who already know these great truths must pass them on to the millions more. If those people who are listening now will ask those millions who are already living Moral Re-Armament how to begin, it will help change the world quickly.

We need now nation-wide thinking and action. We have war because we cannot make peace. We must point to the new era, the new type of personality, the new home, the new industry, the new type of government that, by force of its constructive programme, will outlaw war and industrial unrest. During these days we must develop the framers of the just peace—the peace that will be permanent.

The menace of war makes us rethink all our values. Personal and national surrender to God is a world necessity. Civilisation is at stake.

The future lies with the men and nations who listen to God and obey.

A WORLD PHILOSOPHY
ADEQUATE FOR WORLD CRISIS

Frank Buchman initiated a series of world broadcasts in October, 1939, reaching out to the countries of Europe and Asia across the frontiers of war. Others who spoke with him in this programme included Senator Harry S. Truman, Rear-Admiral Richard E. Byrd, and Mr H. H. Elvin, Chairman of the British Trade Union Congress, 1938. The broadcasts which follow were made from San Francisco and Boston, 29 October, 1939.

I

I AM SPEAKING TODAY to the millions across the world who in these anxious days are increasingly looking to Moral Re-Armament as the one hope for the future. Especially, I am thinking of the men in the front-line trenches, the men faced with the hard realities, the men who know what war is.

Yet where are the front-line trenches today? Today in many countries every civilian carries a gas mask, every garden has its air-raid shelter. It is a new phase in war, where everybody is responsible and every home is a front-line trench.

Our arts of reconciliation have not kept pace with the arts of war. The art of destruction is beginning to outpace the art of living. All our values are slipping as currencies slipped after the last war. As my friend the great Oxford philosopher, Dr Streeter, said, 'A race that has grown up intellectually must grow up morally or perish.'

Today we have reached the parting of the ways. Civilisation, man-controlled, is faced with collapse. The long-endured cycle of moving from crisis to crisis must end. Nations must move beyond crisis to cure.

A new world philosophy is needed, a world philosophy capable of creating a new era of constructive relationships between men and nations. A new statesmanship and a new leadership will ensue from this heightened quality of thinking and living.

This world philosophy will emerge as people begin to get their direction from the living God. It will be within the framework of a hate-free, fear-free, greed-free quality of living.

Think of the cost of hate, fear and greed. Millions of men and women must carry gas-masks today because men the world over have been living behind masks for years. Millions of men and women must grope through darkened cities because the nations have been living in a spiritual blackout. Millions of men and women today must listen to air-raid warnings because nations have not listened to the Voice of God in days gone by.

Times of crisis reveal the bankruptcy of our thought and action. Then we resort to feverish improvisation and expediency. Sheer economy of time and energy, and ultimate bankruptcy may force us to God-control.

Man today is ready to believe that human wisdom has failed. A situation is growing up in which people will want God to speak to them. They will have nothing else between themselves and desperation, as they read the changing, chimerical headlines that no one wants. Men need some adequate voice to interpret and mould events. Expediency must be supplanted by guidance. And dark nights of waiting may prove a blessing in disguise, for guidance is a staple necessity that is not rationed.

The world is awaiting an answer. War is the price of the selfishness of nations. We must have some simple, workable answer available for everyone, and one that can be applied by all. We need people trained not only to make an adequate peace, but also to keep it. Most people are selfish enough to want a peace that permits them to wage their own private wars and foster their own petty indulgences. An American housewife asks, 'Who is responsible for the selfishness and greed in America today? Is it business, or labour? Or is it Mr and Mrs America in a million homes all over the country?'

Without the rise of a new spirit we shall pay heavily for our selfishness. An Army general said to me recently, 'Either I sacrifice my selfishness for the sake of my nation, or I sacrifice my nation for the sake of my selfishness.' And either we sacrifice our national selfishness for the sake of the world, or we sacrifice the world for the sake of our national selfishness.

The chief sin is that we have no adequate philosophy for life. Our conception of living is wrong—easy, soft, protective, indulgent. We need a whole new content and conception of life. The brains and the thinking of the world must have been sabotaged and squandered for a very long time to create such destruction of men and nations. I am reminded of Generalissimo Chiang Kai-shek's forceful phrase, 'If we perspired more in time of peace, we should bleed less in time of war.'

We have tried thinking and living as we want. Now try

thinking and living as God wants. Try living as we want the other fellow to live. Try living as we want the other nation to live. Then our nation will be the spearhead of a new world order.

We need a whole new level of thinking about peace. If peace had demanded as much of us as war, war would have been outlawed long ago.

The world must declare a moratorium on hate and fear, personally and nationally. We cannot make peace between the nations when the people in the nations are in a state of permanent personal warfare. Strikes, labour difficulties and war are inevitable until we change our whole thought and quality of living.

The new peace pact must have as its preamble that all contracting parties, all nations, live on the basis of no hate, no fear, no greed. Someone must always *make* peace. For peace is not an idea; it is people becoming different. Most of us want to make peace by repenting of the other fellow's sins. That is how the world would like to do it. But we cannot permanently go on expecting other nations to repent first. The MRA way is to start by being different yourself.

The necessary prelude to this happier pact is, that every individual, in every nation, begins that new quality of living now and does not postpone it for some future armistice. Then we shall be true patriots. Then there will be law and order in Europe and the world, within your hearts and within the boundary of your nation. Then we shall be able to say, 'Behold how these nations love one another.'

Children see these great truths. I quote from a letter sent me by two children who listen to God each morning with their father and mother. Kennie, aged eleven, says, 'It is now our chance in America. I know how wars start. I used to fight with my sister. It began with arguing and disobeying God's orders and His four standards. Love from Kennie.'

Here is his sister Anne's letter, 'If we want to change the world, we will have to do what God tells us, or He won't give us power to do it. You must start obeying your parents when you are a child, and the four standards. Everybody ought to obey them, even children if they want to change their country. We ought to start now. If we don't, after the war everybody will want their own way. God is the only person who can give us power, and we can get it if we want to.'

My only comment is, 'A little child shall lead them.'

The secret lies in listening to God. Men, unaided, cannot make peace. We must begin to develop the framers of the just and lasting peace of the future—the spiritually rearmed everywhere to be the pacemakers for the peacemakers of tomorrow.

A word of gratitude must go to the men in every nation who have responded to MRA, for what has been accomplished, and for the far-reaching service they have been able to render. These people, far-visioned and sagacious, see that MRA is the highest patriotism.

Moral Re-Armament is bringing a new force into play, an indispensable force necessary for the life of every nation. Moral Re-Armament will be the focal point for the new national unity where God is the constant and final arbiter in every conflict. A truly united nation comes from a directing God. This philosophy will become the mainspring of the spirit of the nation, the magnet that will draw all positive forces together. It will give a new unity to Capital and Labour and bring the answer to industrial conflict and unrest.

It will give the answer to war in the home and to war in the world. It will train that leadership which is adequate for the gigantic work of reconstruction, to rebuild a world which today stands on the brink of ruin.

II

AS I AM SPEAKING HERE, within a fraction of a second I can reach my friends in many countries, my friends in the front-line trenches, the men in the lonely outposts whose only touch with the outside world is through the friendly radio beam which meets all alike, my friends in the far Nordic North, on India's North-West Frontier, on the African Veldt, in far-off Australia and New Zealand, in the Dutch East Indies and the farthermost corners of the earth.

We accept as a commonplace a man's voice carried by radio to the uttermost parts of the earth. Miracles of science have been the wonder of the age. But all those miracles have not brought peace and happiness to our homes and nations. A miracle of the spirit is what we need.

This miracle is undoubtedly the divinely appointed destiny of mankind. Who can believe less than that? Its advent depends on and awaits the emergence in every country of firm and resolute God-guided men, with all the conviction, fire and fervour of early Christians. Their ever-widening influence would be invincible. A new national spirit would soon be born, a new co-operative relationship between the nations, if in every country there would arise a new leadership, free from the bondage of fear, rising above personal and national ambition and responsive to the direction of God's will.

Such a philosophy has been stated as the historic basis for nationhood by the prophets of old and has withstood the test of centuries. The prophet Isaiah says, 'And all thy children shall be taught of the Lord and great shall be the peace of thy children . . . Nations that knew not thee shall run unto thee because of the Lord thy God.'

The man charged with the foreign affairs of a great nation has said that what we need today are men of the type of the prophet Amos. British labour leaders in conference sent a message on MRA to the American capital with these words, 'We need men who will make real the vision of the prophet Micah.'

Moral Re-Armament is recapturing, re-vitalising, re-living the message of the prophets. It is tried. It is true. It is tested.

Television points to a great truth. The ordinary man and the statesman must discover its counterpart—guidance—on the spiritual plane. Just as television is that space-conquering vision on the material plane, so guidance is the far-seeing perception on the spiritual. It is limited only by our capacity for disciplined obedience.

Guidance is when we are in communication with God. The first step in reorientating our minds to God is to listen twice as much as we talk. This is a simple programme of how to begin. Yet here lies the strategy to win the world from her egocentric ways. For immediately self is the centre of the picture, there war has begun, whether in individuals or in nations. Fear is another kind of guidance. People are afraid, and so they will not fight the daily battle against selfishness.

Guidance is an absolute necessity and the irreducible minimum to keep millions spiritually and physically alive. It is the nation's life blood. Without it nations perish. Statesmen living this quality of life will make it possible for the Mind of God to become the mind of nations. Through lack of this quality in their statesmanship, nations sell their birthright. 'If we are not governed by God, we will be ruled by tyrants,' said William Penn.

MRA is the great central revolutionary force. I was personally at war. An experience of the Cross made me a new type of revolutionary.

We are waging the greatest battle of history in this world war against selfishness. Every man to his guns! We must call out the moral and spiritual forces. We need to live a quality of life that will change masses of people. It is because we had no such adequate action during the last decades that we are compelled to make the costly sacrifice of war. The way to outlive the forces of destruction is to build better and more wisely than we are building now.

God has a programme adequate for the world and for each nation, a programme that provides inspiration and liberty for all and anticipates all other political programmes. Our aim should be that everyone has not only enough of the necessities of life, but that he has a legitimate part in bringing about this Moral Re-Armament and so safeguards the peace of his nation and the peace of the world. Thus each individual who has enlisted in this programme can find a job he can do that will affect the civic, industrial and national welfare.

We need a national mobilisation for unemployment on the same scale and carried out with the same personal care that the warring nations have given to everyone who needed to be taken to a place of safety. The unemployed must have the safety and security which comes from knowing that they are needed and that there is a job for them to do. Thus each nation can use all its resources and find its truest security.

Our instant need is for millions to plan for the new world —not only a few statesmen meeting, but the united forces of the world backed by daily living and action that will support them in waging the eternal war against selfishness. Then we can begin to approximate to what is needed.

A national labour leader had the vision of a ten million membership for his organisation. Surely the united forces of reconstruction in the world can think in terms of a hundred million taking their orders from the living God. Thus they will have an advanced knowledge of tactics and a programme that will move men's hearts radically to alter their thinking and living. They will be an incomparable, unconquerable, irresistible army.

Think of the vast forces available—Catholic and Protestant, Jew and Gentile. Think of the spiritually rearmed everywhere who may be the pacemakers for the peacemakers of tomorrow. MRA is open to all and bars none. It is a quality of life. You don't join and you can't resign. You live a life.

The call is to everyone, the ordinary man and the statesman, unitedly to carry the burdens of their country. Responsibility has too often been delegated to the few in the belief that the statesman is expected to do the thinking, planning and living that must become the concern of every man.

We must remake the world. The task is nothing less than that. Every man, woman and child must be enlisted, every home become a fort.

A world philosophy will be brought to power through the cumulative effect of millions of people beginning the experience of listening to God. True, it may be only an initial experience. Enlistment does not immediately make the trained soldier, but we can all begin.

Now is the time to enlist for the duration in this world war against selfishness. We must be fighters ever!

We stand at zero hour on the threshold of a new world order.

Note: Rear-Admiral Richard E. Byrd, the explorer and Commanding Officer of the United States Antarctic Expedition, took part in this broadcast on the eve of his departure for the Antarctic. He said: 'I went exploring because I was fired by those pioneers of history who felt the urge of charting uncharted seas and discovering unknown places. However, today in the crisis which threatens to destroy freedom and civilisation, the most important pioneering to be done is in the realm of the spirit.

'A country's first line of defence is the character of her citizens. Character cannot be taken for granted. If we are going to preserve freedom, it has to be battled for by every man, woman and child— every day and every generation.

'The building of character is Moral Re-Armament. That is the fight of America and of the world. That is the only armament that can stop armament for destruction. On the eve of my departure for the Antarctic I want to say that I believe that this way lies the hope for peace.

'Moral Re-Armament, the fight for a new world, strong, clean, united, should fire the hearts of all red-blooded citizens and stir their wills to action.'

LISTENING MILLIONS

Over the week-end of December 1st, 2nd and 3rd, 1939, through a world-wide series of broadcasts, millions listened to the programme of Moral Re-Armament. On 2 December, Dr Buchman summarised the events in a short-wave broadcast:

I AM VERY GLAD to be able to greet the many listeners, known and unknown, throughout the world who are taking part in this historic December weekend.

Think of the far-flung network of listeners in this and every land—statesmen, Labour leaders, businessmen, sportsmen and workmen, men of vision, united in a common purpose for a common cause. Think what it may mean for world reconstruction—people united in the realisation that human wisdom has failed and that human expediency must be supplanted by divine guidance.

Lord Athlone yesterday in a prophetic broadcast from London gave an inspired lead.[1] In this country we heard the veteran leader of the House of Representatives, Speaker Bankhead, who voiced for America in a moving and dynamic way the ageless truth which Lord Athlone voiced for Britain. The Speaker said: 'I am glad tonight to inaugurate in the Americas the programme for this first week-end of December, when people throughout the world will hear the challenge of Moral Re-Armament.'

After speaking of the new spirit arising in the nation's capital and throughout America, he continued:

[1] See Supplement IV, 5.

'We stand today at a decisive moment in history. Forces of unmeasured strength are on the march. Is there a force which can rally the recuperative powers of mankind and win the race with chaos? There is a force which can outmarch all others and which, if we will, can shape the future. It is the mighty onslaught of a new spirit challenging men and nations to a change of heart. It is the cumulative effect of millions of people who listen to God and obey. Where we have been true to this spirit, man has prospered; where we have neglected it, nations have declined. Now is our chance to re-create for ourselves and for our children the way of true patriotism—the way of Moral Re-Armament. So prepared, we can decide aright the fateful issues of the hour.'

Would that television, with its all-conquering miracle, could have unlimited scope and that each one of you might see before you the moving pageant of the men and women listening throughout the nations today.

In Great Britain alone, I understand, no fewer than 25,000 listening parties have been arranged. Lord Mayors, Lord Provosts, Mayors and Provosts of over five hundred cities, representing more than half the population of Britain, have issued a united call for Moral and Spiritual Re-Armament to their people.

Similar response comes from the British Dominions beyond the seas and from the outposts of Empire. In our great neighbour to the north, there is Dominion-wide interest. The Mayor of Toronto with his fellow Canadian Mayors has issued a proclamation for Moral Re-Armament which is being broadcast throughout the land.

What will be the response of Canada's listening millions? Lady Minto, wife of a great Governor-General of Canada, whose sister the Dowager Countess of Antrim is speaking today from England, has pointed to Canada's future in these prophetic words, 'Canada, united under the Dominion of God, has an historic opportunity to lead the Empire and the nations into the spacious freedom of a world at peace within itself.'

In Holland people have gathered through all the Provinces to listen. There are listening groups in offices and factories, homes and churches. They have taken as their theme, 'National rebirth to become reconcilers of nations.' In Amsterdam, Catholic and Protestant members of Parliament and civic leaders have taken Holland's largest hall so that all unitedly may listen. Later in this hour you will hear the messages not only from the mother country Holland, but from her possessions across the seas where they, too, are listening.

All through these days the Scandinavians have been preparing on a nation-wide scale to have their share in this programme. Everywhere people will be listening, men who have been in the forefront of the cultural renaissance, Labour leaders, authors, businessmen, editors and housewives.

Here I would like to quote a message from the women of Finland, who, inspired by the lead of the Finnish President's wife, recently issued a call for Moral Re-Armament. They said, 'In this way we can, with our own lives, build and fortify our contry's unity and power. It is to this mobilisation that we now call every woman. We, our people, the Nordic North, all the nations of the world, must return to listening to and obeying the living God.'

Those of you who now sit in the comfort of your homes and still enjoy a measure of security must begin to plan to do something adequate to meet the critical situation in your own national life before it is too late. We must give to nations this new weapon of guidance and direction which listening to God brings. The security of a nation is grounded in the strength of her listening people.

In Switzerland, that country great in the spirit of liberty and independence, assemblies of people of different races and languages are taking part in this programme all over the country. A young Swiss, a front-line fighter, whose work for MRA has received national recognition, sends the following:

'The reconstruction of a new Europe is possible only with a realistic knowledge of the problems which are bringing about the death of the old Europe. The future of the world lies in the hands of men of action who give themselves to realise concretely the creative thoughts they receive from the living God.'

In France groups of listeners are meeting in city and village, farm and factory. Political leaders and authors through the newspapers and through radio are calling the people of the French Empire to listen. They ask that all be thankful for what has been received through their Christian civilisation and for what their forefathers and country have given them. They call for an inventory of failures and of gifts, and ask their people to consider each individual's responsibility in bringing about the Moral Re-Armament of their country.

China, land of the teeming millions with their indomitable spirit, is taking part. Three radio stations are broadcasting the message of Moral Re-Armament in Chinese and English. They are planning for the news of MRA in all the great Chinese and English dailies. Posters and pamphlets in Chinese and English are having wide distribution.

These precious moments on the air are all too few and forbid me to take you to all the farthest corners of the earth.

I would just like to give you a picture of what is happening in two American cities—one is San Francisco, the city of the Golden West, where three of these broadcasts have originated, the influence of which has gone throughout the world. The three-day observance was inaugurated in San Francisco at twelve noon on the steps of the City Hall. San Francisco's five local stations also carried their own MRA programme with businessmen, doctors, columnists, shipyard workers and employers among the speakers.

In Los Angeles, Senator Harry S. Truman of Missouri and Mayor Bowron inaugurated that city's part in the programme. The Mayor, who had earlier issued a proclamation, introduced Senator Truman's broadcast. All over America, from coast to coast, people are part of this world audience.

Morally and spiritually, we must enlist and mobilise vast armies of people who are conscious of God as the directing force for their own and for their nation's life. We must rally the forces of right for a great positive constructive advance. The spirit that refuses to hate when men are hateful. The spirit that is just when others are unjust. The spirit that is unselfish when others are selfish. These are the men that can be used by the Prince of Peace to make peace.

Today we are thinking more especially of those for whom this is an initial enlistment and who have yet to learn the discipline necessary to make the answer effective in these fateful days. We are thinking, too, of those who in sheer desperation are crying out, 'Everything else has failed. Why not try God?'

This is the era of the ordinary man—like you and me—

millions of us, a great world family of listeners, remakers of the world.

'Today,' in the words of British civic leaders,[1] 'when our whole world is threatened with ruin, we feel more urgently than ever before the need for that new force of Moral Re-Armament which can create a new world, a world of sanity and order, of plenty and of peace. Amid the failure of human wisdom, there is still one Supreme Source from whom all can draw new power, new hope, new illumination. God speaks directly to the heart of every man and every woman who is prepared to listen and obey.'

George Washington listened at a time of conflict, and gave a nation freedom.

Benjamin Franklin listened at a time of chaos, and brought a nation order.

Abraham Lincoln listened at a time of crisis, and preserved a nation's unity.

Will you listen today?

---

[1] The Civic Heads of 550 cities and towns in Great Britain issued this call for Moral Re-Armament in December, 1939. The *Call to Our Citizens* was broadcast to the nation and Commonwealth by the Earl of Athlone, K.G. (See Supplement IV, 5.)

THE RISE OF A NEW SPIRIT

On the home front in Britain, and in America, fast becoming 'the arsenal of democracy', Moral Re-Armament brought new strength and laid constant emphasis on the basic moral and spiritual issues of the struggle. Frank Buchman saw clearly his own country's needs and threw himself into the battle to meet them. Again and again, as in this New Year message for 1940, his speeches recalled the nation to the sources of her greatness and the faith of her democracy.

The effects of this programme were felt at crucial points in America's war effort as Frank Buchman and his fellow workers dramatised their message on platform and stage, over the radio and through MRA Training Centres and industrial Round Tables from coast to coast in the United States and Canada. Their emphasis on the forgotten moral and spiritual factors began to change stubborn industrial situations.

FOR AMERICA this year is a year of destiny. We have the opportunity of giving the pattern for a new world.

Our task is to enlist everyone in America's war—the war for industrial co-operation and national unity.

Nothing less than this must be our aim. No human plan is adequate for so immense a task. The one essential is the enthronement of a new spirit that will make a new world possible.

In this decisive year we must forge an irresistible force that will change the course of history. Is that America's destiny? Will America be the builder of the foundations for a new world? We have energy, we have resources, we have men. Our one need is the rise of a new spirit—a spirit above party, class, race, point of view or personal advantage. With this new spirit we can build a pattern of industrial co-operation and national unity that will challenge the world and show a way out of confusion.

Men of vision must give a lead. The morally re-armed everywhere will give their support. In home and farm, business and workshop people are awakening to the simple standards of honesty, unselfishness and faith which made our country great. In Moral Re-Armament everyone has a part.

We face either the decline of nations *or* the rise of a new spirit. There is no other alternative. To this task of Moral Re-Armament we dedicate ourselves with all those who would build a new world—united, strong and free.

Note: Gould Lincoln, the Washington columnist, wrote in the Washington *Star*, 1 December, 1942: 'In the United States, long before this country became involved in the conflict, Dr Buchman and his group sought to lay the foundation in home and factory for the tremendous task that inevitably lay ahead.' He went on to quote a tribute from leading Members of Congress of both parties, who said, 'Three years ago there was launched a nation-wide programme of Moral Re-Armament, the value of which was publicly recognised by leaders throughout the country. Since that time the spirit of this patriotic crusade has run like a flame throughout the English-speaking world. It is stimulating personal self-sacrifice, industrial co-operation and national unity so vital to our Allied cause.'

See also article in *The Army and Navy Journal*, Washington, May, 1944, reproduced in Supplement IV, 7.

MORAL RE-ARMAMENT AND NATIONAL DEFENCE[1]

During the war, the work of Moral Re-Armament advanced to a great extent within national boundaries. At the same time, men in the armed forces carried MRA around the world and linked countries and continents together. Later they were the first to re-open the countries of Europe and Asia, and the first to make contact with those who had kept the flame alive throughout the years of war and occupation. Many gave their lives on the field of battle and in the resistance movements. Many won the highest decorations for valour. All found in Moral Re-Armament not only the strength to sustain them in battle, but the hope that they would one day build the world for which they fought.

I AM DELIGHTED to be able to speak to the world-wide family of Moral Re-Armament and to thank you, wherever you are listening, for the good wishes and all the warmth of the greetings which have been coming in from all parts of the world.

We are gathered here from all sections of the United States in this most beautiful city of San Francisco. How I wish every one of you could share with me to the full in the beauty of this place and the happiness of this day.

Two years ago many of us were together in London when Moral Re-Armament was launched. What miracles God has wrought through that group gathered there. Twelve months ago we were in the nation's capital, in Washington. Then we

[1] Broadcast to Asia, Africa, South America and Europe, 4 June, 1940.

spoke to each other in Washington and London, back and forth across the Atlantic. And now in San Francisco I am speaking to you from the heart of the American family of Moral Re-Armament.

In the light of world events all of us must reorientate our thinking. It is imperative that we make certain now that the things we hold dear today will stand the test of tomorrow. Crisis draws us closer together. Every patriot wants to see his country strong and her defences adequate for national safety and security.

The nations need a new kind of defence. The call of the hour is a call to strength. Mr Edison, Secretary of the Navy, whose mother is speaking on this programme with me today, said recently:

'There is one ingredient in national defence that transcends all others. It is born of the hearts of our people and it may be called National Character.

'Without character and a deep-seated moral armament bred into the fibre of our citizens, no matter in what walk of life they may perform their civil tasks, there will be little worth defending.

'The Navy is responsible for the training, welfare and discipline of its personnel. But these are few. A hundred and thirty-seven million others must know why their country lives and is worthy of living.

'To build a citizenry whose roots are deep in the finer traditions of our land—to form a National Character that may some day lead the world back from chaos—to make our country impregnable both from within and without— is not the job of the Navy, it is yours.'

Mr Edison further says, 'Moral Re-Armament shares

equally in importance with material re-armament in these critical days.' He has voiced the real task that faces all of us. It is the conquest of materialism within our borders and within ourselves.

Men's minds are swinging away from the old, selfish, short-sighted materialism that is everywhere proving inadequate in time of stress. Moral Re-Armament is giving them the answers. With lightning speed within the past two years it has girdled the world and brought a new pattern and a new hope to a disillusioned age. Materialism is our great enemy. It is the chief 'ism' we have to combat and conquer. It is the mother of all the 'isms'. There is the battleground. There the warfare must be waged so that we can firmly establish those homely truths of honesty, unselfishness and obedience to God that are the hallmarks of personal and national sanity.

The great Catholic journal and organ of the Vatican, *Osservatore Romano*, after describing the response to Moral Re-Armament in many countries, calls the movement 'a powerful help in the Pope's daily efforts to recall souls and the world to the virtues of the Gospels'. Another Catholic journal, *Italia*, in an article on Moral Re-Armament, states:

'The problem is now to redirect the thinking of all people, to inspire them again with the conviction that God is a living and active force in the midst of us, to persuade them that machinery, technical knowledge, organisation, excellent in themselves, are incapable of solving our problems.'

This is the battle of Moral Re-Armament. Without the conquest of materialism, our nations will decay from within while we prepare to defend ourselves against attack from without.

Materialism and atheism are breeding grounds for corruption, anarchy and revolution. These have their allies in the selfishness that rules our homes, the bitterness that separates class from class, and the spirit of faction that divides a nation.

Here lies our instant danger. If we are fully to understand where our true security lies, we must look to our moral and spiritual defences. Then we must act, resolutely and intelligently to establish those defences.

America must be prepared. But America's security lies not only in planes and ships and tanks, but in men prepared morally and spiritually to make the nation strong. This is our first and foremost need.

A senior Army officer said recently on the radio:

'In recent months I have observed the growth of a remarkable spirit on the West Coast. It is a spirit which is uniting conflicting groups, which is giving to the ordinary individual American a new importance in the light of world affairs, a new sense of participation in his own nation's life. Moral Re-Armament, as it has been called, has spread from man to man, from family to family, and from community to community with such speed and with such effectiveness that it promises to play a major part in the national defence of this country.'[1]

True preparedness—the result of a nation morally re-armed—is the responsibility of every citizen. Everyone must

---

[1] This philosophy was emphasised in the MRA national defence handbook, *You Can Defend America*, with its foreword by General Pershing, of which 1,350,000 copies were circulated in the United States. It was also dramatised in the war revue, *You Can Defend America*, which was shown in twenty States before 250,000 people at the invitation of Governors, Legislatures, Mayors, Defence Councils, industrial and labour leaders. (See Supplement IV, 7.)

take a part in the moral defence of the country. That is our privilege in America—every man bearing his part, every man an essential link in an impregnable line of defence, every home a fort, every worker employed in producing the moral armaments without which democracy must perish from within.

But we are in danger of defaulting on our American tradition. We are failing to bring to our nation today the reality of the importance of every citizen, a reality that gives power and the answer to frustration, personally, domestically, socially, nationally and supernationally. Because every citizen does not feel he has this answer, he delegates the responsibility to the few in the hope that they will have it. Because of our selfishness and our low level of living we delegate to others what should be our own responsibility, and hope that if we give them a large enough appropriation they will accomplish what is necessary for the nation.

It is not enough to understand our danger. It is not enough to say that we need a spiritual offensive against the forces of materialism. The average businessman freely admits that what America needs today is a moral and spiritual awakening. But he quickly adds, '*That* is the business of our religious leaders.' True, but it must *also* be the religion of our business leaders.

We have had gods in business, but they have sometimes been false gods. One of them has been materialism. An important business magazine points out that unless we listen to the Voice of God materialism will engulf us:

'There is only one way out. The sound of a Voice coming from something not ourselves, in the existence of which we cannot disbelieve. Without it we are no more capable of saving the world than we were capable of creating it in the first place.'

But who is to listen to this Voice and become the herald of a new world? Why not the editor? Why not the readers?

Our leaders say that we need a moral and spiritual awakening. Yes, we agree. And we also need a moral and spiritual awakening in our leaders.

The eleventh hour has struck for America. America can no longer be lulled into a false sense of security by dreaming of the sweet by-and-by. We must face the nasty now-and-now. We must plan nationally for the moral and spiritual defence of the nation to create industrial co-operation and national unity.

The country that does not have national unity is licked from the start. We must set up a non-stop assembly line for creating national character. We must break the bottleneck of confusion and division and anticipate the strategy of subversive forces. With the same speed and efficiency that we plan for the production of aeroplanes, we must also plan for the production of men of character.

What if, in an age of force, Moral Re-Armament should be that super-force—the force of an all-powerful God working through men—that will order and rebuild the world?

What would it mean for America to rearm morally? It would mean the uniting of our nation in every part of its life on a constructive plan. We need to find once again the power of a united mind. We must leave our causes, many of them excellent causes, and find this common cause. We shall find the force that will forge amiable individualists into a united nation.

This will come as we set ourselves to eliminate conflict.

Our present policy is, 'Out with anyone with whom we don't agree.' The MRA policy is, 'All of us change and find a new level of working together.' God must be the Arbiter in every conflict whether industrial, national or international. Suppose the foreign policy of nations were based on this thought, 'Let him that is without blame amongst you cast the first stone.'

Try honest apology and find honest peace, in your home, office, city, state and nation. Some of you will try it in your homes and like it so much that you will want to take it to your office. Others will try it out in your offices and find it works so well you will take it back to your homes.

This new spirit which has the answer to conflict in homes, industries and nations is the essential factor in building America's unity.

Our task is to set our own house in order. We waste energy and time trying to persuade the other person and the other nation to change first. We generate so much steam in the process that we become almost apoplectic in our righteous indignation. But events do not change, other nations do not change, because we do not change. So much of our steam never gets to traction.

The task is enormous. We need a super-force adequate to change men and nations. If we have learnt one thing from 1940 it is this, that if we do not listen to guidance, we must listen to guns. The tragic truth becomes more urgent than ever. We must bring the supernatural God to the man in the street. The man in the street must recapture and relive the experience of a supernatural power.

What does it mean to listen to guidance? The prophets of old knew. They listened and they gave their rulers specific direction in national and foreign affairs. They warned about treaties. They warned about invasions. They gave the rulers insight to anticipate disaster.

The fathers of our country knew what it meant to listen to guidance and to obey.

Said William Penn, 'Men must be governed by God, or they will be ruled by tyrants.'

Divine Providence was a reality in their daily lives. That early Cabinet made it the keystone of our Declaration of Independence when they wrote, 'With a firm reliance on the protection of Divine Providence, we mutually pledge to each other our lives, our fortunes and our sacred honour.' They founded a nation. Today we need a rebirth of this spirit, if we in our time are to unite our nations.

Abraham Lincoln knew the secret of God-control. He wrote, 'If it were not for my firm belief in an over-ruling Providence, it would be difficult for me in the midst of such complications of affairs to keep my reason in its seat. I have so many evidences of God's direction that I cannot doubt this power comes from above. I am satisfied that when the Almighty wants me to do or not to do any particular thing, He finds a way of letting me know it.'

The greatest men of our past knew that God-control was the only adequate programme for a nation. Their experience can be our experience. Definite direction, accurate information can still come from the Mind of God to the mind of man. It can come to our nation as men and women everywhere listen to God and obey, as they learn to plot their own course and their nation's course by the four compass points of MRA—honesty, purity, unselfishness and love. But everyone must listen, every last man, in every last place, in every last situation. Not the religious leaders alone, but the business leaders, the cultural leaders, the national leaders.

A listening nation is a secure nation. The only true security is God's power working through the people who obey Him.

Any man can begin today to listen to God. Any man can begin today to bring a new spirit to his home, his city and his nation. The greatest revolution of all time whereby the Cross of Christ will transform the world is enlisting men today. The condition of the world makes it imperative that we enlist now, and to this task we mutually pledge to each other our lives, our fortunes and our sacred honour.

A TRAINED FORCE

Philadelphia, 4 June, 1941

THE AIM OF MORAL RE-ARMAMENT is a nation fortified against attack from within and without. It is a national
necessity.

Moral Re-Armament is a message of the highest patriotism.
It gives every American the chance to play his part.

Moral Re-Armament creates the qualities that make democracy function. It is simple, non-partisan, non-sectarian, non-
political. It gives to every man the inner discipline he needs
and the inner liberty he desires. It calls out and combines the
moral and spiritual responsibility of individuals for their
immediate sphere of action.

It builds for democracy an unshakeable framework of
actively selfless and self-giving citizens, whose determination to bring unity cannot be altered by any beckoning of
personal advantage and who know how to pass along to
others their panic-proof experience of the guidance of God.

The work of Moral Re-Armament to heighten public
morale and strengthen the community's moral fibre is carried
forward by meetings, radio broadcasts, patriotic dramatisa-
tions, books and literature, and by Round Tables where, in
an atmosphere of mutual trust, Labour and Management sit
down together and find the solution to their problems.

Those working with Moral Re-Armament have volun-
teered for this far-reaching patriotic service. Some have been

serving ever since the last war. They possess a special training which they are giving to our nation gladly, freely and not without sacrifice.

The morally re-armed have learned to live under a crisis-proof, fear-free discipline. They are a panic-proof, single-minded and intelligent trained force at the disposal of all who put their country before selfish interest.

These men are true fighters—patriots who have been fighting daily over long periods to bring this needed boon to our nation at a time when hostility piles up between nation and nation, labour and capital, class and class. They are out to break the bottleneck of confusion and division and to antici-pate the strategy of the subversive forces.

The crucial importance of morale has been forcibly brought home to us by the example of Europe, and has been increasingly emphasised in this country by all our national leaders. In showing the essential place of Moral Re-Armament as an effective morale-builder, the Hon. Harry S. Truman of Missouri, Chairman of the Senate Committee for the Investigation of the National Defence Programme, has pointed out:

'I have felt a fresh certainty about the safety and security of America because of the evidence everywhere I go of the spread of Moral Re-Armament. This spirit of true patriotism is solving the internal discord that threatens our national life more seriously than any foreign power.'[1]

---

[1] See also Senator Truman's statement in Philadelphia, 19 November, 1943. (Supplement IV, 6.)

REMAKERS OF THE WORLD

A Christmas Message

MAY THE CHRIST CHILD bring us the birth of a new thinking at this Christmas time and usher in the new world that the statesman and every man want. We need a fourth-dimensional thinking—a gift from God—that will lighten our darkness and bring a speedy answer.

Wise men came from afar, guided by a Star, at that first Christmas. May each one of us, illumined from afar, bring a gift to all mankind that will be more acceptable than any earthly reward.

Trials and tribulations are the furnace which forges prophets. May we have the courage to accept the gift of this fourth-dimensional thinking for which God has prepared us with a common unity of mind to become the remakers of the world.

Ours is the eternal unity of being guided by a Star to give to every man and the statesman the gift of a new world.

> O Holy Child of Bethlehem,
>   Descend to us, we pray;
> Cast out our sin and enter in,
>   Be born in us today.
> We hear the Christmas angels
>   The great glad tidings tell;
> O come to us, abide with us,
>   Our Lord Emmanuel!

IV

DEMOCRACY'S INSPIRED IDEOLOGY

At this hour when humanity is given one last chance to unite and so answer the split atom, Moral Re-Armament is raising up a world force and a world philosophy adequate to reshape our times. I draw strength and hope from the evidence of a new spirit spreading in country after country. Moral Re-Armament is rendering a great service. It is the one hope of the world.

THE HON. NORMAN MAKIN

First President of the UNO Security Council, London, 1946

THE WAR OF IDEAS

As the war progressed, it became increasingly clear that the ultimate struggle in the world was ideological. Frank Buchman, foreseeing that victory in the war would not end this conflict, set out to train the new type of leadership democracy needed. MRA training centres, from 1940 onwards, drew together thousands from all sides of American life and from many countries. Since 1942, these Assemblies have been held each year on Mackinac Island, in the Great Lakes. Mackinac was early described (Grand Rapids Herald, 10 September, 1944) as 'A Laboratory for a New World'. The following informal address was given at the opening of the MRA Training Centre there in July, 1943.

TODAY I want to talk about great forces at work in the world. Sixty and more years ago you didn't hear much about the Communist Party. To begin with there was one man—Karl Marx. Then for a long time only a small group. Eventually world conditions made it possible for Karl Marx to do his work—and Communism is the result.

Think what Russia means in the world today. How large is it? One-sixth of the earth. I remember a time when the Czar couldn't ride unless he had every six feet a man watching him. Even if it was a railway journey of a thousand miles, he always had men posted along the way. It was all part of what helped produce the thing called Communism.

A little while ago the world didn't think much about it. It didn't affect us. We had not come into contact with it. Occasionally there would be a flare-up. Then during the last war there was more and more discontent. There was revolution. And the Communist Party came to power.

Today the Russians are doing pretty well. America is doing a lot for them because just now they seem to be a decisive factor in dealing with Germany, and because they may have a controlling interest in the future.

Now that is one picture. Give it a nice gold frame. Put in as much red as you want. But when you have done that, you haven't done with Communism because it is a tremendous force. Think of the number of people in this country who have been swung by it, who have gone part way and are 'leftist' in their thinking. We are going to meet it all the time.

Now take another force. When did we begin to hear about Fascism? 1921–1922. Again there was a man—Mussolini. I remember when I was in Italy, at Milan. *Viva i Comunisti* was written all over the walls. Soon you saw, *Viva il Duce*, also on the walls—and Mussolini arose as an opposing force to Communism. He marched on Rome. He put himself in power and a Fascist force came into being. For a while there was a growing sense of stability and prosperity. People said, 'Good! Mussolini has come. Fascism has come. The trains are on time. There are no beggars in the streets. We have "good order".'

But today where is Mussolini? Where is Italy? And where is the 'order'?

In those days, back in the 'twenties, Germany was at its lowest ebb. Many had no food—nothing. I remember men of large means taking a hard-boiled egg in their pocket and bringing it out for lunch. For years there was danger of collapse and incipient revolution. The youth were completely out of hand, delinquent, roving the country, with crimes of violence and theft everywhere.

Then along came a man called Hitler who had very definite ideas. He wrote them in a book when he was in prison. When he came out there were mobs, disorders and massacres. The Austrian became a citizen of the German Reich. There was no order in Germany. But this juggernaut comes along and gives seeming order. More and more he took a place in the world. So the German people said, 'Hallelujah!' and *Heil Hitler!* You know the rest of the story.

So we have Communism and Fascism, two world forces. And where do they come from? From Materialism which is the mother of all the 'isms'. It is the spirit of anti-Christ which breeds corruption, anarchy and revolution. It undermines our homes, it sets class against class, it divides the nation. Materialism is Democracy's greatest enemy.

These then were the forces which threatened to dominate the world.

In 1938 the guidance came to me—'Moral Re-Armament', a movement where the moral and spiritual would have the emphasis. The need of the age is the moral and the spiritual. Our task was to bring back these realities to nations that needed them. We initiated this thinking in London's East Ham Town Hall. We took it to the nations. MRA was born that year.

Communism and Fascism are built on a *negative* something—on divisive materialism and confusion. Wherever Moral Re-Armament goes, there springs up a *positive* message. Its aim is to restore God to leadership as the directing force in the life of the nation. Let me recall what I said in Philadelphia on my birthday:

'Moral Re-Armament creates the qualities that make democracy function. It is simple, non-partisan, non-sectarian, non-political. It gives to every man the inner discipline he needs and the inner liberty he desires. It calls out and combines the moral and spiritual responsibility of individuals for their immediate sphere of action.

'It builds for democracy an unshakeable framework of actively selfless and self-giving citizens, whose determination to bring unity cannot be altered by any beckoning of personal advantage and who know how to pass along to others their panic-proof experience of the guidance of God.'

America must discover her rightful ideology. It springs from her Christian heritage and is her only adequate answer in the battle against materialism and all the other 'isms.' But America does not hate materialism. Think of America destroying herself with the very force that she condemns in others. The battle of the ideologies was the granite of the Old and New Testaments. So many people today instead of giving the granite, give the sugar—and so we never cure materialism.

MRA first of all goes straight to the fundamental problem —it recognises sin. Sin is the disease. Jesus Christ is the cure. The result is a miracle. You come to a training centre like this. You may say, 'Oh, I don't like to hear sin mentioned.' Well, that's too bad. It ought to be mentioned, but it ought to be enough just to give a quick picture of it and then move on. And you ought to be so sensitive that you respond immediately and change—and that's one more miracle. That ought to happen today, just as in the old days your grandparents used to go to church on Wednesday night, because they liked a good rugged sermon on sin. That's fine if you have time enough for it—and possibly you need to take time.

Make sure there is no minimum emphasis on sin. Make it maximum. But then quickly make the adjustment. Change, unite, fight. That is the natural sequence.

You will find here the old fundamental truths—but you get them with a mighty, moving crescendo. MRA restores absolute standards in a day when selfishness and expediency are the common practice of men and nations. Take the four absolutes—honesty, purity, unselfishness, love. Perhaps some of you do not put much stock in them any more. But to arm a people you must give them these simple, basic standards.

Take honesty for a start. What do you find in the nation? What about men who have been dishonest, say in war contracts? Graft and the Black Market keep a lot of people busy all the time and cost millions of dollars. In the old days nobody said a good word for dishonesty. Now the successful chiseller seems almost at a premium.

Take purity. You may say that it is just a personal matter. But what is happening to the nation? They tell you that in some war plants impurity is so common that it is even organised among the workers, and especially among the subversive groups who use it as a weapon. They know that when people's morals are confused their thinking becomes confused. People say, 'That's too bad', and keep on going to church on Sunday, but nothing happens. Too few try to bring a great, cleansing force to the nation. What is going to happen to a nation when nobody brings a cure any more? Broken homes, unstable children, the decay of culture, the seeding plot of revolution.

As far as unselfishness and love go, people don't pretend to be unselfish, and they don't expect to be loving.

People have written off the four standards as part of the

horse-and-buggy days. So, naturally, they are the last thing they have in mind for nations. That is why you have the condition there is in the world today. Now if you can get people who will live up to these absolutes and stand for them, then you have a force, a creative something in the community with a strength that nothing will gainsay.

You must have that emphasis on morals plus the saving power of Jesus Christ. Then you experience the dynamic which is almost forgotten—the Holy Spirit, that gives the guided answer and tells you exactly what to do as a clear direct call from God.

That's the programme for the Church today. I believe with all my heart in the Church, the Church aflame, on fire with revolution. We haven't begun to experience the spiritual revolution we need. You need revolution, and then when you come into the clear light of God's Presence, you will experience a glorious renaissance. You will come to see what Christ means this old world to be.

It's one thing to know these realities. But there's a further thing, and that is to make them national.

The trouble with some of you is that you are so idealistic that your hopes never come to pass, even in your own families. That was the trouble with the League of Nations. People were so 'League-minded' they failed to do the thing the League most needed—the spadework with individuals that brings change. There was something left out of the League and that was—God. The League was never God-arched.

Everybody's job is to find the God-arched master-plan. Then we would have a master-plan not only for us, but for post-war Europe. The trouble is, we let the statesmen do all our thinking for us—and then we call it democracy!

Take the great modern cities you come from. You complain of this subversive leader and that one. Yet it is the selfishness of everyone that makes possible the subversive leader. The whole problem is that you endure a thing rather than cure it. You would rather pay than pray. You would rather go on with your confusion, your grumbling, your complaints, than change and have an answer.

The battle for America is the battle for the mind of America. A nation's thinking is in ruins before a nation is in ruins. And America's thinking is in ruins.

People get confused as to whether it is a question of being Rightist or Leftist. But the one thing we really need is to be guided by God's Holy Spirit. That is the Force we ought to study. Then we will have a clear light that ends confusion. The Holy Spirit will teach us how to think and live, and provide a working basis for our national service.

America doesn't have much of her great moral heritage left. Just think, if we fail to give emphasis to a moral climate, where will our democracy go? Some of us have been so busy looking after our own affairs that we have forgotten to look after the nation. Unless America recovers her rightful ideology nothing but chaos awaits us. Our destiny is to obey the guidance of God.

The true battle-line in the world today is not between class and class, not between race and race. The battle is between Christ and anti-Christ.

Choose ye this day whom ye will serve.

THE WORLD PHILOSOPHY

A birthday message, San Francisco, 4 June, 1945

MY BIRTHDAY WISH is that Moral Re-Armament become the world philosophy.

Today we see three ideologies battling for control. There is Fascism, and Communism, and then there is that great other ideology which is the centre of Christian democracy—Moral Re-Armament.

We need to find an ideology that is big enough and complete enough to outmarch any of the other great ideologies. Until that time comes, men will flounder. They will not find their way.

But when the Holy Spirit of God rules the hearts and lives of men, then we will begin to build the new world of tomorrow that all of us long to see.

Note: Rear-Admiral Sir Edward Cochrane, KBE, then a Convoy Commodore, presented to Dr Buchman a book from a thousand Service men and women of the Allied nations. Their message read, in part: 'Through these years of endurance your inspiration has armed us to fight on. As we march into the years of victory, your conquering philosophy is our hope—the fighting faith that will bring resurrection to nations and teamwork to a divided world . . . We stand with you on that world battle-line in the war of ideas. When victory in arms is finally ours we, with you, will battle on to build a sound world, morally re-armed and God-controlled—the world for which we fight.' (See also Supplement IV, 8.)

A REVOLUTION UNDER
THE CROSS

On the eve of sailing for Europe, New York, 23 April, 1946

WE ARE AT THE END of seven years—seven wonderful years. We have learned much. We want to be careful that every single person in this room knows the full truth in Christ Jesus that has been revealed to us.

When I left England a great statesman said, 'I don't want you to leave my country. I want you to stay.' I said, 'My duty is to America.' I came for seven years. Great truths have been revealed to us. I think of those wonderful days in California, in San Francisco, when we spoke to the world and we gave a message that is the answer. It is a great ideology. It is the full message of Jesus Christ. It is putting the message in a way that the world will understand. People didn't fully understand, but the crisis was not as imminent as it is today. Now people everywhere say this is the answer.

These are the two alternatives: Communism and Marxism —and that great inspired ideology that has meant so much for liberty and freedom in the days that are gone.

We are in a global work. Take Australia. A leader of the UNO Conference[1] in London, said, 'MRA is the one hope of the world.' The one hope of the world. Take Rear-Admiral Byrd. In the most momentous meeting that I ever expect to live through in Washington, he sat next to me. He

[1] Hon. Norman Makin, first President of the Security Council.

147

saw that remarkable play.[1] He said, 'I must speak.' Then two other men spoke and he said, 'I must speak again.' And he said, 'This is America's answer.' This is America's answer.

If this is America's answer, then we are in a global effort to win the world to our Lord and Saviour, Jesus Christ. Then the great truths of the Gospel will once more become great and Jesus Christ will be King. There is your ideology. It is the whole message of the Gospel of our Lord and Saviour Jesus Christ. The message in its entirety is the only last hope that will save the world. God's chance is a revolution under the Cross of Christ that can transform the world. The only hope. Our only answer. Go forth with that message united and you will save the world.

And now shall we have a few moments of quiet.

> Oh, Thou best Gift of Heaven,
> Thou Who Thyself hast given,
> For Thou hast died:
> This hast Thou done for me—
> What have I done for Thee,
> Thou Crucified?
>
> I long to serve Thee more;
> Reveal an open door
> Saviour to me.
> Then, counting all but loss,
> I'll glory in the Cross,
> And follow Thee.

The Cross of Christ adequate for a revolution that will bring a renaissance, that will change the world. We pray in Christ's name. Amen.

[1] *The Forgotten Factor.*

THE GOOD ROAD

In 1946, a world training centre for Moral Re-Armament was opened at Caux, Switzerland. In their first ten years, the Assemblies at Caux were attended by 105,000 people from 116 countries, including Cabinet Ministers, Members of Parliament, heads of industries, the elected heads of 60,000,000 workers, leaders of the Church, the armed forces, press and education. The following broadcast was made from Caux, 4 June, 1947, at the request of the Swiss Broadcasting Corporation.[1]

PEOPLE EVERYWHERE are trying to find the good road that will lead them to security. Awesome fear surrounds everyone. It stalks the world. Conference follows conference but peace comes no nearer. Menacing economic problems face both the Old World and the New. The young United Nations sags under the weight of its problems and the lack of the right spirit in which to meet them. People lose faith in their leaders, and statesmen—earnest, able men—toil but see no harvest.

Some people are thinking in terms of another war. I don't believe they are sane if they are thinking of such an answer. But there are men who are willing to submit to all its horrors if that were a way out.

Meanwhile the forces of subversion prey like vultures over man's disillusionment. Even the elements seem to be working with them, giving a red answer to the balance sheet.

On every hand we see disunity. Divisions are the mark of

---

[1] Read into the *Congressional Record* by the Hon. James W. Wadsworth, the co-author of the National Selective Service Act, on 10 June, 1947.

our time. Men oppose other men because they are of another nation, another race, another class, another party, or simply because they hold another point of view.

Everyone longs for peace and order, yet battling for divisive points of view only increases the chaos. What is our greatest need?

Someone in Europe said recently, 'We are hungry, hungry not only for food but for ideas—ideas on which to reshape our individual and national life.'

The truth is that our problem goes deeper than economics or politics. It is ideological. Divisive ideologies strive for the mastery of men's minds. Thousands follow their banners only because they see no convincing alternative. Not all governments have grasped the paramount importance of ideological preparedness. A nation which is materially strong may be ideologically divided against itself, and therefore in danger. Leaders who ignore this fact will sell us short.

There is a road, a good road among many false ways, a good road mankind must find and follow. It is a God-constructed road. It is the great high road of democracy's inspired ideology. It is valid for every nation. It is essential for world peace.

Men today are being stretched consciously or unconsciously into new moulds of thinking. People everywhere ask, 'Have you the answer to Communism?'

It is interesting how fanciful and heroic or even pathetic some people are in trying to find the answer. Others begin to see vaguely that there must be a note of change. Everybody knows somebody, some nation which ought to be different. But most people have not come to the point where they see that they themselves need a radical change. Yet these are days of radical action. And human nature can be changed. 'I thought,' said a military man recently after meeting Moral Re-Armament, 'I thought that I was Major Brown. I found that I was Mr Anyman facing Major Change!'

He had found the good road, the road of a change of heart. As we travel this road miracles happen and renaissance and true security will follow in their train.

A steel worker came to our training centre here at Caux. He had been a Communist for twenty-eight years. He had trained his daughter until she became even more radical than he. Yet that daughter was changed and persuaded her father to come to Caux. Before he left us he read a poem that he had written. These are his words:

> I contemplate, and bow in awe
>   Before God's master Plan;
> I watch the miracle superb—
>   The change in selfish man.
>
> The snows on Dents-du-Midi
>   Are but the robes of grace;
> God has a plan, for every man,
>   And each one has a place.

This steel worker now writes, 'I was a new creature in Christ and the experience at Caux sealed for ever my allegiance to the Highest. This is the first time in years that I have written anything of a spiritual nature, for, for the last twenty-eight years my pen and any talents I possessed were given to proclaiming and proclaiming very forcibly my belief in the materialism of the Marxist theory.'

People summon new hope whenever you give the voice of

faith as a sure and certain answer for even the darkest days. I thank God for the mounting evidence—sometimes in the headlines, more often behind the headlines—that this is true.

I hold in my hand today a report by the noted Associated Press columnist De Witt Mackenzie, which he calls 'one of the most remarkable' in his experience. He tells of the striking new plans which one of China's foremost soldier-statesmen has been developing for his nation. Concerned over the tragic divisions of his country, General Ho, China's wartime Chief of Staff who now represents his country on the United Nations Military Staff Committee, went to a Moral Re-Armament conference in America.

This is the new truth he saw there. He says, 'During the past twenty years of my fight against materialism in China, the method I used was force against force, and organisation against organisation. I have now come to the very firm conclusion that I must fight an idea with an idea.'

General Ho now puts first the moral rehabilitation of China. He believes that along with economic reform must come the moral force that will give new standards to the country. In short, says the General, there is no use trying to reform the Communists by naked force alone. It would be best to solve the Communist problem by moral force. He stresses the importance of raising the moral standards of Chinese society as a whole, including both the Communists and the Kuomintang.

To this end he has submitted to his government detailed plans for sending at once selected groups of his countrymen to Switzerland and America for training in Moral Re-Armament. He specifies that these men must be unselfish by nature, and able-bodied, that they must be men of faith and that they must return to give at least one year's service to the development of this ideology in their country. He concludes with these memorable words. 'To put the world in order, we must first put the nation in order; to put the nation in order, we must put the family in order; to put the family in order, we must cultivate our personal life; and to cultivate our personal life, we must first set our hearts right.'

Here surely is statesmanlike planning, a new approach to the problems of fratricidal strife which menace so many nations today.

At Caux, in the heart of troubled Europe, and at Mackinac Island in America, there are centres for ideological training to which the ordinary man and the statesmen are coming in growing numbers, and they are finding there new hope and the way out of confusion. One of the statesmen from the Paris Peace Conference last summer said, 'At Caux I found the answer to Paris.'

India, a centre of considerable confusion today, sent a distinguished delegation of leaders. One was the Director of Agriculture for the United Provinces. He said, 'Two main ideologies are likely to capture the imagination of the people in India. One is the ideology of Karl Marx. The other is the ideology of Moral Re-Armament.' Indian newspapers got the point. They said it in headlines—'Caux, the answer to Communism.'

Coal is one of the chief problems of the economic world. Every major coal-field in Britain was represented at Caux. In the most critical year for the British mines these leaders went back to settle disputes and raise production. There was more coal because there was a new spirit. These miners have not only increased production, they have happy homes.

A British Member of Parliament said, 'A fresh wind of liberty and goodwill blows from Caux over the ruined nations.' Today he is heading a committee of Parliamentarians who are inviting government leaders from other countries to join them here to plan the moral and spiritual rebirth of nations which will make peace secure. Labour leads in many lands. Labour led by God can unite the world.

Army leaders, too, see a new role for themselves and their forces—to give quickly to their nations the added strength of an inspired ideology.

And thank God there is now at work a world force of people, ideologically equipped, who know how a new moral climate can be produced because of what has happened in their own lives. Workers and soldiers, housewives and statesmen, farmers and industrialists, young and old, they have no new paper plans to offer, but they have experience which cannot be denied. They know that a change of heart is possible. They know that definite, decisive guidance from God is available, today as always.

Two weeks ago I was present in Rome at the ceremonies which proclaimed as Saint a statesman of his day, Nikolaus von der Flüe, who lived in Switzerland in the fifteenth century. Nikolaus had this gift of divine direction. As he exercised it, he became the saviour of his country. He was a farmer who tilled his land well, a soldier, a magistrate. At fifty, oppressed by the problems of a warring world, he gave up much to follow radically the guidance of God. Soon his inspired good sense, knowledge of men and singleness of heart commanded the respect of his contemporaries, not only in Switzerland but in all Europe. He became the most sought-after arbiter in affairs of state. When the bitter quarrels of the

Cantons brought his country to the verge of civil war it was his God-given answer which set Switzerland on the good road that gave her unity. It is most timely that this statesman of five hundred years ago, who listened for God's word and fearlessly passed it on to his generation, should today receive this supreme recognition. Truly he is a saint for our times, a model for the United Nations.

A diplomat led by God—a nation united. Is that the answer?

An Arab Foreign Minister said, 'The world is at the cross-roads. One road leads to revolution and chaos. The other to reaction and despair. Moral Re-Armament is the third way—the way of an inspired democracy that will unite the world.'

Democracy's inspired ideology is a life to be lived, a road to be followed. A whole new order of statesmanship is required. Cabinet Ministers to rule well must change people. Ordinarily Cabinets do not have that art.

As men change, nations find a new level of living that makes problems melt.

As men listen to God and obey His orders, nations find a pattern that makes plain God's Will for government.

Here is the good road. Anyone can travel it. Everyone must travel it—ordinary men and the statesman alike.

As we step out upon it, God becomes real. Fear vanishes and life opens out. There is no need for detours: the good road lies straight ahead.

When ye turn to the right hand and when ye turn to the left, thine ears shall hear a word behind thee saying, 'This is the way, walk ye in it.'

Nations shall run unto thee because of the Lord thy God. And great shall be the peace of thy children.

THE ANSWER TO CRISIS

Opening address at the World Assembly, Caux, 15 July, 1947

ALL THE WORLD wants an answer. We have reached the moment when, unless we find an answer and bring it quickly to the world, not just one nation, but all nations will be overwhelmed.

For too long we have breathed the atmosphere of problems. We move from conference to conference and give up hope of a fundamental solution. We are cynical of success. We have become the slaves of our defeats, personally and nationally.

Nations desire the fruits of an answer without having an answer. We want production. We want peace. We want prosperity. We want a world organisation. We want a united Europe. We want a new national life. But we do not go to the root of the matter.

You cannot continue to cry 'Crisis' without providing an adequate answer. The habit of crisis breeds the habit of apathy. We must lift people to a new level out of the fogs of fear and the bogs of bitterness where today humanity founders.

Nations fail because they try desperately to combat moral apathy with economic plans. Economic breakdown walks as a black threat through the heart of every statesman and citizen. Yet the material crisis may obscure the materialism and moral breakdown that underlie it, so they do not know how to cure it.

Until we deal with human nature thoroughly and drastically on a national scale, nations must still follow their historic road to violence and destruction.

The problem is not just an iron curtain which separates nation from nation, but steely selfishness which separates man from man and all men from the government of God. And when men listen to God and obey, the steel and iron melt away.

A generation ago a group of men gripped by a materialist ideology decided to capture the world with it. They gave their lives to that task. For twenty-five years they have worked—every hour, sleeping and waking, ceaselessly, skilfully, ruthlessly on a world front.

Suddenly the statesmen of the democratic nations have woken up. They rub their eyes as they see what is happening. The world force of materialism has penetrated every nation. It has infiltrated their schools, their industries. It has invaded their offices and government departments. It has influenced their families, their colleagues, and even themselves.

At last they realise the imminence of crisis. They perceive the colossal progress of organised materialism in its march towards world chaos and control. Why, they ask, are we in this situation? How did it come about?

The reason is simple. While many slept, and others busied themselves with their own affairs, the materialists have been working out their revolution with a philosophy, a passion and a plan.

What is the answer? A generation ago the force of Moral Re-Armament began fighting too. On a world front it has been answering plan with plan, idea with idea, a militant godless materialism with a militant inspired ideology for democracy.

The idea caught hold. It remade men. It impacted nation after nation. Now it girdles the globe.

Today at the Moral Re-Armament Assembly at Caux we see this force in action with the answer, available for service. At a time when statesmen realise the lateness of the hour, it freely offers the fruit of twenty-five years of toil. A force in the war of ideas, with the training and experience which, under God, can equip the statesmen and the ordinary man with an ideology adequate to remake the nations—now.

A new message goes out from Caux to a stricken world. At Caux the answer has been found. It has been given legs and it is on the march. Here at Caux we are reaching the end of the age of crisis and pioneering the era of cure.

Take the great world problem today—the production of coal. Test this answer. Britain must produce more coal, or, as Cabinet Ministers say, the midnight hour will strike for her. This week the Coal Board announces the output of coal nationally is considerably short of the target set by the Government. But where miners have been trained at Caux, in coalfields where the Moral Re-Armament drama *The Forgotten Factor* has been shown, there is a different picture. In one mine the six-day target was reached in four and a half days. In another the target was passed so often the miners have asked for the target to be raised. In one area absenteeism dropped in twelve months from 20 per cent to 3 per cent.[1]

Paper plans will never raise production. Only new men working together in a new spirit with the fire of an ideology

[1] In the *Spectator*, London, 6 June, 1947, Janus wrote in 'A Spectator's Note book': 'Tribute should be paid where tribute seems to be justly due. I heard this week of a striking impetus to coal production. The manager of one of our larger mines happened—I don't know how or even when—to

will raise production, build teamwork that springs from happy homes, and set the nations on the path to recovery.

Test this answer again. A great Indian labour leader was with me at Caux last week-end. He told me two problems dogged India—racial bitterness and class bitterness. He saw no solution. After one day he told me he had seen the answer. He came again. He says: 'Moral Re-Armament is the answer because moral apathy is the problem. I have seen here the way of life without tragedy. As I make this way my own my life can be effective and I can make others effective. This is our chance. One of us can make many. Thousands can make millions. The world can be saved from tragedy.'

see a performance of the Moral Re-Armament movement's play *The Forgotten Factor*, at the Westminster Theatre. He was so deeply impressed that when he got back he called together a group of his sub-managers to consider the situation as he had come to see it. Interest in the affair percolated down, and some 300 men from the pit went up to see the play—at their own expense; the fare was over 30s.—returning late, just in time to go straight on the night shift. The result, I am assured, is that the pit regularly tops production for its region. Let me add that the story comes to me from no Moral Re-Armament quarter, but from someone who knows the pits and pitmen of that area particularly well.'

This play, which Mr Truman called 'the most important play produced by the war', develops Frank Buchman's philosophy in an industrial setting. At its Washington première, 5 May, 1944, the audience included 300 Members of Congress, and many leaders of labour and industry, and the armed forces.

The Forgotten Factor has played to over one million people in twenty countries, in twelve languages. In 1947, 100,000 saw it in London at the Westminster Theatre. It has played in German to 120,000 in the Ruhr; in French in Paris and the industrial areas of the north; in Italian in industrial Lombardy; in Finnish in Finland, where a film was based on it. It has been played by a Japanese cast in the Imperial Theatre in Tokyo, and by Burmese railway workers in Rangoon. It was enthusiastically received by 100,000 of all races in South and East Africa. When it was invited to tour New Zealand by leading members of Government and Opposition, the Foreign Minister said on the opening night, 'Here is something more important than the atom bomb'. It has since been filmed.

His words are the key to statesmanship that can save the world. He shows us where to begin, because Moral Re-Armament is for everyone everywhere. Human nature can be changed. That is the basic answer. National economies can be changed. That is the fruit of the answer. World history can be changed. That is the destiny of our age.

Let us be honest and face the facts. A new conference is no answer to a false philosophy. A new theory is no answer to a militant ideology. Plans fail for lack of inspired people to work them. Yet we multiply plans. Caux produces the inspired people who will make plans work.

A statesman came to Caux. He is President of the Board of Trade of his nation. For years life had been governed by a hatred of the British so powerful that he had sworn never to speak the English language publicly again.

He was involved in incidents which brought his country to a crisis that, in his own words, 'could very easily have led to civil war.' He spoke in English as he told us: 'I have experienced myself that a hatred which at times used to flash to white heat can be removed in an instant through willing-ness, although I did not know God or believe in Him, to learn His miracle-working power.' He learned the secret that an honest apology leads to honest peace. Civil war was averted. Change in this statesman and the guidance of God turned him from a divisive element in his nation to a pioneer of teamwork and taught him to live effectively for other races as well as for his own.

A change of heart. Inspired statesmanship. The answer we are all seeking?

Moral Re-Armament offers the world and the statesmen of the world a force, trained and on the march, that has the answer to individual and national selfishness. It is the chance for everyone everywhere to step today into the fresh dimension of a new age. It is not a theory but a way of life, tested and tried in every circumstance. It is a force that has the power to save and re-create a society on the brink of collapse.

On his return from the Antartic, Admiral Byrd summed up his own conviction about Moral Re-Armament: 'I want to say with all the emphasis at my command that it gives you the chance you have been looking for to go into action to save civilisation.'

Men born again are bringing renaissance to nations. Industry with this force of Moral Re-Armament at its heart will produce enough for the needs of all. Homes with this force in everyday life will secure the next generation from chaos. Armies with this force will give new standards of moral training to their nations. Cabinets and diplomats with this force will be totally effective for they will have the power to turn their enemies into friends. Europe will arise, the world will arise from the sleep and defeat of apathy and dis-illusion. This is the only possible hope for world reconstruction.

'Men must be governed by God or they will be ruled by tyrants,' said that great American, William Penn.

It is the new day, and a new way.

THE ANSWER TO ANY 'ISM'
—EVEN MATERIALISM

June, 1948, marked the tenth anniversary of Moral Re-Armament. Dr Buchman presided over a World Assembly in California. His opening address, on 2 June, is given below.

From France, the Foreign Minister cabled, 'I salute in Moral Re-Armament one of the animating forces at work for inspired democracy which must re-establish the supremacy of all spiritual values at the heart of our tormented humanity.' Five Ministers-President wrote from Germany: 'Germany is ready for your message. The ideology of Moral Re-Armament is an indispensable foundation for the reconstruction and peace of Europe and the world.' Simultaneous assemblies were held in Denmark, France, Germany, Switzerland, Australia and Britain.

EVERYWHERE MEN LONG for peace and prepare for war. They long to rebuild and prepare to destroy. They plan for new prosperity and expect fresh disasters.

What is the missing factor in the planning and the statesmanship of the world today?

It is our lack of an ideology for democracy. We say, we are democrats, we need no ideology. We almost feel it is a sign of weakness to talk about an ideology.

So we try to meet the united plan and passion of alien ideologies with talk and with lip-service to high ideals and with a last resort to force. And we hope to live as we have always lived—selfishly, comfortably and undisturbed.

We have all lived too long in an atmosphere of imagining

that security, prosperity, comfort and culture are natural to man.

We forgot the eternal struggle between Evil and Good, victory in which brings the blessings of security and prosperity. But defeat in this struggle, and even ignorance of it, brings poverty, hunger, slavery and death.

It takes more than diplomacy to exorcise evil. It takes more than lip-service to fight for God. Statesmen talk about the answer. They talk of union. But disunity increases. They talk of moral values. But immoral policies prevail. They use these words which the hard logic of events has proved true. But it remains words. These men do not face the cost in their own lives and the life of their nations of giving an answer.

An extreme of evil must be met with an extreme of good. A fanatical following of evil by a passionate pursuit of good.

That is why democracy fails. Only a passion can cure a passion. And only a superior world-arching ideology can cure a world divided by warring ideologies.

We Americans have been lulled into a false security by believing that all the 'isms' are across the sea.

'Isms' grow from unsolved problems in the life of men and nations. One man's hate kindles a million hates. One man's suspicion explodes a million suspicions. It spreads like a prairie fire. Or it creeps like a flame underground to burst out unexpectedly in a hundred places.

Is America free from hates, fears, suspicions, greed?

Why is our record of broken homes so high? How about industrial strife?

Are we victims of the greatest 'ism' of all? Materialism.

Is materialism the mother of all the 'isms'? Is materialism becoming our national ideology?

We stretch out generous hands to help Europe and Asia economically. But materialism frustrates our best intentions. Prices rise, money is worth less. Troubles in industry cut down the supply of goods. At the moment when our strength is most needed abroad, we may find ourselves in our greatest crisis.

The other 'isms' are banking on that. They wait their time. They know that money, food and clothes alone will not save Europe; that material things may make nations just strong enough materially to become their tools in their ideological conquest of the world.

Ten years ago Moral Re-Armament was born. In this very Hollywood Bowl the crowds gathered to see the preview of a new world order.

What have we learnt in these ten years?

We have learnt that democracy without an ideology can win a war but cannot build a peace; that ideological preparedness is the task of the whole nation, and is the one sure basis of national strength, moral, military and economic.

Today MRA offers the democracies and the whole world the superior armament of an ideology, without which armies are out-fought and statesmen are out-thought.

MRA has grown in ten years to the stature of a world answer to any 'ism'—even materialism. It has restored for millions the simple sanctities of home and honour, and given hope for a new world. It has built the world organism that can make a reality of this hope. In the words of a British coalminer, 'Moral Re-Armament is the answer to every "ism" ever invented.' It is for everyone everywhere.

Let me cite a few proven facts of the past twelve months. One hundred and fifty leading Germans came to the World

Assembly for Moral Re-Armament in Caux, Switzerland. General Clay in Berlin and Lord Pakenham in London made their visit possible. These Germans found the answer to nihilism and to an ideologically broken nation. An Allied official, Military Governor of Cologne, said, 'MRA is the ideal solution for Germany.' A leading German Socialist, a former Minister-President, said, 'If Europe is to be saved, it must be saved in the spirit of Moral Re-Armament.'

The first democratic handbook by Germans giving the answering ideology was produced by these men. It is going out far and wide even behind the Iron Curtain. Sweden gave 100 tons of paper because she saw her security lay in a new spirit in Germany.

French industry—battlefield of the ideologies—has found a uniting force. An employer, heading an organisation of employers of 600,000 workers, fought Labour. The head of all the Socialist women of France mistrusted Management. These two saw the new battle-line—for or against democracy's inspired ideology. They met. They changed. They apologised, and are working together. Thousands rally to them. They speak not of revolution, not of reaction, but of renaissance—the rebirth of a nation, the rebirth of a continent.

Italy—focus of an anxious world. Two hundred Italians, including twenty-six Members of the Italian Parliament from five different parties, came to the MRA Conference last summer. The Christian Democrat and the Socialist learned to work together. A Socialist said, 'It is a miracle. Our parties can get together in the same way as we have.' Is that one of the secrets of the Italian elections?

Britain—production is returning. But what is her greatest problem today? After seeing the Moral Re-Armament programme in the coalfields of Britain a mine manager said, 'Moral Re-Armament fills the emptiness and gives the dynamic we need.' Lord Nuffield, the genius of Britain's automobile industry, sent this message to the MRA programme at the time of the British Industries Fair, 'We must be prepared to face man-made problems which beset us by bringing into our personal, family and industrial lives in full measure the principles of truth, integrity, unselfishness and compassionate understanding of the other man's problems.'

What is the common factor in all this good news? It is *union*—the almost forgotten solution to all our problems today.

Division is the mark of our age. Division in the heart. Division in the home. Division in industry. Division in the nation. Division between nations.

Union is our instant need.

Division is the work of human pride, hate, lust, fear, greed.

Division is the trademark of materialism.

Union is the grace of rebirth. We have lost the art of uniting because we have forgotten the secret of change and rebirth.

Moral Re-Armament is the good road of an ideology inspired by God upon which all can unite.

Catholic, Jew and Protestant, Hindu, Muslim, Buddhist and Confucianist—all find they can change, where needed, and travel along this good road together.

I called on a great leader in his time of deep sorrow. He gave me these words of Fulton Sheen, 'What the world needs today is not to plead for religious unity so much as to plead for the unity of religious people.' Those are the words of a great Catholic leader.

The Jew has his pristine contribution in the words of the great prophet-leader Isaiah, 'Nations shall run unto thee because of the Lord thy God,' and 'Great shall be the peace of thy children.' And in the words of the Psalmist, 'Great peace have they which love Thy law; and nothing shall offend them.'

And what does Islam say? The Foreign Minister of Pakistan, Sir Zafrullah Khan, sent me this word, 'Among my friends of MRA I have been delighted to observe the constant striving after discovering God's plan and purpose and putting their lives in accord with it. I am convinced that it is only through sincere and sustained effort in that direction that mankind can win through to its true redemption.'

Is that the medium of approach for the Palestine problem?

It is so easy to have these great truths lost in prejudice. 'Behold how these brethren fight one another,' says the world. But it should be, 'Behold how these brothers love one another.'

Prejudice shall not keep any of us from the maximum leadership which our nations demand.

The Bishop of Tammerfors in Finland came to see that great ideological play *The Forgotten Factor* in his own land and language. He was afraid a play might not be the right medium. He came. He wept. He said, 'This must go to everyone.' After the first act he telephoned a well-known industrialist who came straight to the theatre. As a result the cast was asked to show the play for a whole month.

What a joy must have possessed this Bishop who warily and almost against his will decided to come, and found the thing he most longed for for his nation—an over-arching ideology.

And what does India say? The Minister of Labour in

Bombay Provincial Government, took this word back to the leaders of his country and to the millions of India's workers, 'Here is the force that can change selfishness and greed and all that is wrecking the spirit and soul of people. Until I met Moral Re-Armament I had not felt confident that there was an idea which could be applied universally as an adequate answer.'

Labour here in California says the same. They see this great principle of changing and uniting on the level of an answering ideology. It led a group of labour leaders to go to management and offer their services free for the filming of our play *The Good Road*. I didn't ask them to do it. They saw a tremendous part they could play and they took the initiative. Isn't this the freer atmosphere in which we all need to move? Isn't this the dignity of labour?

Think of strikes today: 75,000 men—100,000 men. No one thinks much about strikes. True, the President says they may have national repercussions. Economists give us grave warnings. But do we see that strikes can be the entrance for one of the 'isms'? Is it materialism in the thinking and living of both management and labour—and of you and me?

Think of America destroying herself with the very thing she condemns in others.

And how about France? Italy? The Po Valley? Do they understand the language of an answer to strikes?

And what does the employer say? The representative of one of the greatest aircraft manufacturers in California told us, 'Until I saw your work, I thought the answer to materialism was dead with St Francis.'

Now make no mistake. I do not say that this message will be wholly popular. It stirs the conscience. That is uncomfortable. It will always be open to misinterpretation by those who wish to escape it. But it comes as illumination to those who are ready.

Let me tell how it came to me. Just forty years ago I was divided. Just as nations today are divided. Materialism was winning its battle in my heart. I went to Europe to try to escape. But my battle came with me.

One day, in England, God showed me the cost of my pride and my materialism. I admitted it. That is the first step. Get honest.

I said, 'Sorry'—first to God, then to those I had wronged. That is the second step.

I learned to listen to God. I accepted His commission to bring an answer to men and nations. That is the third step.

God is calling men everywhere to be the instruments of union. It comes not by conferences, not by laws, not by resolutions and pious hopes, but by change.

Change is the heart of the superior ideology.

As individuals change, a new climate comes to the nation's life. As leaders change, policies become inspired and the nation's life-blood flows again. As statesmen change, the fear of war and chaos will lift. The most difficult will respond to the firm, united but humble voice of reborn democracy.

Why should there be catastrophe again when, with God, renaissance is inevitable?

This is the new pattern of freedom for all nations. Shall it be a new Dark Age for Europe and the world? Or shall it be world-wide Renaissance of the moral and spiritual forces everywhere, bursting into life and bringing at the last moment a miracle to mankind?

Which shall it be? The decision lies in your hands.

IS THERE AN ANSWER?
THERE IS

In October, 1948, on the invitation of the Ministers-President of North Rhine-Westphalia, Wurtemburg-Baden and Bavaria, and other German leaders, Dr Buchman and a task force of 250 from twenty nations travelled from end to end of Germany. They took with them the musical play, The Good Road, *which drew tens of thousands in city after city. Early in 1949, the MRA industrial play,* The Forgotten Factor, *opened in the Ruhr with a German cast. In the following months 120,000 from the mines and heavy industries came to see it, among them life-long members of the German Communist Party who found in Moral Re-Armament a superior ideology.*

In the world broadcast which follows, given at the opening of the World Assembly at Caux, 4 June, 1949, Dr Buchman spoke of the results of this action.

IS THERE AN ANSWER? There is.

It came during an afternoon's walk I had in the Schwarz-wald of Germany. God spoke—'A moral and spiritual renaissance, Moral Re-Armament.' There lies the hope of the future.

Moral Re-Armament has found a million feet. It has the vital message for the millions. It meets the needs of statesmen. Foreign Minister Schuman says, 'Now we need to give ideological content to the lives of the millions of Europe.'

The worker, too, finds that there is enough in the world for everyone's need, but not enough for everyone's greed.

Moral Re-Armament has the tremendous uniting power that comes from change in both East and West. It gives the full dimension of change. Economic change. Social change. National change. International change. All based on personal change. It creates a personal opinion that can change the fate of nations. It presents a force adequate to remake the world. It shows how to unite nation and nation, and creates inspired democracy in families, industries, cabinets and nations. It is the inspired living that makes nations think and live. It has God's mind.

It works in Germany. It becomes the policy of Minister-Presidents. Karl Arnold, Minister-President of North Rhine-Westphalia, says, 'The real answer to any ideology must be a superior ideology. Germany needs an inspired ideology to support her new democracy. Moral Re-Armament is the spiritual road to a new Europe. In our cabinet we have already begun to see the fruits of this ideology at work. This is the ideology which can bring us the moral and spiritual healing we need in our nation and provide a real basis of peace with other nations. When the nations of the world seek the good road with conviction and passion, then I believe there is a new beginning for the world.'

His colleague, Minister-President Ehard of Bavaria, echoes his thought when he says of Moral Re-Armament, 'This is what the world can be. This is what the world should be. This is what the world must be.'

This works for everyone everywhere. What man wants is security—a hate-free, fear-free, greed-free world. The bottle-neck is that people say human nature cannot change. But human nature does change, and the nature of nations can change too.

In the battle for new men, for new nations and a new world we must have adequate weapons. The plays *The Good Road* and *The Forgotten Factor* have spoken to their thousands in many lands and languages. Now they are being filmed and will speak to their millions. People marvel at the irresistible power of a God-given idea. A German Marxist in Baden-Baden said after seeing the play, 'It was as if I had been toiling up a long hill and had suddenly seen a city of light.'

A French official said, 'I was overwhelmed by the power of this play. If it had been given four years ago there would have been no difficulties between the French and the Germans. I am determined to see this spirit is applied in my administration and in my own life.'

Reinhold Schneider, the great Catholic writer, said, 'This is what the whole world must hear.'

What is the response of German industry? One hundred and fifty of the Ruhr industrialists met at the invitation of General-direktor Kost, head of the German Coal Board, to plan how the spirit of Moral Re-Armament could be brought right through the industry of the Ruhr. Someone said that if a bomb had been dropped on that room, production would have stopped in the Ruhr. They heard industrial and trade union leaders from a dozen countries speak. Mr Kost gave the keynote: 'It is not for us to wait for Labour to change. Change, Gentlemen, is demanded of us.' And he further said, 'It is not a question whether we change, but how we change.'

Dr Hans Boeckler, Chairman of the Trade Unions of the British Zone, was at this conference. He says, 'If men are to be free from the old and the outmoded, it can only happen as they set themselves a new goal, and place in the forefront humanity and moral values. I believe that Moral Re-Armament can bring about a definite improvement for mankind in many areas of life. When men change, the structure of society changes, and when the structure of society changes, men change. Both go together and both are necessary. The goal which Moral Re-Armament strives to reach is the same as that for which I am fighting as a trade unionist.'

We have had half of the twentieth century. Who has the key to the second half? The nation whose youth finds the answer to nihilism and apathy.

A Heidelberg student editor said, 'All of us students have come to a dead end. Moral Re-Armament is the only thing that gives an answer.'

The Forgotten Factor was given in Bonn. The Rector of the University, a Catholic priest, welcomed the play by saying that what St Francis had done for the crisis of the thirteenth century a similar movement, Moral Re-Armament, was doing for the yet greater crisis of today. He saw his students respond in their hundreds and, as a result, the Rector comes to Caux.

In Freiburg a student came to *The Forgotten Factor* when all the tickets had gone, and pleaded to be let in. He said he had come from the East Zone of Germany for a short visit and had to go back the next morning. He said, 'Everyone in the East Zone speaks about Moral Re-Armament. They do not all quite know what it is, but apparently it is our only hope. My friends told me to make sure to find out what it really is, and I won't go back without having seen it in action for myself.'

Everyone feels Moral Re-Armament has the answer for

Germany, but not everyone realises that a reborn Germany would have the answer for them. The fate of Germany is the fate of Europe.

Dr Peters, Professor of Law in the University of Berlin, in his recent book on the *Problem of German Democracy*, describes seven forms of democracy in history and concludes with the 'Inspired Democracy' of Moral Re-Armament as the answer to the failure of democracy in our day.

A Trade Union President of 170,000 workers in Berlin says, 'How do I find the peace in my heart that enables me to know what is the right thing to do? You need apostles: I will be one. You are bringing this message like a storm to humanity.'

Is there an answer for Paris? Is there any other answer? A leading German Socialist says, 'Any unity in Europe must have Moral Re-Armament.'

A French woman, Madame Laure, former head of the Socialist Women of France, replies, 'I had good reason to hate Germany when I came to Caux. But a miracle happened. When I found Germans who lived Moral Re-Armament, my hatred died. A common ideology is doing for France and Germany today what sentimentality never did between the two wars. Now we have this firm ground to stand on from which both sides are honestly striving to build the bridge of understanding.'

These words find response across the world from the Deputy Prime Minister of New Zealand, Mr Walter Nash, who says, 'MRA is bringing a new note between person and person, employer and employees, government and government. What they do must prevail. It is the most powerful agency in the world. How long it takes depends on us.'

Nations can find a new spirit when men begin to work together. It does not take many. The East gives us an example. The front page of *The Burman*, Rangoon's daily paper, carries this headline, 'Nationwide spiritual advance. We want an idea that will lift us above every prejudice, all faction-feeling and self-seeking.'

What lies behind this story? National leaders came together in Burma's dark hour to light the torch of a moral and spiritual awakening. In a call to the nation they wrote, 'The reason why we have hitherto all failed to find an answer may be that we have not looked for it in the right place. We need a loan. We need money. We need almost everything. We need most of all an idea that changes people —a change of heart that will enable us to trust one another. Then we would begin to live as we want the other fellow to live. We would begin to live what we believe.'

Is that the new note in government? Is that why the editor of *The Burman* is on his way to Caux?

People respond when statesmen give a selfless lead. General Ho Ying-chin, China's soldier Prime Minister, sends me the message that he will never compromise on moral principles. Does your nation act on principle, or on expediency?

India hears the call of Moral Re-Armament. Mr G. L. Nanda, Minister of Labour in the Government of Bombay, presents a pledge to the people of India which contains these words, 'The strength of an individual and a nation depends on the virtues of love, purity, unselfishness and honesty.'

'Moral Re-Armament is the ideology that will answer hatred,' says the Marxist. 'It has taken away my hatred of the white man,' says Louis Byles, gifted singer from Jamaica.

Why is Moral Re-Armament the answer? Because it deals with the fundamental problem. A Mid-Western farmer said, 'I used to wonder, when I read my Old Testament, when God stopped talking to people. When I met Moral Re-Armament I realised He hadn't stopped talking; people had stopped listening.'

Someone has said that the modern man is not worried about his sins, but the result is that he is worried about almost everything else. Moral Re-Armament takes sin seriously. And it takes Christ seriously. Bishop Wurm of Germany writes, 'In Moral Re-Armament people do not talk so much about the Cross of Christ, but they live by the power of the Cross of Christ. All come under its influence. That is why they can unite people of different parties, nations and confessions.'

'It is the one sure hope for a crumbling civilisation,' says Glasgow's Catholic former Lord Provost, Sir Patrick Dollan.

A labour leader sums it up, 'Moral Re-Armament is not a new trade union. It is not a new religion. It is not a new political party. It is the remedy in the common fight for a new world.'

Is there an answer? There is.

All we need is the millions who say, *Yes, I will.*

THE DESTINY
OF EAST AND WEST

On 28 May, 1950, an Assembly was held in the Ruhr at Gelsenkirchen, on the invitation of leading German personalities. The Federal Chancellor, Dr Adenauer, said in a message to Dr Buchman, 'Moral Re-Armament has become a household word in post-war Germany. I think of the great success which has been achieved with The Forgotten Factor *in the Ruhr . . . I believe that in view of the offensive of totalitarian ideas in the East, the Federal Republic, and within it the Ruhr, is the given platform for a demonstration of the idea of Moral Re-Armament.'[1] Dr Buchman's address was broadcast by Radio Berlin and other stations in West Germany and throughout the world.[2]*

MARXISTS ARE FINDING a new thinking in a day of crisis. The class struggle is being superseded. Management and labour are beginning to live the positive alternative to class war.

Can you imagine Marxists so different that their employers say of them, 'They are our best friends'? Can you imagine an industrialist so different that the workers ask to see his passport before they will believe the miracle? These things are true. They are happening. They are the one hope of finding unity for all. Is there any difference between West and East when this becomes a fact?

[1] This Assembly coincided with a much publicised Communist demonstration in Berlin. Next day the headline in a German newspaper read, 'Berlin washout—Moral Re-Armament the basic answer'.
[2] Two days before the Ruhr Assembly, the French edition of Dr Buchman's speeches appeared with a foreword by Robert Schuman,

Is change for all the one basis of unity for all? Can Marxists be changed? Can they have this new thinking? Can Marxists pave the way for a greater ideology? Why not? They have always been open to new things. They have been forerunners. They will go to prison for their belief. They will die for their belief. Why should they not be the ones to live for this superior thinking?

Two Marxists came to Caux. A third was sent after them to bring them home. He, too, came back changed. People cajoled him. They tried to trick him. But he has become an outstanding example to Communist and non-Communist alike of this new thinking. He goes to the Prime Ministers of the North. They are interested because they are looking for a hope akin to this one, a hope that a mighty miracle is possible on a large scale, reaching the millions in this day and age.

This Marxist met one of the great leaders of the North, a man of different outlook and tradition. But he saw in that man one who lived the eternal sense of brotherhood. 'There's a real man,' he said. It bridged for him a gulf in his mind.

Change soon becomes the talking point of a nation. The diplomat who has all the answers at his fingertips, but is confused about this one, comes to talk about it. He begins to invite in his friends and they talk about it. It is a wonder to them that Marxists should have this new thinking that is the answer to division.

In a country which is one of the world's hot spots the

Foreign Minister of France: 'Democracy and her freedoms can be saved only by the quality of the men who speak in her name,' said M. Schuman. 'Dr Buchman has declared war on materialism and individualism, twin generators of our selfish divisions and social injustices. May he be heard and followed more and more in all nations of the world by those who today still clash in fratricidal hatred.' (Supplement III.)

divisions are so apparent that everyone says, 'They certainly need to change.' They have all the thinking, all the tradition, all the outward trappings of religion which could make an answer possible if they were willing. But they have been sitting there like encased mummies until one seemingly frail woman, a Member of Parliament, takes some of the principles of Jeanne d'Arc and leaps into the fray. Naturally they oppose her at first. They hold a solemn council and tell her she will lose her job. She gives them the truth she knows. She had seen with her own eyes how Marxists had discovered the secret of this new thinking. She found a response. Prejudices were removed. She was the satisfied inquirer who could give new truth. Everywhere she went she found people wanting it for their own lives.

She came to Northern France. There she found the workers in wool and in textiles, the employers, the socialist Mayor, the conservative industrialists, all beginning to find a solution they had not dreamt of before. They were impressed to learn that their Foreign Minister had said, 'Here is something we must look into. It has the hallmark of reality. It has the old truths. It doesn't deny the old truths. It makes them live.'

This is the same wise statesman who says, 'We must find something that overarches all our differences and gives us unity.'

In Italy in this Holy Year one finds a deep desire to advance to a new level of national and international living. One of the greatest Italian industrialists speaking to his colleagues said that MRA was the way to a better world. His words were echoed by the guest of honour, the leading industrialist of France, who said, 'All our pacts and all our economic arrangements will be successful only if they are undergirded by the spirit of unity I saw in Caux.'

Today we must know how to reconstruct nations. Not your own nation perhaps. Some may say, 'We won the war.' But take a nation like Japan which lost the war, and is in the throes of struggling to her feet. There are many forces at work. There are those who are bitter because they have lost their privileges, and there are Marxists who have not yet found this new thinking that can avert crisis. They need to be won. They divide a nation. Just as in Eastern and Western Germany there is bitterness because of division, so also in Japan. And there are statesmen who are finding their way, fighting against opposing tendencies, and they need the unity that comes as the grace of rebirth. It is not easy in countries like these, but it is the only possible way.

But Japan has met this new thinking. Thirty-seven of her leaders came to Caux last summer—the first Socialist Prime Minister, the former Minister of Finance, the representatives of the two great newspapers, the former Ambassador to Washington, members of the Mitsui family. And now leaders in national life, heads of newspapers, whose task is to mirror for a nation its true destiny, the workers on the railroad, those who work that others may ride, from the least of them to the man who is their president, all are being reached. In a leading article the *Nippon Times* writes:

'Moral Re-Armament is affording the Japanese people a chance to live and to practise democracy. Democracy can become an even greater force for good in Japan as in other nations if the people translate into action what is now too often mere lip-service. MRA works on the simplest of formulas. Its basis is the individual—from all walks of life and from any nation. He is asked to observe in his daily activities the basic tenets of honesty, purity, unselfishness and love. His spiritual regeneration will affect and influence others around him and by spreading from one person to another would permeate and move a whole nation.[1]'

MRA works for all—for every man everywhere. The Chief Justice of Japan, probably the leading Catholic layman, writes, 'I am expecting much from Moral Re-Armament.'

And what of Southern Asia where teeming millions came to independence only to find their new-won liberty threatened by their own disunity? A Foreign Minister from that part of the world says, 'Moral Re-Armament is as important as the atom bomb.' He sees that it opens the door to a new unity—between different races, different classes, different nations—based on an experience of change for all.

A great statesman in the East said, 'I am deeply in sympathy with the basic concepts of your work.' He spoke of the failure of character to keep pace with knowledge and of the need for leadership. 'Some place the theologians missed the boat and the timing became wrong,' he continued. 'Some-

---

[1] In June, 1950, seventy-six leaders of Japan arrived in Caux. They came with the active support of the Prime Minister, and included Members of Parliament from all the main parties, seven Governors of Prefectures, the Mayors of Hiroshima and Nagasaki, and leaders of industry, finance and labour. On their way home they were received in Washington in both Houses of Congress, an event unprecedented in history. Their spokesmen addressed both Houses, apologised to the American people, spoke of Moral Re-Armament as the greatest hope for the future of Japan and the Pacific countries, and were received with a standing ovation from both the Senate and the House.

Before returning to Japan, the delegation issued the following statement in London (22 July, 1950): 'We came to Europe, where Communism began, to find a positive answer to Communism. We found it at Caux, in the ideology of Moral Re-Armament . . . We realise that Japan has caused

times the forces that could help, give the most difficulty. In some countries newspaper writers make their livelihood by character assassination. They destroy a man's confidence in himself, and then they destroy public confidence in him, and they feel they have no responsibility themselves. In other countries it is the whole system of life that cripples leadership.'

That is the problem. The Press must become the inspirer of statesmen and the herald of a new world. The system of life must change so that every man everywhere takes responsibility and feels himself part of a mighty plan for the remaking of the world. As it is, our thinking is awry. We expect to differ instead of to agree. Yet wherever MRA goes it creates unity. It averts conflicts. It settles strikes. Instead of the news that a strike has broken out, I receive a telegram from a great industrial city to say that the head of the union and a leading employer propose that management and labour celebrate my birthday together on a city-wide scale. That could be normal because that is the result of change.

A nationalist leader from Africa came to Europe. Bitter political quarrels have divided the leaders of his own people. He feels he has to choose between East and West for his country's salvation. In London his fellow-countrymen tell him of Moral Re-Armament. He changes his plans and

great suffering through her pursuit of false ideas and false roads. We hope in future as a nation to show by our deeds that we have found a change of heart and that we can make our contribution to the remaking of the world.'

The statement concludes, 'Russia has advanced in Asia because the Soviet Government understands the art of ideological war. It fights for the minds of men. We appeal to the governments and people of the West to do the same, to make themselves expert in the philosophy and practice of Moral Re-Armament, which is the ideology of the future. Then all Asia will listen.'

comes to Caux. He finds an answer that unites East and West. Before he leaves for Africa he cables his political enemies at home to meet him at the airport. They are the first people he greets. They find he has changed and they want to work with him. Six months later one of his close friends says of him, 'A new atmosphere has been brought into our national politics since he became reconciled with his political enemies and has shown the truth of not who is right, but what is right in his leadership.' The five newspapers he owns can carry this new spirit to the whole nation. Division is beginning to change into unity for thirty million people.

Across the world the docks are a battlefield because who controls the docks controls the lifeline of nations. Management is baffled. Governments set up inquiries. Trade Union leaders call in vain for discipline. But the trouble goes on. Men are dissatisfied and their dissatisfaction is exploited by the forces of division. Then Moral Re-Armament comes into the picture. Here is the word of a dock leader, the editor of a docker's paper, and one of the men responsible at the time of the big London dock strike of last summer. He has found the answer. He writes, 'Just a letter to let you know what MRA ideology and guidance with God has meant to me in the past ten months. Guidance has been the means of settling two dock disputes in this time, and what a difference guidance means to myself, my wife and family! I have a great partner in my life, Nellie my wife, who is a great fighter, and by taking guidance with her we have got over many a difficult problem. Take, for instance, the dispute in Tooley Street where I was guided to take a hand in it myself. After the employer, union and workers could not agree, I went to the employer and stated the truthful facts. He invited me into his office, and I proved to him not who is right, but what is right, and by us talking together on the MRA ideology, he called the Union officials in, and within an hour of our meeting the strike was settled.

'You may have read of the recent dock dispute. You can rest assured that it was chaps like myself who, with the guidance of God, got the men to go back to work. Had we not had guidance the strike would have still been in progress. When you have guidance with God you see a different light. If only the governments of the world took guidance with God as I have taken guidance in the past ten months, we would have a world at peace in our time.'

A few weeks ago an old friend of mine died. He was a Frenchman of the Frenchmen. He had a beautiful home in Alsace. For the last twenty years he had lived to bring unity between his own country and Germany. As he lay dying his thoughts were clouded by a sense of the division in the world and he said in French, 'I am afraid of what I see coming.' Then he was quiet, and then in a strong voice he spoke in German, and these were his last words, 'There must come reconciliation between the nations. There must come unity between the nations.' His family wrote me that he died with a smile of Heaven on his lips and that his face was like a young man's.

Everyone agrees that unity is our one hope. It is the true destiny of France and of Germany today. It is the destiny of East and West. The alternative is divide and die. Moral Re-Armament offers the world the last chance for every nation to change and survive, to unite and live.

WHAT ARE YOU LIVING FOR?

On Dr Buchman's birthday, 4 June, 1950, a reception in his honour was given at the Hans Sachs Haus in Gelsenkirchen, attended by many hundred miners and their families, by leaders of industry in the Ruhr and representatives from all parts of Germany and many other countries. At this reception Dr Buchman was invested on behalf of the French Government with the Order of Chevalier of the Legion of Honour, in recognition of his contribution to better understanding between France and Germany.

TWELVE YEARS AGO I walked in the woods of the Black Forest near Freudenstadt. The world was on the edge of chaos. Just as today, everyone longed for peace and prepared for war.

As I walked in those quiet woods one thought kept coming to me—'moral and spiritual re-armament, moral and spiritual re-armament. The next great movement in the world will be a movement of moral re-armament for all nations.'

A few days later I was in London in the East End where the British Labour Movement began. The workers responded. Moral Re-Armament went to the world. The newspapers carried it, the radio. Today, twelve years later, in many parts of the world people are gathering to plan for the Moral Re-Armament of their nations. The London workers are meeting in Poplar Town Hall with the dockers. In Birmingham Town Hall labour and management from the British heavy industries and the coal-mines are celebrating the day, and in Glasgow the Clydeside shipworkers.

In America my friends will be speaking on a two-way telephone conversation, giving us news of the advance in America and hearing the news of what you have been doing here in Germany.

Messages have been coming in the last few days from Australia and New Zealand, from India, South Africa, America, from all parts of Europe, from Japan and the Far East.

Typical of many is the following from the executive head of the Government Planning Commission of India, Gulzarilal Nanda:

'Greetings from those of us who have pinned our faith on MRA to cure the ills of the world. Each year MRA is growing in world significance and in power. MRA will not have done its job till the ideology it represents becomes the most significant and the most powerful factor in political, economic and social thought and action in every part of the world.'

What is the secret behind the triumph of a God-given thought? What is it that has enabled an ordinary man like myself, and hundreds of thousands of men and women across the world, to do the extraordinary thing?

Only the very selfish or the very blind person is content to leave the world as it is today. Most of us would like to change the world. The trouble is, too many of us want to do it our own way.

Some people have the right diagnosis, but they bring the wrong cure. They reckon without God and without a change in human nature, and the result is confusion, bitterness and war. Other people are quite sure they have the answer in theory, but they always want somebody else or some other nation to begin. The result is frustration and despair.

186

When the right diagnosis and the right cure come together, the result is a miracle. Human nature changes and human society changes.

Let me illustrate this with a personal word, because it happened to me one day forty-two years ago. For the first time I saw myself with all my pride, my selfishness, my failure and my sin. 'I' was the centre of my own life. If I was to be different, then that big 'I' had to be crossed out.

I saw the resentments I had against six men standing out like tombstones in my heart.

I asked God to change me, and He told me to put things right with those six men. I obeyed God, and wrote six letters of apology.

That same day God used me to change another man's life. I saw that when I obeyed God, miracles happened. I learnt the truth that when man listens, God speaks; when man obeys, God acts; when men change, nations change.

That was the revolutionary path I set my feet on forty-two years ago, which millions are treading now, and on which I challenge you to join me today.

What are you living for? What is your nation living for? Selfish men and selfish nations can drag the world to total disaster. A new type of man, a new type of statesmanship, a new type of national policy—this is our instant need, and this is the purpose for which Moral Re-Armament has come to birth.

A young Swiss engineer, successful in his profession, with family, friends, position and wealth, died this spring.[1] He had discovered this same secret of investing his life and his possessions to create a new world based on change. He gave

---

[1] Robert Hahnloser, one of the founders of Caux.

himself with his wife, who is with us today, and with his children, to make Caux the world centre it has become for all nations. Suddenly people have realised that in five short years he accomplished more for the world than many men in their whole lives.

This young Swiss followed in the steps of another young man who, seven hundred years ago, put aside fame and career and gave everything he had to change the world. He brought a new life to Europe and his life has inspired countless millions since then. He was St Francis of Assisi. This young Swiss engineer, so his wife tells me, kept constantly by him these words of St Francis; and they are the secret of how to change the world:

Lord, make me the instrument of Your peace.
Where there is hatred may I bring love;
Where there is malice may I bring pardon;
Where there is discord may I bring harmony;
Where there is error may I bring truth;
Where there is doubt may I bring faith;
Where there is despair may I bring hope;
Where there is darkness may I bring Your light;
Where there is sadness may I bring joy.

O Master,
May I seek not so much to be comforted as to comfort,
To be understood as to understand,
To be loved as to love;
For it is in giving that we receive,
It is in losing our lives that we shall find them,
It is in forgiving that we shall be forgiven,
It is in dying that we shall rise up to eternal life.

TURN ON THE LIGHT

An address at the opening session of the World Assembly for the Moral Re-Armament of the Nations at Mackinac Island, Michigan, June, 1951.

THERE IS CHAOS and confusion in the world today. There are wars and rumours of wars. There is a strong militant force that is out to win the world. You encounter it everywhere—in the mines, in the docks, in far-away Korea, in Malaya, in Indonesia, in Australia. It is a global conflict. And people are really worried. Fear grips them. They haven't an answer.

What can a man say and do in thirteen short minutes? This is my job, to try and give you the answer.

All people, I know, want to live happily together. We don't want to be disturbed. But we have to be. It is a thing that affects our taxes, and things that affect our taxes touch everybody. And when they go high enough, we try to work out something; rightly or wrongly we try to find an answer.

Everywhere people are dissatisfied. In Milan I saw signs on buildings, 'Long Live Communism.' What is the other sign to put up? 'Long Live—what?' People aren't much united yet on the answer.

Party lines don't hold the way they used to. Democrats and Republicans, it doesn't seem to make much difference. Some are good and some—not so good. But what is so hard to find is the leadership, the type of man to be in Washington, the universal type of man that really meets people's deepest needs. There are so few in whom the people place their full confidence. It used to be a fairly easy job to be in Washington, wrought with honour. But now with the divergent views it is beginning to be a considerable nuisance, unless a man has the art of giving something everybody wants. Today we need men who take God into their consideration and make Him dominant without piosity. Men who forgive their enemies. Men who can clearly decide.

In Britain it is some of the dockers who are giving this leadership. They used to be a problem. They caused strikes and turmoil. But they changed and they are the ones who sent to all the Members of Parliament, not only the Commons, but the Lords, a book about Moral Re-Armament which seems to them to have the answer. They sent it not only to the Labour Members, but to the Conservatives, and a man high in that Party acknowledges with eagerness that these dockers have what he hasn't had. Other people were not aware that he didn't have it. They thought it was enough that he was a Conservative, but he said, 'You have shown me that class is wrong, and no class or person of any class is always right.'

This is such a difficult lesson to learn, each thinking the other fellow better than himself. People are so filled up with their own importance that there isn't room for much more. We need a new altitude of living, something above what we have seen as yet. It is acknowledging the right and yielding the wrong. And it brings illumination.

We have lived in darkness so long. Thomas Edison once said to me in a conversation which lasted way into the hours of the morning, 'Is Heaven lighted up?' I told him, 'Of course. You don't have to bother about that. It's been lighted up long since. You did your job in lighting up the earth.'

Everything can have light. Why shouldn't politics have light? Then our disputes would have more light and less heat.

Turn on the light. More light. That is the answer to confusion. There is no reason for not seeing clearly.

We have all the modern means of having more light. We have electric light which Edison first gave to the world by lighting up one house. We have radar which penetrates fog. We have X-ray which enables us to look inside. But we are not using all God has given us. With all this light the world seems to be marching in vast columns to darkness.

Our faith must be illumined, must have light. So different faiths, all faiths, need this supernatural gleam. 'Lighten with celestial fire.' 'God is my Light and my Salvation, of whom shall I be afraid?' And this light needs absolute moral standards to spotlight where we and our nations need to change. These are the additions to our Christian practice that need furbishing and burnishing. These need to be activated. Lived by every man they are the secret of success.

Here in the State of Michigan the laboratory of Thomas Edison has been given a permanent home in Greenfield Village by that other great American, Henry Ford. Why are the names Ford and Edison such a galvanising force in modern life? They were far-seers. Is that the element we lack in modern-day statesmanship?

Henry Ford sent me this message, 'Moral Re-Armament gives me hope for the future of our country and the world, because of the results that are being achieved.'

Mrs Edison, too, understood Moral Re-Armament. She said, 'This light, like my husband's, must go into every home.' And the son, Charles Edison, as Secretary of the Navy, said, 'Now more than ever I am convinced Moral

Re-Armament shares equally in importance with material re-armament.'

These men were pioneers of the new industrial age. That is why they understood Moral Re-Armament, this new spirit alight in the world.

World circumstances now may compel us each to strike a flint and each one will have to get it for himself. And that is our hope.

Take the Ford plant at Dagenham in London. The Superintendent in charge of the Assembly Building says, 'In the unsettled state of affairs after World War II, I tried the tough way with the men. One day the shop-stewards asked me if I would meet them to discuss our problems on the basis of the four absolute standards of Moral Re-Armament. These meetings have had nothing but the best results. We are getting production without having to drive men. The Building is running more economically today than ever before. Our efficiency was 99.43 per cent in April—better than anything we have had since the war.'

This Assembly gives witness to the fact that an illumination is spreading to the whole world. We are practical people. If a new gadget is to be put into the house, we will put it in. It may be television. Why not this far-seeing vision, this new illumination in every home?

What is it that makes Members of the Senate and House support this work? What is it that makes members of the Foreign Affairs and Foreign Relations Committees cable to the capitals of the world? There is a whole new level of statesmanship wrapped up in this. It is a statesmanship that turns our foes into friends. When Communism comes in, darkness follows just as night follows day. But a Cabinet

Minister who had seen this happen in his country said, 'If Communism is darkness at noon, Moral Re-Armament is sunshine at midnight.'

That is why a founder and anchor man of the Communist Party of Norway, thirty-four years a Communist, is sitting in our midst today. Labour leaders, formerly Communist, from the Ruhr, from the London docks, from France and Italy, leaders in management from Europe and Asia, people of every creed and no creed, of every race and background find here the essence of truth, something they all accept and say, 'This is better than anything I have known before. It works.' The industrialist says, 'This is the thing the worker wants,' and it is something, too, he finds he wants for himself, and enjoys.

Men who have been constantly wrestling with problems see where they themselves have been wrong. The problems and strife melt away. There is nothing left for them to do. One CIO leader said, 'Now I can go to bed and have a good night's sleep. The problem is solved.'

Men are here today who through change have become exponents of the new order. They have seen this revolution on the march. A year ago I was invited by the German Chancellor, Dr Konrad Adenauer, to lead a meeting in the Ruhr to offset the Berlin Communist demonstration. One of the German newspapers came out next morning with the headline, 'Berlin a wash-out. Moral Re-Armament the basic answer.'

Robert Schuman acknowledges this force in Franco-German relations. The Socialist, for six years Mayor of Milan, says, 'Moral Re-Armament is the only arm by which no one is conquered and all are conquerors.'

General Ho Ying-chin, who was Commander-in-Chief of the Chinese Armies, spoke recently in the Upper House of the Japanese Parliament. He said, 'Moral Re-Armament is the only basis for lasting peace for China and Japan. It is priority.'

This world-wide advance is in process of mighty development. A book, *The World Rebuilt*, which appears in twenty countries and ten languages, is eagerly read by all and is understandable by all.[1]

Only last January I said in my statement to the press, 'The airlines will lead the way.' The fact that five delegations from the airlines with special planes are attending this Assembly shows how wonderfully this guidance is being fulfilled. A few days ago Captain Eddie Rickenbacker, speaking to 2,500 of his employees in Eastern Airlines, said, 'Unless we grow morally, mental and financial growth won't last. If you and I can take the one fundamental principle of Moral Re-Armament, honesty, and live up to that, the other three will follow. Our ambition is to build leadership of the quality Moral Re-Armament is teaching. If every one of us could overnight put the spirit into action it would guarantee America would be sure to survive.' These were Captain Rickenbacker's words.

My deep personal wish is to have every American free under the direction of God to fight for America; so to fight that America really be free, free from the tyranny of sin, under God's direction, the unseen but ever-present Power. I wish this no less deeply for everyone in every nation. I don't want our sons, especially our fighting sons, to go about without an answer. It simply enslaves them. It is not good

[1] *The World Rebuilt*, by Peter Howard, 1951, Blandford Press, London Duell, Sloan and Pearce, New York.

enough. It will drive them to the same philosophy that rules our opponents. We shall never create an inspired democracy that way. Men must learn to have a faith that will create the right revolution. If we can spread this revolution fast enough we can save America and the world. Unless we have this revolution there will be a revolution of chaos.

It needs this stronger dose. Sin leaves us with such a dull, heavy thud. 'The blood of Jesus Christ His Son cleanseth us from all sin.' That is the discovery everyone is looking for. That is the answer.

Then you will have a wonderful example that the whole world will want to follow. You will have an America to which the wise and honest can repair. And that is what the world expects today of America. You will have a battle-cry of freedom, and that is what America wants. You will have a democracy that is really inspired.

Then our young men and our old men will fight as Lincoln fought of old. Our young men will know what to fight for and our wars will be won. And we shall be at peace with all men and the whole world.

Note: Dr Adenauer in a message conveyed by his personal representative, said: 'Nations cannot enjoy stable relationships until they have been inwardly prepared for them. In this Moral Re-Armament has rendered great and lasting services. In recent months we have seen the conclusion of important international agreements. Moral Re-Armament has played an unseen but effective part in bridging differences of opinion between the negotiating parties, and has kept before them the aim of peaceful agreement in the search for the common good.'

WHAT WE NEED IS SOMETHING
ELECTRIC

*Dr Buchman opened a World Assembly at Mackinac Island in June,
1952. The invitation was issued by the Chairman and members of the
Senate Foreign Relations Committee and of the House Foreign Affairs
Committee.[1] At a reception in the United States Senate for the overseas
delegates to the Assembly, 12 June, 1952, Mr Richard Nixon of
California said: 'There is no question that in the final analysis the
great struggle in which we are engaged in the world, between the forces
of freedom on the one side and Communism, dictatorship and totali-
tarianism on the other side, will be decided in the minds and hearts and
souls of men. The Moral Re-Armament movement is one of the greatest
factors which is winning that struggle.'*

WHAT WE NEED is something electric—a shock that brings
men and nations to their senses before it is too late. Something powerful enough to weld unity out of the hardest
elements.

I remember the first electric light. It revolutionised our
living. It altered men's thinking about the future. Is there
today a discovery that can go into every home in every
nation and unexpectedly bring an answer to our darkest
problems?

Our job may be to cure the maelstrom of disorder and

[1] In their invitation, they said, 'We need such a demonstration of united
strength in the field of inspired moral leadership, without which our
common military, political and economic efforts to save the free world
will certainly be less effective. We are impressed with the practical evidence

196

have the answer to a panic throughout the lands. Is that your conception of your part in world statesmanship? That is the purpose of Moral Re-Armament. Here is the answer that enables all of us to work together for something really big.

A man from Washington came to see us. At the end of the evening he said, 'I and my experts discuss everything except the point. Moral Re-Armament deals with the point.' Next morning he got up early and telephoned to his superior in Washington. He apologised to him for a resentment against him which he described as the deepest resentment of his life. He said on the telephone, 'What is the use of us talking to the world about unity when we have division right here in our own offices in Washington? I was resentful because I was self-righteous. I have not been fully honest with you. I am sorry.'

A European who heard this said, 'Here is American statesmanship that will win everybody. It's the secret we are looking for.'

Everyone everywhere can make contact with the source of power and illumination that changed the thinking of the man from Washington and told him what to do.

The short-circuit is human selfishness. It breaks contact. It is the source of darkness and loss of direction. When selfishness is crossed out, every home and every Cabinet can be power stations radiating an answer that works.

of what such active moral leadership has accomplished to establish democracy as a working force in danger areas that affect the future of your country and ours. We recognise the opportunity this Assembly offers to proclaim to the world an inspired experience of democracy, based on moral standards and the guidance of God, which is the greatest bulwark of freedom.' Senator Alexander Smith, of New Jersey (*Congressional Record*, 12 June, 1952) introduced on the floor of the Senate the Members of Parliament attending the Assembly. The Vice-President, who recalled his earlier visit to Caux, welcomed the guests on behalf of the Senate.

We need to bring the reality of this answer quickly to the eyes and ears of the world.

We have just seen a film—made in Finland—forged from the experience of men eight hundred yards from the Iron Curtain. Its effect is electric. It is called *The Answer*. It is industry's answer. It is democracy giving a sure answer with a united voice. An American, whose business it is to show films, said, 'This is the finest film I have ever seen.'

Is that what we need? Something in our movie theatres which gives the answer to a steel strike? This film does. It shows the answer to the self-will in management and labour who are both so right, and so wrong.

The play which inspired this film has been seen by over a million people in sixteen countries around the world. In recent weeks it has been showing in the industrial North of Italy and drawing thousands. In real life one of the two men who played the part of management and labour is the personnel head of 55,000 workers. The other is one of his workers and a former Communist. The change in these two men has electrified Milan. The nation began to realise that when management is ready to change and make sacrifices for an idea that can unite the world, labour responds.

It works in America too. The Personnel Superintendent of one of the great airlines states that three years ago there were four hundred and ninety-one grievances outstanding between labour and management in his company. Then Moral Re-Armament went to work. Men changed. Men got honest. Last year there were only seventeen grievances in that company. So far this year there have been three.

As the head of the Textile Workers of France, a former Communist who was electrified into a positive force by

Moral Re-Armament, said, 'Honesty in the factory and the government equals prosperity in the nation.'

Take one city. It has a stormy industrial record. Subversive elements have skilfully worked for division and control. Men from the airlines who apply Moral Re-Armament were invited to bring their evidence. The next day the labour leader in the dispute said, 'What has happened to management, they are different? We can negotiate with men like that.' Management said, 'We hardly recognised the labour leader today. He is different. He is a pleasure to do business with. We are ready to agree with him on what's right in this issue.' Two days later a leading financial paper carried the headline, 'Strike Threat Resolved after Visit of MRA Employer-Labour Team.'

We need something electric. Something that sparks men's hearts and minds to a new way of doing business. A positive force which can magnetise a whole community. When that happens it makes news for the millions.

I have in my hand an article by Rear-Admiral Richard E. Byrd. It arrived yesterday. It is on the news stands today. It will be read in millions of homes across America and Canada. Its title is 'Preview of a New World,' the story of Moral Re-Armament. Say the editors of the journal which publishes the article, 'It's a great piece of writing. It's authoritative. It reads like the wind.'

Admiral Byrd says, 'MRA is above party, class or point of view. It is not an organisation you join, but an ideology you live. Not a new religion, but a new dynamic force. It starts when you start with yourself to live out the four absolute moral standards of honesty, purity, unselfishness and love.'

Another Admiral was invited by the Governor of an island

to dine at Government House and afterwards to give news of MRA at a public meeting. Introducing him to the audience, which included government officials, mayors, newspaper editors and trade unionists, the leading figures of the island, the Governor said, 'I have been a scoffer, but I went to an MRA assembly and I have changed my mind. MRA is something of tremendous importance for us all. It is a terrific power for good throughout the world.'

It is amazing how speedily even scoffers get the point. It is split second transmission. It leaps from man to man. It brings unity to classes, races, nations.

Take South Africa. At a pan-African assembly for Moral Re-Armament, all the different communities and races were represented. A member of one of the oldest Boer families in South Africa stood up and said, 'As I grew up I accepted superiority to the African as my right. When I met MRA I knew it was the answer for me and for South Africa. I saw where I needed to change. I lost my superiority and I want to apologise to the African people for my previous attitude.' A young African barrister said in reply, 'It is not easy for a South African or an Englishman to say "sorry" to us. But we Africans have to say "sorry" too. We are prepared to work with anyone who accepts this spirit.'

African leaders summed up the assembly in these words: 'We have seen history being made here as Africans, Asians and Europeans find the secret of unity through change, absolute moral standards and the guidance of God. We believe this to be the only true road for the new Africa, and we pledge ourselves to fight along with you to bring Moral Re-Armament to the whole continent and the world.'

As I speak to you I have beside me representatives from the

Far East. The Prime Minister of Siam says, 'MRA is the best thing for Siam. Siam must give its best for MRA.' There has just arrived at our world headquarters in Switzerland five tons of the best Siamese rice. The shipping lines and railways delivered it free to the door. It is a gift from the Prime Minister. He knows the work of Moral Re-Armament in the East. He has read full-page articles of its world effect in his leading newspaper. He knows what the Burmese and Japanese are doing. They and members of the Cabinets of India, Pakistan and Ceylon have invited Moral Re-Armament to bring this answer to their countries. That news is electric. An answer that unites East and West.

A delegation of leading citizens from Siam is with us here in Mackinac to equip themselves to take MRA to their nation.

And men with this answer are answering the needs of the nations. Think of the struggle for South America. Recently forty-six trades union men from Brazil went for three months' training to Moscow. That is the problem. What is the answer?

A French Count who served in his country's resistance force during the war; the son of a French Marxist seaman, whose mother was Secretary-General of three million Socialist women; a former football star from America, and a young Swiss born in Egypt, have been working together with tremendous effect in Brazil. These four men were responsible for a mass meeting of Santos dockers. There were twenty speakers. The president of the dockers was in the chair. Among the speakers were top management and former Communists who in the force of MRA had found a revolutionary philosophy, a new passion and plan which is the answer to the bitterness of the Left and the hardness of the Right. Men of all classes are here from Brazil to learn together how to give this force to all of South America.

We are in the midst of the breakdown of our civilisation—war in the home, war in industry, war between the nations. What is the future? Further disintegration, chaos, anarchy and dictatorship? Or the birth of a new society brought about by a revolutionary change in human nature? The Holy Spirit is the most powerful Force in the world today. Man can split the atom. The Holy Spirit is uniting humanity through men who listen to Him and obey. It needs to be a daily experience. It is practical. It works.

The basic struggle is for the wills of men. That is the ideological struggle. It goes on in your heart and mine every day. Armies and pacts and economic assistance are necessary. But the deciding factor is whether as men and nations we are guided by the voice of materialism or the Voice of God.

V

AN IDEA
TO WIN THE WORLD

Hearts and minds of Asians and Africans have been gripped by Moral Re-Armament. This is the one ideology in which Eastern and Western countries can unite. MRA challenged me to apply to my own life the standards which my grandfather applied to his. I have decided to give all I have with this force which is turning the tide of history.

RAJMOHAN GANDHI

Grandson of the Mahatma,
June, 1957

BREAD, PEACE, HOPE

In October, 1952, Dr Buchman left for Asia with a task force of 200, invited by the leaders of a number of Asian countries. He has known the peoples of Asia and their leaders since 1915, when he was welcomed to India by Mahatma Gandhi. The MRA force arrived in India in November, after a visit to Ceylon which, in the words of the Prime Minister, 'left an abiding impression in the hearts of the people.' In New Delhi Dr Buchman was invited to address both Houses of Parliament. An All-Asian Assembly opened in New Delhi in January, 1953. Dr Buchman's New Year message to the people of India follows.

MEN ARE HUNGRY for bread, for peace, and for the hope of a new world order.

Before a God-led unity every last problem will be solved. Hands will be filled with work, stomachs with food, and empty hearts with an ideology that really satisfies. That is what Moral Re-Armament is out for. It gives faith to the faithless, but also helps men of faith to live so compellingly that cities and nations change.

A nation where everyone cares enough and everyone shares enough, so that everyone has enough, will pattern a new social and economic order for this and all future generations.

A nation at peace within itself will bring peace to the world.

A nation which makes *What is Right* regnant in personal, industrial, political and national life will pioneer the next historic step of progress and destiny for all mankind.

THE NEW STATESMANSHIP
TO END CONFUSION

After his visits to Ceylon and India, Dr Buchman visited Kashmir, Pakistan, Iran, as the guest of His Imperial Majesty the Shah, and Turkey. On returning to London, he gave the following address on his seventy-fifth birthday, 4 June, 1953.[1]

PEOPLE DON'T SEEM to see eye to eye. It is so difficult for them to have a common mind. They have their own ideas and are prone to push them on others. And to begin to think of a new statesmanship that will end confusion will demand a history-making decision.

We lack a mighty positive programme which can win all men and all nations. We produce a myriad conferences and schemes that add nothing to the solution of our problems. Leaders are prone to do it in their own selfish way. They say it is for the good of the country, but it is mostly for the good of themselves, and that is the reason they miss the bus.

But there is a new statesmanship abroad in the world. Conferences which give this great positive have the cure.

Last month an inter-racial Assembly for Moral Re-Armament took place in the heart of strife-torn Africa. Sir

[1] Senator Wiley, Chairman of the Foreign Relations Committee of the US Senate, said in a message to Dr Buchman, 'On your historic mission with your great task force through Egypt, Ceylon, India, Pakistan, Iran and Turkey, you have been not only an ambassador of goodwill, but you have been the light of Asia, an ambassador of the highest order . . . I am grateful for the untold work of you and your task force.'

Gilbert Rennie, Governor of Northern Rhodesia, in his opening address said, 'The aim of this Assembly is to find a common goal towards which all can work together without suspicion, without fear and without bitterness. Moral Re-Armament is based on change. Change in ourselves is the first step towards better relations. I hope and pray this Assembly will help us to achieve that change.'

A South African, a member of one of the oldest pioneering families, responded to the Governor: 'I wish every statesman in every land might have heard your words, for you represent a new kind of statesmanship.'

The Assistant Secretary for Native Affairs evaluated the results. He said, 'I came sceptical. I go away convinced. We know these Africans well and they are obviously changed. They must be asking now, "Show us changed Europeans."'

In January a similar Assembly attended by thirty-four nations was held in the capital city of India. An Indian Cabinet Minister summed up the results, 'It has opened a new chapter in the long history of Delhi.'

Last October in Colombo an experienced United Nations diplomat attended a Moral Re-Armament Assembly of Asian and Pacific nations. He said, 'I have seen more true unity and peace produced here in two weeks than in all my years at Lake Success.'

What if this were the spirit of the next Three-Power or Four-Power conference?

I am just back from seven months in the East. A force of 200 from twenty-five countries travelled with me. We took this message to Ceylon, India, Kashmir and Pakistan. We were honoured guests in Egypt, Iran and Turkey. One thing is certain. These countries are united in their response to

Moral Re-Armament. As one of their statesmen put it, 'Moral Re-Armament is the great future. It is destined to save the human race.'

It was Jinnah, the founder of Pakistan, who invited me to his country. On the one free night he had in London, he went to see our play *The Forgotten Factor*. He came tired and worn after a busy day, feeling he had not reached his objectives. He sat in silence until a line in the play described the hard-headed industrialist who would not change his mind, in these words, 'Will not budge.' Jinnah laughed, and from then on he was living in a new climate. He came to my home afterwards for dinner and said, 'I want you in Pakistan. You have the answer to the hates of the world. Honest apology— that is the golden key.' Those were Mr Jinnah's words.

But who will put that key into the lock of history and open the gates of the future for all men everywhere to enjoy peace on this earth?

Kashmir, land of charm and beauty, knows those ancient truths of simple honesty, and if she applies them nationally she will give the answer to the world. Sheikh Abdullah, the Prime Minister, said to me, 'It will take patience, but you have the answer to India and Pakistan.'

Throughout these countries the press has indeed been the herald of a new world order. *Dawn*, the newspaper founded by Mr Jinnah, gave the headline, 'A New Basis for Co-operation—MRA the answer to world problems.' It reported the new unity that Pakistanis and Indians are finding through Moral Re-Armament.

One of the largest newspaper chains in India, *The Express*, along with *The Hindustan Times*, edited by Mahatma Gandhi's son, Devadas Gandhi, carried this message of mine to the nation: 'Men are hungry for bread, for peace, and for the hope of a new world order. Before a God-led unity every last problem will be solved. Hands will be filled with work, stomachs with food, and empty hearts with an ideology that really satisfies. That is what Moral Re-Armament is out for.'

The editor of the great Indian newspaper *The Hindu* was so impressed by the evidence that he issued a ten-page supplement on Moral Re-Armament and distributed it to the nation. In America Admiral Byrd and a national committee including the Speaker of the House, the Chairman of the Senate Foreign Relations Committee, the Chairman of the Senate Labour Committee, the Vice-President of the Hearst Newspapers and the Executive Vice-President of the CIO, sent it out to the 3,000 editors and publishers of America.

This Executive Vice-President of the CIO, who represents five and a half million men, is giving this new statesmanship to American labour. He says, 'I have taken my decision to live by the four absolute moral standards of absolute honesty, absolute purity, absolute unselfishness and absolute love, and under God's guidance for the rest of my life.' He found unity in his home. He now negotiates on the basis of *what* is right, not *who* is right. Here is his new thinking for American labour: '1. To set the pace for unity in the nation by achieving unity within its own house. 2. To create with industry a pattern of teamwork that will sell democracy to the millions. 3. With the united strength of labour and industry, to back the government in a foreign policy that will win all nations.'

What do the nations need? My mind goes to Japan. They say, 'We have a new constitution. It is like an empty basket. What will we put in it? We need an ideology that will make democracy work.' Three hundred leaders of the new

Japan have come to Moral Re-Armament for training in this ideology. They have begun to set it to work nationally.

In my lifetime I have seen two history-making discoveries. The discovery of the *atom* as a source of untold energy and its mobilisation. That has given us the atomic age. The other discovery is of *man* as the source of untold energy and his mobilisation. That has given us the ideological age. It is the key to events around us.

While statesmen plan for armies and conferences and alliances, the disruptive forces win a dock worker, a civil servant, a scientist, a soldier, a schoolteacher. They mobilise the grievances, the bitterness, the righteous longings for a better world in the hearts of these men. They set them on the march with a total commitment to capture the world with their idea. So while Cabinets call for more production, there are 'slow-downs' in industry. While statesmen call for another conference, vital secrets are betrayed. While everyone calls for unity between nations, disunity grows within nations.

What is the answer? The statesmanship which can set the ordinary man on the march with a vision, comradeship and plan to remake the world.

In 1938 there came to me while walking in the woods in Freudenstadt the simple thought, 'There will be a mighty movement of God's Living Spirit throughout the world. It will be known as Moral and Spiritual Re-Armament.' That seed thought has taken root among the leadership of the world.

Sometimes we are tempted to wonder if there is another way. Everyone in every nation seems to have his own solution based on personal and national advantage. But the secret is, 'Not my way, but God's way. Not my will, but God's will.'

This is the cure for confusion—making God the decisive authority—not saying 'Yes' with our lips only, but also with the discipline of our lives. It makes you natural, it makes you real. You need never try to appear wiser or better than you really are. This is the sort of person people will flock to and follow.

Confusion comes from compromise. Clarity comes from change. The moral change that illumines the darkest motives and mobilises the latent powers. If only we could see our nations as others see us, then we would want to change.

Absolute moral standards are the well-spring of inspired statesmanship. We talk of peace and unity, but forget that no man who harbours ill-will can solve the hates of nations. We criticise stubbornness in others, but ignore the selfwill which our children are so familiar with in ourselves. We talk of divine guidance, but forget that it is the pure in heart who see God. It is not those who talk, but those who listen who receive guidance. The key to new statesmanship is new statesmen.

This is my seventy-fifth birthday. I have long experience in many lands. It all comes back to basic moral truth, to absolute honesty, absolute purity, absolute unselfishness and absolute love, to the guidance of God and the total commitment to His Will. Without that experience we have nothing. With it, we have everything. A new world spelt out in new men. That is our only hope. The evidence is conclusive.

'MRA is the ABC of the answer.' Yes, the African chief was right when he said, 'MRA is the ABC of the answer.'

FOR ALL MEN EVERYWHERE

In December, 1953, a task force, sixty strong from fifteen countries, left for Africa on the invitation of leaders of South Africa, the Rhodesias, Nigeria and East Africa. In nine months they travelled 20,000 miles through Central, South and West Africa. An Inter-racial Assembly in Johannesburg was attended by 563 people of all races and all parts of Africa. Leaders of the countries advancing to independence welcomed MRA as the basis for their national life and the unity of the continent.

Dr Buchman's personal links with Africa go back over fifty years. In 1929 he led a task force to South Africa. In 1941 the Deputy Premier, the Hon. J. H. Hofmeyr, stated that this visit 'was of national significance and started a major and continuous influence for racial reconciliation throughout the whole country.'

THIS BROADCAST was written in Morocco,[1] a land of warriors through the ages, a land which, like all the African continent today, faces the problems of a new age and poses statesmenship with its greatest test. Is there an answer to division?

Six months ago a special plane took a force of sixty from Europe to Central Africa. Among them a British Admiral, a former Governor of Khartoum, a Colonel of the Black Watch, a former Communist from Germany, a Scottish

---

[1] Two years later, in June, 1956, His Majesty the King of Morocco, said in a message to Dr Buchman, 'I thank you for all that you have done for Morocco, the Moroccans and myself in the course of these testing years. My desire is that your message of Moral Re-Armament, founded upon the essential moral values and the Will of God, reaches the masses of this country. We have complete confidence in the work you are doing.'

Marquis and a French Marxist united in this answering force of Moral Re-Armament. They join with people from many parts of Africa to carry this programme to a whole continent. They move with a passion and a plan through the country.

A historic event takes place in Cape Town. This is how the *Cape Times* arrestingly headlined it, 'White, Black on MRA Platform.' The newspaper describes an Assembly where more than 2,000 people pressed into the City Hall and crowded the doorways and aisles. It says:

'Dr William Nkomo, founder and first president of the African National Congress Youth League, said he formerly "believed that the hope for the African lay only in a blood revolution." He then described his visit to an MRA conference in Lusaka last year at which, he said, "I saw white men and black men change, and I myself changed." His words drew the biggest ovation of the evening.' *Die Burger*, the Government newspaper, headlined it: 'Moral Re-Armament freed him from hatred of Afrikaner.'

George Daneel, former Springbok rugby football player, speaking after him in Afrikaans, said, 'It is impossible not to feel anxious about the way that the differences between the races are being exploited by certain negative forces out to undermine the civilisation of Africa. That is why my wife and I have decided to fight together with this force to find God's plan for this land and for all races.'

These two men created a sensation. They pledged themselves to fight for the remaking of South Africa on a new dimension under the direction of God.

The Mayor of Cape Town said, 'You are taking the city by storm.' A Cable and Wireless operator said he was glad he wasn't on duty after the meeting that night. 'Two clerks had to work overtime,' he said, 'and it seemed as if every newspaper man in town was filing a story.'

Natal experienced the same impact. Two thousand thronged the City Hall with all races unsegregated for the first time. The theme was, 'Durban the beacon light for the unity of Africa.' Here Dr Nkomo said, 'I saw something greater than nationalism at work. I saw an ideology which is superior because it is an ideology for everyone, everywhere. I believe this is the one road which will be the best road for my people and for South Africa.'

John Ngcobo, Zulu baritone on the BBC, just back from England, sang. The vast crowd insisted on an encore. The next day two of the MRA force visited his mother sixty miles away in the hut where she lives.

The large Indian community of Durban invited this force to the Community Centre at Phoenix founded by Mahatma Gandhi, and to the Gandhi Memorial Hall. Among them was Lady Hardinge of Penshurst. The Secretary of the Indian cultural society, in an official vote of thanks, said, 'We have merely attached the name of Mahatma Gandhi to our hall. But you have inscribed his ideals in your hearts and lives.'

All parts of Africa respond to this message. Nigeria, fitting itself for the task of self-government, turns to Moral Re-Armament. An invitation signed by three central and five regional Cabinet Ministers and other Nigerian leaders says, 'We are doing this with the realisation that a self-governing Nigeria must be built on a firm moral foundation, and with the conviction that MRA by its performances in Europe, Asia and other continents can give to our people and country the moral revolution which is the only basis of survival in a world of conflict and chaos.'

'Nigeria needs nothing but the best,' the invitation continues, 'and that is why we believe in a world-wide force such as MRA which is above party, class, race, creed or colour and has its roots in the guidance of God and the love of our fellow men.'

Africa, too, has its share in the Moslem world which stretches from Morocco to Indonesia. The Rector of El Azhar University in Cairo says, 'MRA is working to spread the principles of peace, love and sound morals without individual and national differences. We ourselves will co-operate to establish this sound, God-inspired ideology.'

Bangkok was the scene of a New Year's Assembly for Moral Re-Armament which drew delegates from all parts of South-East Asia, Australia and Japan. The Speaker of the Malayan Legislative Council said, 'This ideology with its unifying influence will be needed to help bring about the birth of a united Malayan nation and a God-inspired democracy. Our delegation to Bangkok,' he said, 'is a multi-racial one—Malay, Chinese, Indian and Briton. Personally I have made up my mind to bring this superior ideology of MRA into the Government councils of my country.' Those were the words of the Speaker of the Malayan parliament.

Here is something for all men everywhere, but most of all for the men in government and industry who need to make it the policy of their nation.

The head of an Asian trade union asked a prominent American labour leader about Moral Re-Armament. He replied, 'The question is not how MRA fits into the labour movement. MRA fits you for the labour movement, and MRA's four absolute moral standards are labour's true basis. MRA fits you as a labour leader to do your job.' The Asian leader replied, 'Can you not come on the next delegation to our country? This is what our labour movement needs.'

The Regional Secretary of the Tea Plantation Workers of South India, who was trained in Caux and who has applied MRA with considerable success to the tea industry, says, 'MRA is a constructive force, whose influence benefits the workers and industrialists. It changes people as well as the social system. This idea transcends geographical divisions, racial distinctions, party differences and class conflict.'

Continents are linked by this answer. For the opening performance in Rhodesia of Peter Howard's ideological play, *The Boss*, came a cable to Sir Godfrey Huggins, Prime Minister of the Central African Federation. It was sent by the Mayor of the steel town of Firminy in France who had been for four years his nation's Minister of Reconstruction. The cable read, 'Great success of *The Boss* in Firminy. Shakes workers and industrialists and makes them think. Opens the eyes of the blind and the hearts of the sceptical. Moral Re-Armament gives to all men the means of uniting and rebuilding the world in peace.' The leaders in Firminy speak with conviction because faced with unemployment and some of the worst housing conditions in France, the latest word from the Managing Director of the steelworks is that there will be no unemployment, and the Mayor says that the spirit created by the play has immeasurably helped in his fight for better housing conditions for the city.

The French Socialist paper, *La Tribune de Saint-Etienne*, commenting on the play writes, 'To pose the immense problem of the happiness of man, and then to answer it in an indisputable fashion in barely over an hour, is something to which the completely convinced spectators will be able to testify, and which they will never be able to get out of their minds.'

Small wonder that these French employers and labour leaders are together carrying this message to other countries —to Germany, Holland, Italy and North Africa. Among them is the Secretary-General of the French Textile Workers (Force Ouvrière). He is one of those responsible for the new agreement in his industry, which former Prime Minister Antoine Pinay, in a series of articles on France's problems in *Figaro*, described as one of the first solid achievements in the change of attitude which he feels essential to the economic survival of his country.

What is the secret of uniting men? The Vice-President of a national labour organisation of five million members in America was called in to settle the problems of a union that was divided by political and personal ambitions. He told the workers that the only way to unite the world is by change—personal, social, national and supernational. Afterwards an international official of the union said to him, 'John, can I drive you the 450 miles to the airport? I want to talk. I was shaken by what you said. I would like to know what the answer is. How can I unite my home? How do I get the answer to drink? How can I unite the union?' John told him about his own change and how he had started, and how to find the guidance of God. His decision was to go back to put things right with his local union leaders, to be honest about his underground political activities, and to put things right with his wife and family. That man is now a force for unity.

Asked how he found the power to unite men and meet their needs, John will reply, 'I always wanted my wife Rose to change and to be a perfect wife, to be where I wanted her to be and do what I wanted her to do, always. I never thought I should change a little too. That did not occur to me, but when I took a good look at myself in the mirror I found out where the nation's sins were. You start with yourself, John. The kind of teamwork you create with Rose and the children from the quiet time in the home in the morning and reading the Bible, is the kind of teamwork you can create with management and labour and take into your office, conference rooms and negotiating tables.'

His wife Rose says, 'When I met Moral Re-Armament I saw I was responsible for the failure of our marriage. I had been a fashion model who took an hour to make up my face. I had spent my evenings at drinking parties. I felt I had hindered the settling of a national strike because I had given my husband nothing but censure and blame. I learned the secret of listening to God for His guidance. The first thought that came was to apologise to my husband for the failure of our marriage. The divorce was called off. Now, together, we are out to pioneer the idea of selfless living and giving.'

What is the answer for a divided world in which men have developed points of view they cannot overcome and forces of destruction they cannot control? The answer lies in labour leaders, industrial leaders, the ordinary man and the statesman finding John's experience. Such men bring confidence to the conference table. Conferences on the current pattern will never solve the problems and needs of people and nations. That can only come from heart speaking to heart. That ends confusion. That brings the cure. The fate of our nations depends on how speedily we seize this answer and apply it.

THE ELECTRONICS
OF THE SPIRIT

In June, 1955, the Moral Re-Armament World Mission of 250 from twenty-eight countries, travelled across Asia, the Middle East and Africa. In the course of their 35,000-mile journey they were the guests of the governments of eleven countries. They took with them the musical play The Vanishing Island. *The final preparations were made at Mackinac where Dr Buchman gave this world broadcast, May, 1955.*

I FOUND something new in Los Angeles.

I found it at a dinner.

And I found it in a man. His name is Lee de Forest. He is a pioneer of the new science of electronics which is leading us into an age beyond the atom age. He says the time will soon come when the world will work a four-day week and a six-hour day.

My old friend Thomas Edison came to mind as I listened to this pioneer. Edison gave the world illumination, electric light. I saw it happen. It opened up something new for the whole world. Mrs Edison, also, flew out with me to California to fulfil her conviction when she said, 'Moral Re-Armament, like my husband's light, must go into every home.'

Now electronics is a new science. Spirit has been known for a long time. It's an old science. But linked with electronics, it hitches the world to a new dimension of life and thought. Millions can speedily, automatically yield to this new practice, the Electronics of the Spirit.

We can scarcely grasp what the Electronics of the Spirit means. We just faintly glimpse it. Think of the veritable instantaneous reaction whereby a thought can travel across America in less than one-fiftieth of a second. And now, with electronics, in a flash you not only hear the voice but the time you speak is registered and you get the bill at the end of the month, all without any human aid. No words of mine can explain it.

Then take the Electronics of the Spirit. It works with an Infinite Mind. It circles the globe instantly. It taps resources hitherto unexplored and forces hitherto unknown. Take the whole question of guidance—God's Mind and my mind. The thought that slips in any time, day or night, can be the thought of the Author of mind. We are dealing here with facts that no one can measure.

A thought comes—maybe just an arresting tick. One responds to it. And millions can be the richer if it is effectively carried out. It may apply to someone who crosses our path— some friend, perhaps, who may be the link which can reach cabinets, which can prevent nations from taking the wrong turning.

It was the results of the Electronics of the Spirit to which Congressman Harry Sheppard, dean of the California delegation to the United States Congress, referred when he said a few weeks ago, 'What MRA is doing is the pinnacle of human achievement—bringing people together.'

Take Nigeria, a nation of thirty-three million people, pivotal for the whole of Africa. A full-page article in the Colonial Review of the London *Times* describes how Dr Azikiwe, Prime Minister of the Eastern Region, met Moral Re-Armament in 1949 and decided to apply it to Nigeria.

The Prime Minister and the Leader of the Opposition, who had fought a long libel suit against each other, came together on the opening night of an MRA play in Nigeria. The theatre was crowded. Hundreds had to stand. Dozens more peered in through the windows and listened outside.

The Leader of the Opposition came to the play four times. During the presentation of the Budget, when Parliament and all the galleries were crowded, he crossed the floor of the House to greet the Prime Minister, and paid a generous tribute to him. He said, 'Our greatest problem, greater even than grinding poverty, is spiritual confusion.'

The Prime Minister and Leader of the Opposition together gave a reception for the House of Parliament to meet the whole MRA task force. They sent out an invitation on gold-engraved cards. The two men chaired the reception like old friends. The Prime Minister had all the guests repeat after him the four standards—absolute honesty, absolute purity, absolute unselfishness and absolute love. The issue of unity in Nigeria is crucial because the bitterness is intense. One Member of Parliament made an experiment of the Electronics of the Spirit between God's Mind and his own. He said, 'I have divided the nation, and spoken bitterly in public. I must change and work to unite the nation.'

In South Africa, too, a force is at work powerful enough to unite even the bitterest enemies. The *Eastern Province Herald* quotes a well-known Afrikaner, 'Moral Re-Armament has brought together those who were poles apart in the task of building a new South Africa. It has brought the answer to hatred in the country's heart.'

In India, the *Hindusthan Standard* in a special ten-page supplement tells how this electronically heart-spanning force spreads from continent to continent. This is the eleventh of the great Indian newspapers which have published special supplements on the work of Moral Re-Armament.

Its front-page headline is 'Asia and Africa—New Era of Constructive Co-operation.' Manilal Gandhi, editor of South Africa's *Indian Opinion* and son of my old friend Mahatma Gandhi, whom I met on my first visit to India in 1915, is one of the contributors to this special supplement.

The Speaker of the Indian House of the People, Mr Mavalankar, says, 'Moral Re-Armament is the old, ancient way of the East. It has given our old philosophy a new orientation and given it wings.'

A Leader of the Opposition in the United Provinces Legislature, member of the State Executive of the Praja Socialist Party, says, 'I have learned more from MRA in two and a half days than in twenty-five years of political life. One day's living of the four standards is worth more than a thousand hours of lectures.'

The Electronics of the Spirit certainly saves time—and it comes out with the right answers. Some people spend twenty years and more in politics, but still do not seem to have all the answers fully right.

For twenty years of politics does not always produce a new type of man. But the Electronics of the Spirit produces new men who are effective at the heart of nations.

Two Australians, who had spent a lifetime in political opposition, and who had greatly suffered when their country was at war with Japan, went together to Tokyo. They brought an electronic answer which had freed them from bitterness and hate. One of them told the Japanese Prime Minister, 'We came here to work with you to make Dr

Buchman's vision "Japan the lighthouse of Asia" a reality.' They were received by the Japanese Cabinet Ministers. They were welcomed at a reception in the Diet. They spoke to the Left and Right wings of the Socialist Party. Within recent days the Prime Minister had a special showing of one of the Moral Re-Armament plays in his official residence for Cabinet and Government leaders which press, radio and television covered nationally.

And Dr Ichimada, the Japanese Finance Minister, said, 'The spirit of MRA is permeating the life of our country. We pledge ourselves to fight that a fresh illumination shall come to Japanese political life, by making MRA the basis of our policy.' This represents the fulfilment of the vision I had when I made the first of many unforgettable visits to Japan forty years ago.

The Electronics of the Spirit is available for everyone. It is not only necessary but normal for all men everywhere. The *Afro-American*, most respected national Negro newspaper in America, caught the joy of this basic answer given at the Afro-Asian Conference with its bold headline, 'Moral Re-Armament urged in Bandung.' The story reads, 'Dr Jamali, chairman of the Iraq delegation, speaking at the opening of the conference called for "moral re-armament as the need of the world today". He received a vigorous, sustained ovation.' The speech concluded, 'We must work on the basis of moral re-armament. The world would then turn into one integral camp with no Eastern or Western camps.'

These truths are readily perceived and speedily acceptable to the far-flung Moslem world which can be a girder of unity for all civilisation. My ancestor, the scholar Bibliander, was the first man to make the riches of the Koran available for Europe when he translated it into German 413 years ago. Today the Secretary-General of the Arab League says, 'The Arab world hails the advent of Moral Re-Armament as one of the most significant factors on the world scene.'

The Prime Minister of Egypt, in a message to the Washington Assembly for Moral Re-Armament early this year, said, 'The problems of government which confront the statesmen will not be solved without this secret of a change of heart which you are giving back to the world. It will lift men everywhere above the hates and jealousies fostered by selfish interests and recall them to the creative inspiration which comes from obedience to the Will of God.'

A book called *Where Do We Go From Here?* which with pictures and colourful phrases that all can understand gives the secret of the change of heart of which the Prime Minister speaks, was translated into Arabic by the Director of Information in the Egyptian Ministry of National Guidance.

Plays as well as books can bring this electronic answer to millions. Twenty-seven casts are giving the Moral Re-Armament plays in eight languages on every continent. In Hollywood, leading directors of screen and music, as well as actors, technicians and designers, have given of their genius to help create a new musical, *The Vanishing Island*, which has a captivating answer that reaches the heart of every man.

Ole Olsen of Olsen and Johnson says of this musical, 'This has something a man can understand and live. The music of this show is terrific. It is an ideological atom bomb that will have repercussions around the world.'

We have reached a point where man must either solve his problems or be destroyed by them. Politicians in every country are beginning to discover that the human mind, however able and sincere, cannot solve the problems created by the human passions of hate and greed and fear. It needs an electronic intervention, an experience of the Spirit. It needs the new dimension that can usher in a new age. This experience must go into every department of life in every land.

How to catch this new dimension? St Francis of Sales says the secret is to listen to the inner voice. He says that half an hour a day is a basic minimum, except when you are exceptionally busy. Then a full hour is necessary.

An Italian priest declares that writing down the thoughts which come from the Mind of God to the mind of man is advisable. He says, 'What you do not write down, you will forget. So you might as well never have thought it.' He adds that we reach the Presence of God when and only when our wills are touched and crossed.

The Electronics of the Spirit, so simple, so natural, and so fundamental. Herein lies the key to a new age.

Statesmanship without the Electronics of the Spirit, without guidance and without change, is like flying an aircraft in stormy weather over uncharted territory without choosing to use radio, maps or compass. It is both unnecessary and criminal. It is recklessly selfish. It leads inevitably to disaster.

With the Electronics of the Spirit, renaissance becomes inevitable—and it can happen fast. The statesman, the business man, the labour leader, the workers, the housewife, the family—all have their part to play. Guided by God, all can build unity and answer the frustrations and divisions of our times. The Electronics of the Spirit holds the answer to the second half of the twentieth century.

It is an answer that works.

NATIONS
THAT WILL NOT THINK

In 1956, Dr Buchman visited Australia on the invitation of the Chairman of the Olympic Games Committee and other leaders. He also visited the Philippines, Japan, Taiwan, Viet-Nam, Thailand and Burma as the guest of the heads of government. In Japan he was decorated with the Order of the Rising Sun, in Taiwan with the Grand Cordon of the Brilliant Star of the Republic of China, and in Bangkok, with the order of Knight Grand Cross of the Crown of Thailand. In June, he was invested with the Legion of Honour, with Gold Medal, of the Philippines. This world broadcast was given from London, 4 June, 1956.

STRANGE THINGS are happening in the land. A new perspective is being revealed. Old concepts are breaking down. Democracy is on the defensive. Armaments no longer guarantee security. Pacts lose their purpose as new forces arise. Old loyalties break down in the face of new emergencies. The new alignment in the world is between the nations who think and the nations that will not think.

The united thought of a nation with a purpose is the greatest force in history. An idea invades without the formality of declaring war. It makes men prisoner without firing a shot and captures countries while parliaments are still debating. It cannot be stopped by weapons alone. It cannot be deflected merely by economic aid. It can be redirected only by a better idea, a stronger purpose and more dedicated living by leaders and by led.

Plans alone are not enough. The trouble with many of the planners is they do not think adequately. They think of plans but not of what is essential if a bond is to be built between East and West, between black and white, between rich nations and poor. They do not think of changing the motives of men; or changing the purposes for which men and nations live. It takes an ideology to do that.

A Norwegian Trade Union leader told political and industrial leaders of his nation recently, 'Moral Re-Armament's job is to arm statesmen and peoples with an ideology that makes it possible for them to see what is happening in the world. Democracies are faltering because they do not have the ideological fuel they need. Many of our statesmen are suffering from a very advanced stage of ideological undernourishment.'

That is why nations without an ideology are being outthought by those with one, and why men who have a superior ideology are succeeding where both Communism and non-Communism fail. The superior ideology is multiplying a new type of man with new motives—men who are solving the difficulties.

One of the largest newspapers in Japan wrote of my recent visit that I had arrived in Tokyo at a critical time. The Diet was in a turmoil of deadlock and seemingly irreconcilable division. Each member took endless time to walk up and cast his ballot. They called it the 'cow's walk'. It frustrated and infuriated. Sleep and tempers were short. A new factor was needed. Leaders of Government and Opposition arranged a lunch in the Diet for me and the friends with me, men and women who live an ideology that unites. Said members of Government and Opposition afterwards, 'It was a miracle.

You brought sanity where there was insanity. A solution was found. There was no riot. We found a way to solve our problem not on the basis of a party's will, but on what was right.' Now, it wasn't me. I didn't do it. It was the power of an ideology to change the thinking of men and women of the Diet. At the root of our problems are people. With a superior ideology people can be changed.

Says a leading banker, a recent Japanese Ambassador in Washington, 'Moral Re-Armament is the greatest force in the moral and spiritual reconstruction of post-war Japan.' And the Prime Minister wrote in the Press, 'As I face the scene in the Diet I cannot but long that the spirit of Moral Re-Armament would permeate the lives of every single member of the Diet. When the people of Japan and of the world live the spirit of MRA real peace will come.'

When I landed in Manila I was greeted by a large group of men, workers from the docks, with huge placards, 'Welcome Moral Re-Armament. Workers unite the world.' It was an unexpected welcome, but it was the vital voice of those workers who control the life-line of nations from Manila to London, from Hamburg to Sydney, from New York to Yokohama. The next morning one of their leaders breakfasted with us at the President's table. President Magsaysay has the supreme art of knowing men and of keeping the human touch. He said to us, 'Most people load me down with problems. You bring answers.'

Everywhere Communist and non-Communist, East and West respond to men who have the thinking and living of a superior ideology.

A British miner who has worked for thirty years at the coal face, says, 'Moral Re-Armament is to the heart of man what coal is to a furnace. It gives it power. If we want more coal, we must have more Moral Re-Armament.'

On the eve of the Italian elections I passed through Milan. On the station platform to meet me was a cross-section of the nation—industrialists, the manager of a large plant with a member of his works' council, the national secretary of one of the great unions, and men and women from 'Little Stalingrad' where Communism holds sway. One of the men, a Communist leader of the 12,000 tramway workers of Milan, was there. His sister, a bitter Communist, had changed. She became a new type of revolutionary woman and her brother had been captured by her freedom from bitterness and her power to create unity. He was seriously ill but said he must come to the station to tell me his determination to fight at my side. 'I only want to live for my children's future and the new world of Moral Re-Armament,' he said.

Also on the platform was the brother of the Communist newspaper editor. The editor, like the tramway worker, had found this superior ideology. He told the whole city about it in a ten-page supplement to his paper. He now carries this answer to the political leaders of Europe. His wife, his brother, his friends and former enemies follow his lead. He faced the years of bitterness against his Church and put it right. He has begun to live a revolutionary faith. He has accepted the discipline of meditation to find the direction of God instead of following the drive of human passions and materialism.

No wonder Gabriel Marcel, the great Catholic philosopher, writes in *Figaro*, 'Moral Re-Armament is a hope—perhaps even *the* Hope.'

A European statesman who was Chairman of NATO said,

'We will certainly commit a very great error if we think that Communism is the only problem and that the answer is a negative opposition to Communism. A materialistic philosophy is now rooted in democracy. Even if there were no Communism, Moral Re-Armament would still be essential to the future of humanity.'

Chancellor Adenauer and members of his Cabinet in their invitation to the Moral Re-Armament World Mission to come to Germany said, 'In this time of confusion we need an ideology which can bring clarity and a moral force to shape international relations as well as our own national life.'

Western Germany by her energy and genius has recreated the industry of a nation. She has secured prosperity. But her leaders now face the fact that prosperity alone can never cure bitterness, build unity, or create an answer to Communism.

Nations who will not think shed blood and money and breed bitterness and disaster. But men who think have a superior statesmanship. I have just heard from Mohammed Masmoudi, Minister of State in the Tunisian Government. He says, 'But for Moral Re-Armament our country would be involved in a war without mercy.'

Take Morocco. The unexpected happened. One fiery young leader spoke of his great enemy as the Devil incarnate. A man skilled in meeting the needs of his fellow men talked with this young leader. He decided to listen, not to the voice of hate or of prejudice, but to the still small voice that said, 'You are as near to God as you are to the man from whom you feel most divided.' He went in trepidation and met the old statesman he called the Devil. He apologised, not for his convictions, but for his hatred. Even right convictions can become a negative force when they are employed by prejudiced minds or by men or nations who do not think. The old man wrapped him around in his arms in affection and forgiveness, and two days later publicly changed his policy and united the nation on a new course. Today Morocco is independent and finding her direction.

Who are the men in France who will apply this new effective way to Algeria before it is too late?

I was received in Viet-Nam by that man of destiny President Diem. He said, 'We welcome Moral Re-Armament. It perfectly responds to the longing in the heart of Asia for a change of heart in the West.'

In Thailand Field Marshal Pibulsonggram took the exceptional action of inviting the Buddhist leaders to attend the ideological play *The Vanishing Island*. Their verdict was unanimous: 'The ability of Moral Re-Armament to change men is proof that it has the power to unite the world.'

In Taiwan I met an old friend, General Ho Ying-chin, who is a close adviser to President Chiang Kai-shek. General Ho said, 'If we leaders of China had had the unity of Moral Re-Armament the history of our country would have been different.' President Chiang Kai-shek said, 'This is the most valuable form of aid we could have been sent.'

Premier U Nu of Burma has expressed his gratitude for the new direction given by this ideology to the students of Burma. The Rector of the University said, 'Moral Re-Armament is a magic word in Rangoon University.' U Nu spoke to me of the universal message that the world needs that can disarm the suspicions of the East and rearm the moral integrity of the West.

The *New Times of Burma* commented, 'Moral Re-Armament is, in fact, the only practicable way out of the morass in which man has landed himself.'

Men like U Nu and the other Asian statesmen I have conferred with in recent weeks realise more clearly than many Western leaders the need today to give priority to ideology in the affairs of their nations.

Says a distinguished American scientist, 'I have seen enough of what we call "high level staff" in Washington to know that the ideological answer is not going to come from a paper prepared by a planning staff in a government department or any place else. It is not going to come from an executive order. It is going to come from human beings individually, from your heart and mine. The fault is with us, and the answer will not come unless we are different.'

Communist and non-Communist have one fundamental weakness in common. They are not creating a new type of man. Consequently both lack the one essential for creating a new world. But there is a superior ideology which is giving men new motives, new character. It works! It is a new thinking forged by living absolute standards, absolute honesty, purity, unselfishness, love. With this ideology nations will begin to think. They will solve all their problems. Families will be united. Youth will find a purpose more dynamic and compelling than lawlessness.

This is the new statesmanship, a life commitment adequate to change the thinking, living and daring of the whole world. For everyone everywhere this is the future. This is normal living.

THE UNEXPECTED SOURCE

A Christmas Message

E'en the hour that darkest seemeth
Will His changeless goodness prove.

NATIONS that will not think have become nations that walk in darkness.

To them at Christmas from the unexpected source comes the light of an answer.

At the first Christmas, wise men came from Arabia and Africa to acknowledge the hope of the world.

Today Arabia and Africa may be the unexpected source that gives the answer to chaos.

Africa today has sent its men to the West to show the true meaning of freedom for mankind. They speak in a play and a film called *Freedom* that has been named the boldest and most audacious approach to the fundamental problems of human relations of our time.

It is the moment for a miracle. A Moor came to worship the Babe; Egypt sheltered the Child Jesus and an African carried the Cross to Calvary. The voice of this Africa can speak to every humble heart everywhere.

Where meek souls will receive Him still,
The dear Christ enters in.

IDEAS ARE GOD'S WEAPONS
FOR A NEW WORLD

In June, 1957, a World Assembly opened at Mackinac Island in the new Assembly buildings, built during the two previous winters. The Assembly was attended by 5,000 people from seventy-six countries, including 100 leaders of the Japanese Youth Organisation, the Seinendan, and a delegation of 100 from Taiwan, as well as political and industrial leaders from Asia, Africa, Europe, South America and Australia. The following world radio and television broadcast was given by Dr Buchman on this occasion.

A GLORIOUS ANSWER has come to the years of costly failure in the Pacific.

'Pacific Relations' was an idea that caught the imagination of the world, but it was the wrong idea. It brought no peace, nor did it improve relations. Like all false ideas it threw up a mountain of chaotic debris that dammed back unity and freedom for millions. Today that debris is being swept away by the force of a God-given idea.

Magsaysay of the Philippines experienced it. He said to us, 'Most people weigh me down with problems. You bring the answers.'

General Ho Ying-chin of China defeated the Japanese in battle. The mainland of his nation is enthralled by the wrong idea. He has been a friend of mine for many years. Recently in Magsaysay's country at the Moral Re-Armament Assembly of Asian Nations, he said, 'What we have failed to achieve in ten years of postwar diplomatic effort has been accomplished at this Assembly.'

Mr Hoshijima, Supreme Adviser to the Japanese Government, declared at this Assembly, 'Here we have been able to find the road to unity between Korea and Japan.' He was a signatory of the Japanese Peace Treaty in San Francisco. That was the time Robert Schuman said to me after the signing, 'You made peace with Japan two years before we statesmen had the courage to sign it.'

Korea I have known for many years. Take Mrs Park, a former Cabinet Minister, who had been deeply humiliated, and whose husband has been bedridden for more than eighteen years as a result of Japanese imprisonment. She said at the Assembly, 'Through change in my own heart, I have lost my enmity. Only on the basis of Moral Re-Armament can permanent peace be achieved in Asia and the world.'

Also at this Assembly was the great-grandson of the founder of modern industrial Japan. Viscount Shibusawa was my host when I first went to Tokyo in 1915. His great-grandson is a typical postwar young Japanese business man. He saw that the choice for Asia was Moral Re-Armament or Communism. He made his choice. He changed. He found a faith. He has given up his business. His father, a postwar Minister of Finance, had young Shibusawa speak to fifty of his intellectual friends including economic professors and younger business men. At the end the father spoke. He said his son's great-grandfather had left his home and plunged into the Meiji revolution. He had felt history was being made and that he must have a part in it. Now the great-grandfather's blood was surging in the great-grandson's veins. He believed

Moral Re-Armament is a new factor in history and that he must give everything for it.

The youth organization of Japan, the Seinendan, 4,300,000 strong, is asking, 'Which way will youth go?' They are finding the idea of Japan's future at the Moral Re-Armament assemblies in Europe and America. Now Moscow offers a hundred of them a free trip to Russia. They turn to us—can we answer this strategy? And so one hundred from Japan are coming to an Assembly at Mackinac Island and a proportionate number from the rest of Asia.

Not only Japan, but the youth of Taiwan, the Philippines, Viet-Nam, Indonesia, Burma, Malaya, India, Ceylon, are asking the same question, 'Which way shall we take— Moscow or Moral Re-Armament?'

U Nu of Burma while in America heard that in his University in Rangoon an idea had gripped the youth— taken them away from the wrong idea that obsessed them, and given them the right idea. His message to the Asian Assembly was, 'This ideology is above race and class because it answers the needs of the heart. It seeks to change men, their ideas, their motives, their aims.'

The Rector of the University's older brother, Foreign Minister U Tin Tut, said, 'The one unfailing light in this dark world is the light of Moral Re-Armament.' As the younger brother, the Rector, told us he had always reserved the right to disagree with his older brother, but he, too, now says, 'Moral Re-Armament is a magic word in Rangoon University. It marks the beginning of a new era.'

The widow of President Magsaysay is caught by this same spirit that won her husband, She invited the Colwell brothers to her home to meet her son. They are the three

Americans whom Magsaysay specially wanted to be at the Philippines Assembly. He put their songs on the national radio. They have laid aside all worldly advantage. The Asian leaders at the Assembly declared, 'They have played a vital part in creating the spirit in which unity is being forged between our nations.' The Colwells arrived at 4 o'clock. The Magsaysay family kept them till 11.30, such was the radiant response. Mrs Magsaysay twenty times called for their songs.

Then the Colwells travelled sixty miles to a Philippine village fifteen miles from the territory of the rebel Huks. The Mayor, the Chief of Police, the Deputy Mayor, were among hundreds who gathered beneath a spreading acacia tree beside the main street for an hour and three-quarters to hear the Colwells and their friends. They were introduced by the Medical Director of the Far Eastern University, Dr Gutierrez, who cares for 28,000 students. Traffic was repeatedly blocked in the street as people crowded to listen. They said there were Huk rebels in the crowd. At the end the people refused to disperse until there were two more songs from the Colwell brothers. Said Mrs Gutierrez, also on the staff of the Far Eastern University, 'You are doing what made Magsaysay so loved among his people. You have gone to meet them in the villages.'

The Chairman of the Philippine Senate Committee for National Defence is quick to realize the meaning of this for the nation. He said, 'For reasons of national security, I want Moral Re-Armament to take root here and be a force. It can be a very practical and realistic bulwark against the infiltration of Communism.'

In our frantic efforts to buy security, let us not sell ourselves short by overlooking the one real security—the idea which can remake men and unite them to remake the world.

Ideas are God's weapons for a new world. And man has the capacity to receive ideas from God. When men act on these ideas they find new direction for themselves and their nations. Now I believe that we should so live that God can speak to us at any hour of the day or night.

And it was in the night that I had the compelling thought, 'Africa will speak to the world.' I was at the World Assembly at Caux at the time and with me there were Africans from all parts of the continent. The Africans responded. They wrote a play on the theme closest to their hearts—*Freedom*.[1] The German Ambassador in London saw it. The same night he telephoned Bonn to tell his colleagues they must see it. That play went through the capitals of Europe. Now it has been made into a film—the first film made in Africa, written by Africans and played by Africans. Walt Disney's European cameraman sacrificed his contract to make the picture. Men of many nations gave money, time and skill. The première

---

[1] *Freedom* was written and produced by African leaders from all over the continent at the Caux Assembly, 1955. In the course of 1956 it was filmed in Africa. The world première took place in the Egyptian Theatre, Hollywood, on 12 February, 1957. At the subsequent Washington première, in the National Theatre, Manasseh Moerane, Vice-President of the ten thousand African teachers of South Africa, who plays the Prime Minister in the film, said, 'The real battle for Africa today is ideological. In that struggle manpower, munitions, money and military strength, important though they are, are not by themselves an answer. Without an ideology all these things will be in vain. We need an ideology fundamental enough to deal with the problems raised and roused by hate, fear, greed—both in individuals and nations. We need an ideological answer to Communism. We need this ideology big enough to unite men above race, colour, class. A false ideology came to Africa. Men brought an answering ideology—Moral Re-Armament. That is the ideology the whole world needs today. A man with an ideology is the truest patriot. A force trained in democracy's ideology is the most priceless national possession.'

was in Hollywood. 'A picture that may change my life,' wrote one critic. 'It made me feel the soul of Lincoln was still with us,' wrote another. 'If we act on it, we may save all we value in civilisation.' And a Nigerian political leader commented, 'For our present generation of vipers "Freedom" is the bible which people will read today.'[1]

'Africa speaks to the world'—Washington queued up four deep for half a mile outside the National Theatre twice in one day to see it. Leaders of nine Asian nations at the Asian Assembly cabled the Speaker of the United States House of Representatives and the Chairman of the Senate Foreign Relations Committee, 'This overwhelming film is providential for our nations at this critical time and must reach the millions of Asia now. Its ideology is the only true basis on which East and West can unite.'

Men of science understand that weapons can only buy time. An idea must win the world. And the youth of a scientific age respond to Moral Re-Armament because it is the idea that answers the basic divisions of race, class and ideology.

An American university student leader was won by this

---

[1] The *Eastern Sentinel*, Nigeria, in a special Royal Visit edition on the occasion of the arrival of Her Majesty the Queen, wrote two editorials, the first headed 'Welcome to the Queen', the second '*Freedom*—A Great Play'.

The editorial on *Freedom* states in part: '*Freedom* points out the highroad to unity. The play deals with the basic issue—not the attainment of self-government, which for us is assured, but the quality of self-government that is to be practised. These men of MRA are pioneers of a new battle that has to be won—the battle for unity and honesty in public and private life, and for democracy based on absolute moral standards.

'Many of our leaders from all parts of Nigeria owe much to Caux, for the influence of Moral Re-Armament since 1949 has been greater than anyone can assess. It has produced the stability in this country without which the Queen's visit would not have happened.'

idea. He began by putting right what was wrong. He went to the home of the president of the 16,000 students of his university, a Negro. He apologized for his bitterness and his dishonest politics. It was at Christmas time. The president held out his hand. 'This is really going to be a happy Christmas,' he said. The two of them joined forces. They brought 700 of their fellow students to see the film *Freedom* including members of the faculty, the staff of the university paper and the members of the student council.

Then they went together to the Asian Assembly. Declared the president through the *Los Angeles Sentinel*, 'Moral Re-Armament is the only real solution to the race problem in the United States. This answer is needed in the Negro community. Only the ideology of Moral Re-Armament can answer racial prejudice because it is the only force that can challenge both black and white to change and build a new world.'

Senator Alexander Wiley on the Floor of the Senate introduced the story of the Asian Assembly to the *Congressional Record*. He spoke of the ideology which had produced these results. He said, 'If we in America live that ideology we shall find a response in Asia that money cannot buy. It could be the turning point. The signs of a response to these deeper realities at this Assembly are a source of hope for us all, and a challenge to us to examine our policy and our practice in the light of these truths.'

A book has just been published. The idea for it came to me early one morning. It was a God-given thought—*America Needs an Ideology*.[1] William Penn expressed the heart of

---

[1] *America Needs An Ideology* by Paul Campbell and Peter Howard, published by Frederick Muller Ltd., London, June, 1957.

this ideology, 'Men must choose to be governed by God or they condemn themselves to be ruled by tyrants.'

When man listens, God gives him ideas. And when man chooses to be governed by these ideas, he becomes a new type of man. It is an experiment which can be tested by anyone, anywhere, at any time. It works.

The challenge of our time is simply this. Will the scientists, the statesmen, the men of the factory, school and farm, face these facts? Test them? Act on them and live accordingly?

Ideas quick and powerful to reconcile nations, to conquer all hearts and wills, to inspire a world-wide renaissance, are instantly available, immediately applicable.

For God's ideas are weapons for a new world.

And every man, if he will, can listen to God.

GOD IS THE ANSWER
TO THE MODERN CONFUSION
THAT DOGS US

A world broadcast on the twentieth anniversary of Moral Re-Armament, and Dr Buchman's eightieth birthday, Mackinac, June 1959.

WHEN THE PRIME MINISTER of Japan was in Washington he telephoned me on Mackinac Island to thank us for what Moral Re-Armament had done for his country. A hundred revolutionary Japanese youth were with me there who, instead of going to Moscow in their search for an ideology, had come to Moral Re-Armament on Mackinac Island. I was able to tell the Prime Minister that they had found a policy for the youth of Asia, and were going not to the Left, nor to the Right, but straight. On his return to Tokyo the Prime Minister declared this to be the policy of his government.

Following Prime Minister Kishi's visits to a number of South-East Asian nations, including the Philippines, President Garcia welcomed delegates from these countries to the Moral Re-Armament Assembly at Baguio with these words: 'As well as strengthening our economies and defences, we need to encourage an association of Asian peoples which is not directed against other nations but founded on the sure basis of a moral ideology.'

What a revolution it would be if confused statesmen in

every nation had this conviction that God has the answer. Today people just expect and live in chaos. The tragedy is that they accept leadership confused by compromise, when there could be the executive genius that comes when people normally listen to God.

Russia launches a dog-carrying satellite. The whole world tunes it ears to listen to a dog. That is important in our conquest of space. But it does not help us to settle our confusion on earth. If we were willing to tune our ears to God we could simply settle our earthly confusion and even perhaps move nearer our conquest of space.

The Foreign Secretary of the Philippines, after having presided over the SEATO meeting in Manila, came to our Assembly in Baguio. 'With this,' he said, 'we can change the world.' What had moved him to say this? He saw an Asian force in action and he saw an ideological weapon—a play. One such play had been written by the Japanese in Mackinac. They played it throughout Japan. It showed how a man, a family, a community can go not Left, not Right, but straight. Members of the Imperial Family, industrial and labour leaders, shipbuilders, miners, farmers and youth acclaim it. They say it is the answer for Japan.

Philippine leaders invited this play to their country. In the heart of the old city of Manila, where tens of thousands of Filipinos had died in Japanese prisons, this Japanese play was given at the request of the Filipinos. A former Philippine guerilla fighter and a former Japanese officer introduced it. The crowd would not stop applauding the play until the Japanese stepped before the curtain and told of the answer they had found in their own hearts. Wounds were healed. Unity was born.

One member of the cast is Mr Sumitomo. His industries employ more than half a million men. He has been called the 'Rockefeller of Japan'. He takes the part of the poorest man in the play, a tenant farmer. At first he met opposition from some of the heads of Japanese industry. Some of his own directors at the Osaka plants, which dominate the life of that great city, were against him. But the firmness of Mr Sumitomo's conviction and the world-spanning size of his idea won them. And the labour leaders, too, say they can work with Mr Sumitomo for he is more revolutionary than they are.

Moving with these weapons throughout Asia is a group of Asian leaders. Koreans, Chinese, Burmese, Filipinos, Indians and Japanese are among the seventeen nations represented on this force. Premier Kishi understood their effectiveness and cabled, 'I cordially invite you with your plays, believing that the idea that you bring is the most needed at this crucial time in our history.' Costly sacrifice sends them on their way. At Baguio, Dutch and Indonesians stood on the same platform in forgiveness of the past and pledged to bring a new future in the Pacific. Indonesian and Philippine women gave their jewels. Europeans and Americans gave their capital. Such a spirit prompted the French philosopher Gabriel Marcel to say after a visit in Tokyo, 'Thinking men in the West understand the full value of this tremendous bid to restore genuine relations between men, such as the spirit of truth demands.'

Who are these men who are bringing this answer to Asia? When I first went to Tokyo in 1915, I was received by Baron Shibusawa, a founder of modern industrial Japan. Today his great-grandson is with that force, and the great-great-grandson sends me the message, 'I am praying for Uncle Frank'. In India in 1915 I was for the first time with Mahatma

Gandhi. Today his grandson is also with that force and leading Asia to Moral Re-Armament. It is the commitment of his life. He says it is chaos or MRA for Asia's millions. A high American official from Washington was in Baguio. He said to the young Gandhi, 'I knew your grandfather. He gave his life to create a nation. You are giving yours to save a nation.'

The descendant of one of our great American Secretaries of State is another. He and a Philippine editor, respected and welcomed in Washington for his knowledge of South-East Asia, arrived in Tokyo. The Prime Minister sent his son and an *aide* to the airport to meet them. He received them next day and told them that MRA had been the key factor in bringing to birth and fostering the negotiations between South Korea and Japan. This Philippine editor says, 'Material re-armament is necessary. But Moral Re-Armament is indispensable because it will unite Asia.' His conviction is that the Japanese play can bring light to Peiping. He also adds that a billion people in Asia and Africa can find this answer to their modern confusion.

Prime Minister U Nu of Burma, receiving this force in Rangoon, said: 'More than anything else the world needs to rearm morally. In the course of my travels abroad I have continually urged my friends of both ideological blocs to rid themselves of fear and suspicion of each other. But when I have myself been beset with fear and suspicion I realised how difficult it was for others to swallow the advice I had given them. So it is that certain things are easy to preach but extremely difficult to practise. This is the big challenge of Moral Re-Armament.' What is our part? We need this new factor if we are to find an answer. And the world awaits it, too, from us.

Take the answer that came in a theatre in Atlanta, the hub of the Southern States. A white and a coloured person were mounting the theatre stairs to the exit, side by side. They had just seen the musical, *The Crowning Experience*, inspired by the life of Mary McLeod Bethune, with its stars Muriel Smith of Broadway and Covent Garden fame, who sings like a bird and Ann Buckles, who made her name with her Broadway and television successes. These two gave up all their contracts this last season to take this MRA play to the South. Said the white man, 'On this basis our two peoples could work together.' Replied the coloured man, 'Yes, I believe they could.'

An Atlanta attorney said, 'In all my forty years in public life I have never witnessed anything that has called forth such a depth of feeling or such a mighty response. You are having a tremendous influence and changing the notions of people. Some of us have had the answer but have not had the courage to put it into practice. You are living it and demonstrating it. It will reach from Atlanta to the whole country.'

Said another Atlanta leader, 'We have been listening to the tick of the time bomb in Atlanta but you have taught us to listen to the tick of the Holy Spirit.' A newspaperman's conviction is, 'You are doing what the Communists boasted never could be done in the Southern States of America.'

The European and African press heralds this miracle in Atlanta as the 'answer to Little Rock'. It is what the world hopes for and rightly expects from America.

Africa points the way. The African film, *Freedom*, has been shown in this past year on every continent. At its New Delhi première the press wrote, '*Freedom* has been seen by the maximum number of India's most important personalities.'

Said the great Indian producer S. S. Vasan, 'Wonderful! Wonderful! It must be put into every language of the world.' It was shown to officers and men in the NATO Headquarters at Fontainebleau and is being taken by the Government of the Sudan through the length and breadth of their country. The Speaker of the Canadian House of Commons, introducing *Freedom* to a première audience of political and diplomatic leaders in Ottawa before its nation-wide distribution, said, 'In this film our friends from Africa are heaping coals of fire on our heads.' Africa has produced in *Freedom* a voice for a continent which in the words of President Tubman of Liberia is 'destined to remake the world by shaping the lives of all who have seen it and all who will see it.' And he adds, like the Indian film producer, 'It is a wonderful, wonderful film. It must go to the whole world.'

An Algerian journalist who had suffered at the hands of both French and extremists in his own country said, 'I am determined to get *Freedom* in Arabic to North Africa as quickly as possible. That is what our nationalist movements need.' A colleague added, 'Conferences alone do not bring a solution to conflict. The only solution is to listen to God and for each to do as God directs. This film will render a great service to North Africa and will bring in a new era of peace and brotherhood among all peoples there.'

People have been teaching the great truths in the wrong way. They lack the dominant passion to hear the plan that God has for their nations and the conviction to follow it. They lack the training that helps them to live for their nations and to remake the world.

Mackinac and Caux are schools of statesmanship where statesmen, workers, industrialists are trained to meet men who have a materialist ideology and to win them to a superior idea. One European expert on Russian affairs, who went with the head of his nation to Moscow to advise him in the negotiations, says that the work of men who have had this training has three times been a decisive factor in recent history. First at Bandung, where Moral Re-Armament was declared to be the one way to unite the East and West; then in the industrial heart of Europe, the Ruhr, where MRA-trained men broke the hold of materialist ideologies and saved Europe; and thirdly, in the Pacific, where at the Baguio conferences, Japan, Korea, the Philippines and other South-East Asian nations found unity through a moral ideology. These are solid achievements of trained men who live fully convinced. A uniting ideology is the essential pre-condition of any successful Summit conference. Governments as fully convinced of Moral Re-Armament as Moscow is of Communism will lead the world immediately into a new era of unity, peace and plenty, the God-given heritage of the millions of every nation.

In India they asked me what is Moral Re-Armament's programme for the millions. My reply was, 'Empty hands will be filled with work, empty stomachs with food, and empty hearts with an idea that really satisfies. That is Moral Re-Armament—for East and West.'

Take our youth in America. A young man found this answer. He had been part of a New York street gang that drank and drugged. He had smashed up three cars in six months. He found in Moral Re-Armament a purpose big enough and the idea that satisfied. He said, 'This is what the kids where I come from really need—and want.'

A young American girl from a home of privilege gave

herself wholly to healing the hates and hurts of the world. She was a modern girl with the secret of patriotism, a modern Joan of Arc for the youth of the nations. She said, 'Every day is a new adventure. There is nothing that holds me.' She was only twenty-two when she died this year, but her life, too, was fulfilled and satisfied.

American labour lost a great leader in the passing of John Riffe, former Executive Vice-President of the CIO, whose fight for unity between the unions sprang from his own experience of change and unity in his previously very divided home. At Mackinac last year he was seriously ill. One day he had just one God-given thought for a Senator who was at the Assembly. When the Senator came to his room, John slowly said, and then repeated, these words, 'Senator, you must tell America that when Frank Buchman changed John Riffe he saved American industry five hundred million dollars.'

Could that be the answer for inflation? Is that the way our nation's wealth could be saved from the waste of selfish conflict to be invested in the strength and unity of our people?

A man of eighty is speaking to you. A man who has often been beset by confusion and gradually learned to know the answer for a nation. In every baffling problem of the statesman and the ordinary man the answer is given to those who listen. Only there must be the willingness to obey. It is not what we expect but what we allow God to give us. With all the sincerity of my eighty years and impelled by the urgency of the critical world situation, I say God is the answer to the modern confusion that dogs us. Go all the way with God and you will have the answer. Go all the way with God and you will bring the answer to your nation.

THE WRONG WAY AND
THE RIGHT WAY

Given at the opening of the Summit Strategy Conferences for Moral Re-Armament at Caux and Mackinac Island, 4 June 1959.

'WE ARE NOT ready to live in the world that faces us.' The man who says this is a production genius in charge of 400 scientists and 35,000 men who launched Atlas in answer to Sputnik. There is a wrong way and a right way of launching a rocket into space. There is a wrong way and a right way of living on earth.

Dr Douglas Cornell, Executive Officer of the National Academy of Sciences, says, 'Science has made it possible for the world to be destroyed between lunch and the cocktail hour. But the problem does not lie in science, it lies in man. It is modern man who needs to be remade.'

There is a wrong way and a right way to meet the challenge of Communism. An American general who trained the army of an Asian nation, says, 'I tried to fight Communism with an army and with economic aid. I trained good soldiers. But I was unable to equip them with a world idea superior to Communism. Moral Re-Armament is the idea I was looking for. It is the right way to do it.'

We have been living the wrong way for so long that we have come to accept it as normal. Broken homes, disrupted industries, divided nations, deadlocked conferences—these things are not normal. They are the inevitable outcome of doing things the wrong way. Many people condemn Communism. But could it be that the hate, greed, fear and selfishness which create confusion and division in our own society, are the strength and essence of Communism? Millions who would never join the Communist Party, make its advance inevitable by the way they live.

Admiral William H. Standley, who was United States Ambassador to Moscow and Chief of Naval Operations, sees this issue clearly. In a thought-out statement which has gone all round the world, he says, 'The choice for America is Moral Re-Armament or Communism.'

An Air Force general in charge of 8,000 men who are part of the Strategic Air Command and for two years have been on a fifteen minute alert, says, 'The young men who are sent to me don't know what democracy is about. They live as they please. As for Communism, that doesn't concern them and they won't trouble to understand it.' While arming against atomic attack from without, we have already surrendered within ourselves the basis of our defence—moral character.

The right way is not 'my way'. It may not even be 'your way'. The right way is God's way. Some seem to think that freedom and democracy mean 'do as you please'. Each man decides and goes his own way. Fathers and mothers do as they please and then they are alarmed when their children follow their example. It is estimated that more than one million youth will go through the juvenile courts this year in America. Broken homes spread disillusion throughout the nation.

A play called *The New American*, written and produced from their own experiences by a group of young Americans, is capturing the mind of America with an answer to delinquency, divorce and subversion. At the invitation of the Commanding General it was shown at one of the largest Marine Air Stations in the world, and at command performances for Air Force bases, and in high schools. At one of these bases a newspaper described it as 'a great driving force which is awakening the free world from complacency.' The Mayor of one city where this play was shown, said, 'It is the soundest, most down to earth thing that ever came to our community.' The Mayor of another city said, 'It must go to every school and college throughout America.'

There is a wrong way and a right way in statesmanship. A high official of the German Foreign Office, former Ambassador to Canada, told the press, 'The most astonishing event of post-war European politics is the reconciliation of Germany and France. A major factor in the birth of an apparently permanent friendship between these former enemies is Moral Re-Armament.' And Dr Adenauer, the German Chancellor, in a letter to me says, 'Unless this work of Moral Re-Armament is extended the peace of the world cannot be preserved.' The Chancellor talks of Moral Re-Armament as the unseen but effective force in achieving international agreements.

A diplomat who has been at the heart of the great international conferences that have taken place in the last fifteen years writes to say, 'Three events in recent months have amazed the diplomats.' In each case the answer has been found through men who have changed.

The first was the Lebanon crisis. This issue which divided the world was solved by ten Arab nations who united to bring an answer to East and West. The man most responsible for this was the Secretary-General of the Arab League, who was in Egypt when he heard the news of crisis. He had the compelling thought which he believed came from God, to fly immediately to New York. He obeyed. He found the Arab States divided amongst themselves, and all the other nations divided against each other. There was a real risk of war. Early one morning a further thought came to him, that the Arab nations were meant to be a bridge and not a battle-ground. He brought them all together in one room, and they stayed together until they found a resolution on which they all agreed. When it was put to the United Nations, the vote was 80-0.

The Times of London said, 'Overnight an almost magical transformation has come over the scene.'

The second event was the new unity being brought to birth through Asia. A token of this was the visit of the President of the Philippines and his reception in the Japanese Diet. Little more than a year ago the feeling between those two countries was so intense that such an action would have been political suicide. The man who, as Speaker of the Japanese Diet, received the Philippine President, and was one of the plenipotentiaries who signed the Peace Treaty for his country, says that in the last two years Moral Re-Armament has brought reconciliation between Japan and the Philippines, wrested control of the largest single political organisation in Japan from Communist hands, established new relations with Indonesia and Viet-Nam, ended a dispute with Free China, and is now in process of healing the division between South Korea and his country. The President of the Philippines says, 'The bitterness of former years is being washed away by compassion and forgiveness.' *The New York World-Telegram* comments, 'This visit of the President of the

Philippines to Japan may mark an historic turning point in post-war affairs.'

The third most recent event is the Cyprus settlement. An Asian Ambassador in Washington was in my home. He had been chairman of the committee that vainly tried to bring an answer to Cyprus in the United Nations. He told us, 'Cyprus unsolved would have shattered European unity and could have led to European war this year.' The answer was brought by men—British, Greeks and Turks, who through Moral Re-Armament honestly faced the fact that they had been doing things the wrong way. A British Member of Parliament went to see some of the Cyprus leaders and was honest about the places where he felt he and his country had made mistakes. A Greek leader expressed his sorrow to the British leaders in London for the situation of bitterness and bloodshed in Cyprus. A Turkish editor went to Athens and in an article which appeared throughout the Greek press, said that his country and Greece were meant to live as brothers and not as enemies. *The New York Times* called it 'a resounding success for enlightened statesmanship.' Is not this the answer for our overworked and under-inspired statesmen?

A diplomat of world experience says, 'In Africa today they are saying everywhere to the white man, "How soon can you leave?" But to the Moral Re-Armament men and women they are saying "How soon can you come?" ' My friend Dr Azikiwe, Premier of Eastern Nigeria, recently entertained Premier Nkrumah of Ghana on a State visit. He took the occasion to show him the Moral Re-Armament film *Freedom* through which Africa has spoken to the world. Written by Africans and acted by Africans, it shows how a young nation threatened with destruction through division and Communism in its own ranks, can find the secret of unity and the right road. Afterwards Premier Azikiwe spoke to the nation of 36 million Nigerians and said, 'We must build a hate-free, fear-free, greed-free Africa, peopled by free men and women.' The newspaper of Ibadan, the great Nigerian city where the largest university in West Africa is situated, came out with the headline, 'MRA is our only hope.'

In the great cities of South Africa *Freedom* has been showing to packed audiences. In Cape Town the manager of the theatre himself introduced the film and said, 'We believe this is the most effective weapon in the free countries today to win the world to the right idea.' At the end of the film the man who plays the part of the Prime Minister in it, the former President of the African teachers of South Africa, steps in front of the screen in the glorious robes which he wears in *Freedom*. He speaks to those audiences, which is an unprecedented event in the life of South Africa. For probably all the white people in that theatre it is the first time they have ever listened to an African speaking. Afterwards night after night he is surrounded by those who want to find from him the secret of how to get their own lives and the life of South Africa on the right way.

The Colwell brothers sing at each performance. These three young Americans are playing a major part in this revolutionary answer in South Africa. They have given up Hollywood contracts and over the past years have had a profound influence on the leadership of Asia and Africa. In South Africa they won thunderous applause by their commitment and their songs sung in national languages that few South Africans have ever tried to master. Of them the

255

Mayor of their own city in California says, 'These three are securing and undergirding the defences of America.' They tell the South African audiences that they are giving their lives to the answer they feel Hollywood is meant to interpret to the world.

A battle is being fought for the mind of the world. Think of the mothers in Asia, Europe, Africa, yes, even America, who weep because their children are learning the wrong way to live from the motion pictures we make in the West. Rickard Tegström, the brilliant Walt Disney cameraman, who went to Africa to film *Freedom*, spoke of the films he saw in Africa. He says, 'From white screens against the blue-black African night, the dregs of Western civilisation's film production were poured out over defenceless young Africans night after night.' Now this cameraman is lending his genius to put the answer on celluloid. He is at present completing the filming of *The Crowning Experience*. It is inspired by the marvel of the life of Mary McLeod Bethune, born of slave parents, who rose to be the adviser of Presidents in the White House, and who said of Moral Re-Armament, 'To be a part of this great uniting force of our age, is the crowning experience of my life.'

The Crowning Experience showed in the South as a play for four months last year and then broke the 123-year attendance record at the National Theatre in Washington. Of its effect a leading newspaperman of Atlanta said, 'This is the greatest news story to come out of the South this year.' Rickard Tegström adds, 'Filming must be in the hands of men who understand the need of the world today and the deepest need of mankind. The statesmen who realise this in time can save the world from disaster.'

U Nu, Burma's great statesman, recently visited me. We talked of the need for statesmen to be able to read men as we read a page of print. We spoke of their need to diagnose and cure every corrupt and subversive influence, and so safeguard our nations from going the wrong way. We dealt with the urgency in the ideological struggle for the men who lead to be incorruptible and to create around them men and women with clean hands and pure hearts. U Nu together with the Prime Minister of Japan and the Presidents of the Philippines and Viet-Nam has just welcomed the Moral Re-Armament Assembly of Asian peoples in Japan. Said he, 'It is giving a clarion call to one and all to read the writing on the wall.'

The objective of the Assembly is to clean up the nations from bottom to top. One of the instruments is a play called *Shaft of Light* written by the great-grandson of the founder of modern industrial Japan. This play deals incisively with men at the Cabinet level, with politicians of all parties, with industrial and labour leaders who can be bought with money, tempted by position or by indulgences which make them vulnerable to Communist strategy. The play is being nationally acclaimed because it deals fearlessly with the primary need and gives the answer.

What is the answer? The author of this play, Masa Shibusawa, spoke recently in Washington at the farewell service for a great American patriot, Priscilla Cornell. For the last few years, with her family and through the weakness and pain of cancer, she has fought for a clean-up in the leadership of America, Europe, Asia and Africa, and helped create the good news of a world changing. Said Shibusawa, 'It is up to us to carry on what she lived. With the Cross of Christ lived in reality, which means a change at the very root,

America can save the world. This is the revolution which takes the Communists' breath away and changes them.'

That's it. The whole-hearted, single-minded, completely dedicated commitment to provide our nations with leaders who are fear-free, hate-free, greed-free, men and women who know the strategy, the power and the unity that comes when the will is totally given to God for the building of a new world.

There is a wrong way and a right way for statesmanship. MRA has conclusively demonstrated in some of the most critical national and international deadlocks that when the fear, hate and greed in man is changed, solutions are rapidly achieved. This is the panorama before us—so simple that many miss it, so fundamental we cannot do without it.

A HURRICANE OF
COMMON SENSE

*On Dr Buchman's eighty-second birthday and the opening of the
World Assemblies at Caux and Mackinac Island, June 1960.*

THERE IS A HURRICANE of common sense sweeping
through the world. 'A Hurricane of Common Sense'—that
was the headline in a newspaper read by the leaders of
Washington. It refers to the manifesto *Ideology and Co-
existence* which in the last six months has gone to 73,000,000
homes throughout the United States, Canada, Scandinavia,
Germany, Italy, France, Great Britain, The Netherlands,
Greece and Turkey, as well as India, South Africa, South
America, Australia and Japan. It has already been translated
into 24 different languages, and will be read by the millions.
It puts squarely to the modern world the choice—Moral
Re-Armament or Communism.

My old friend General Guisan, wartime Commander-in-
Chief of the Armies of Switzerland, wrote the foreword to
the Swiss edition. In it he said, 'On the ideological plane
neutrality can be dangerous, for refusal to fight for what is
right plays the enemy's game. The training centre at Caux
is a unique instrument that has changed the conduct of
nations. I long that our whole people should face realistically
the forces which confront each other today, that we draw
from our traditions a relentless determination to safeguard
at all costs the freedoms we inherit.'

This was the last public statement General Guisan made. When he died 300,000 citizens of Switzerland stood in silent tribute to the man who was regarded as the saviour of his nation. His widow wrote to me, 'General Guisan was gripped by the idea and the might of Moral Re-Armament. In the evening of his life it was a great girder of support to him.'

Moral Re-Armament is a hurricane of common sense sweeping irresistibly through the heart of nations. It is smashing down the barriers between nations and races, dispersing the fogs of hate that threaten humanity and bringing a mighty wind of hope to the millions of the earth.

Hope—Hoffnung—is the name of the play God put in the mind of a miner from the Ruhr. He is a worker at the coal-face. He had never thought of writing a play. He changed. He found an answer to division in his home, his nation and the world. Chancellor Adenauer heard of this play and sent for this Ruhr miner and his friends. He asked them to go to Britain and France to prepare the way for his own visits to those countries. 'Many of us Germans,' he said, 'do not realise how deep are the wounds in other countries which were caused by what we did through having the wrong ideology.' In an exclusive article in the *New York Journal-American* headlined 'Adenauer Calls MRA World's Hope' the Chancellor said, 'A nation with an ideology is always on the offensive. A nation without an ideology is self-satisfied and dead.'

In Britain *Hoffnung* was like a hurricane. It shifted the prejudices of years. In the spirit of Moral Re-Armament men like James Coltart, executive of the British Press and Television, took inspired and fearless action to prepare for

Chancellor Adenauer's visit. His time in Britain was hailed as a triumph. Back in Bonn the Chancellor at a meeting of the Christian Democrat Party referred to the mistrust between Britain and Germany which had been swept aside, and said, 'We have to thank Moral Re-Armament for that.'

In Paris, French audiences stood and cheered. Some were in tears as the German miners sang the *Marseillaise* in French.

There is a shrine at Mont Valérien where during the occupation 4,500 Frenchmen of the Resistance met their death. To Mont Valérien went those Ruhr miners. They were escorted by the wife of the General at the head of the French nation's defence, and the niece of President de Gaulle. They were the first Germans to go there in fifteen years. They gave news of an idea powerful enough to unite nations separated by generations of hate. They expressed their sorrow for the past and their resolve to lay down their lives to rebuild Europe and the world. The columns of *Figaro* gave the news of this event to the French nation.

Vaterland, leading Swiss Catholic newspaper, reported the response to the miners' play in the monastery schools of central Switzerland under the headline, 'Catholic Colleges Hail MRA Play.' *Vaterland* reported Rektor Scherer of Schwyz as saying, 'We can all subscribe to the principles of MRA. To recognise absolutely the dominion of God, or to bow down under the domination of human tyrants, that is the alternative which should unite us all, whether we are Catholics, Christians, or non-Christians.' *Vaterland* also reported how Father Rektor Thommen of Kollegium Niklaus von der Flüe in Sarnen declared, 'Because you live what you believe, we can whole-heartedly accept this ideology.'

In Luxembourg, where the German miners were Government guests, the Prime Minister, Pierre Werner, said, 'The moral and spiritual values on which your actions are based are the ideology that can save the Christian West from its enemy.'

The hurricane blew into Kerala and its 16,000,000 inhabitants, the first major state in the world to vote itself into the Communist camp. Night after night vast crowds flocked to hear the evidence of Moral Re-Armament. Mannath Padmanabhan, father of his state, leader of the Hindu majority in Kerala, had found at Caux the secret of uniting with Christians. The Governor of the state, the Cabinet Ministers, trade union leaders, industrial men and students in their hundreds and their thousands came to hear the news of an answer.

Archbishop Gregorius of Trivandrum said, 'History will record our permanent gratitude to Mannath Padmanabhan not only for having ousted the Communist regime in Kerala, but for creating the unity of all the communities following his return from Caux.' The Governor of the state, Ramakrishna Rao, then said, 'All our problems, political, economic, individual, must be solved in the spirit of MRA. It has an essential appeal to every man.'

Men changed in Kerala. The leader of 38,000 students made the experiment of listening to the voice of God. He said, 'I am going to end impurity in my own life and clean up the student body. It is through moral compromise among the students that Communism has gripped us. I see that the choice for India is Moral Re-Armament or Communism, and I choose Moral Re-Armament.'

Rajmohan Gandhi, grandson of my old friend, Mahatma

Gandhi, whom I met on the first of my nine visits to India in 1915, said, 'Without Moral Re-Armament the new government in Kerala might already have fallen. Moral Re-Armament will save India and Asia and the world from Communist take-over.' When Chou En-lai arrived in India for his conferences with Prime Minister Nehru, the *Times of India* and the *Hindustan Times* carried full pages with the double-banner headline, 'Moral Re-Armament—the next step for Communists and non-Communists alike.'

These pages challenged the two men who today lead 1,000,000,000 Asians to find a new way of doing things for the sake of all men everywhere. They said in part, 'Communism has failed to produce the new type of man—the unselfish man who can develop and run the unselfish society. The ideology of MRA changes people. That is why thousands of former Communists all over the world are fighting the battle of Moral Re-Armament to restore the world on the basis of absolute moral standards.' It was a *real* hurricane, and it *was* common sense.

When Chancellor Adenauer arrived in Tokyo for the state visit, he was welcomed at the airport by his miners from the Ruhr. He spoke to a joint session of the Japanese Diet calling for a moral ideology that could unite East and West and answer Khrushchev's challenge to take over the world. Next day in the Japanese Diet a Cabinet Minister said, 'Chancellor Adenauer proclaimed Moral Re-Armament to Japan.'

The miners had come to Japan in response to an invitation from Japan's Prime Minister and other leaders of the country and they were the guests of the Japanese throughout their six weeks' visit. A special train was put at their disposal by

Governor Sogo of the Japanese National Railways in gratitude for the sanity of the news they brought.

Prime Minister Kishi said, 'You are giving a moral backbone to the whole world. I wish to express my gratitude for
the massive impact MRA has made on this nation during
the past six weeks. The reports which I have received from
all over Japan have convinced me of the effectiveness of this
mission in giving ideological clarity and a moral answer to
our people.'

A leader of the Japanese Socialist Party at a crisis point
early this year played a key part in healing a fresh split in
their ranks and prevented Communism from taking over. A
leader of the Seinendan, a political organisation of 4,300,000
youth, cabled me at Easter saying that MRA had once again
won every seat from the Communists at the annual election
in spite of the Communists' outpouring of manpower and
money in the last twelve months.

A trade union leader tells how through Moral Re-Armament the President of one of the great mines of Japan was
changed and as a result of his change, 3,500 miners, who
needed 3,000 armed police to keep them from attacking the
President, went back to work satisfied that their just claims
were being met.

At the Miike mine where workers had fought workers at
the pithead, one man had been killed and hundreds injured.
The leader of the organised women of the mine said, 'You
brought us the answer to hate. Without it more would have
been killed and injured. MRA is the answer to every injustice
and human hate.'

And one of the great men of Japan, primarily responsible
today for the security of his country, said, 'For the first time

since the end of the war you have given me hope. Moral Re-Armament is restoring a sense of destiny to a hundred million Japanese people. You are talking straight to us and cleaning us up in homes and politics. You are saying to us what no one else has dared to say.'

A movie is going out to the millions which says what needs to be said in a way that the modern man understands, accepts and follows. It is a full-length musical in Technicolor called *The Crowning Experience*, which in the words of Arthur Baker, for twenty-one years Chief of the Parliamentary Staff of *The Times* of London, is of 'indescribable beauty. Its message is so deep that it needs to be seen again and again and yet again. It answers all the hunger and hurts of nations.'

When Spyros Skouras, President of 20th Century Fox, saw this movie, he threw his arms in the air, saying, 'Fantastic! Fantastic! Fantastic! This must go to every movie theatre throughout the world.'

S. S. Vasan, President of the Indian Film Federation, said of it, 'A thousand times wonderful. You have shown me not only how to make a film, but how to live a life.'

And the leadership of the nations of Africa are clamouring for *The Crowning Experience*. They say it will blow like a hurricane through the hearts of the Africans and heal the hating of a continent. Dr Azikiwe, the man to whom 35,000,000 Nigerians say they largely owe their freedom, says, 'I spent many years in America where I was fed with the bread of bitterness. It took me fifteen years to find an answer to my spirit of revenge. I found that answer at Caux.' He added that *The Crowning Experience* attacks with tact and subtlety the social inequalities that have created wrong ideologies between men and gives definite promise of a cure.

And he says, 'Moral Re-Armament was the secret of independence for Nigeria.'

Jasper Savanhu, Parliamentary Secretary for Race Affairs in the Federal Government of Rhodesia and Nyasaland, says *The Crowning Experience* must be seen by every African, black and white, this year. He says, 'Winning political power will not by itself secure the future of the African. We can throw off the foreign yoke and then find African leaders who live only for personal advantage. Unless leadership is inspired by Moral Re-Armament, there is no future for the people. Moral Re-Armament is the solution to the greed, ambition, selfishness and competition in high places all over the world.'

Leaders for the 40,000,000 French-speaking Africans eagerly demand *The Crowning Experience* for their people. They say its message could bring the bloodshed in Africa to an end. Gabriel Marcel, the world-famous French writer and philosopher, said after seeing it and talking with leaders from Africa, 'I came to Caux in despair. Here I have found a transfusion of hope. A deep confidence flowed back into my being.'

White and black leadership in South Africa want their Cabinet and the whole country to see this movie. They say it holds the secret that alone can cure the racial divisions that are tearing South Africa apart, dividing her from other countries, and undermining her economic life.

Mrs Daisy Bates, Negro leader of Little Rock, Arkansas, known all over the world for the part she played in the battle with Governor Faubus over racial integration in the schools, saw *The Crowning Experience*. She said, 'Magnificent! It must go everywhere. It is essential in the South, but MRA is now needed throughout the world. It will soon catch the imagination of the whole world. Nothing else on the scene can do it.'

Mrs Bates, and her husband, as publisher of a newspaper, came to our training centre in Mackinac Island, Michigan. There Mr Bates said, 'For the first time in my life I have lost my hatred of the white man.' On her return to Little Rock, Mrs Bates invited some of the leading citizens of her State, white people who had also been to Mackinac, to dinner in her home. They came—the first time in the history of Arkansas that such a dinner-party had been possible. After dinner, Mrs Bates suggested a time of quiet in which together they should seek God's way of ending the deadlock. The thought came that Mrs Bates should visit Governor Faubus, the man who for years had been pictured to the world as her bitterest enemy. She trembled, but she went. She said later, 'The Governor could not have received me more graciously if I had been the President.' They shook hands, and the picture of that handshake went round the world. Governor Faubus had previously said, 'Moral Re-Armament is sowing the seeds that will prove to be the salvation of us all.'

Mrs Bates told an audience in Washington, 'Without Moral Re-Armament it would have been impossible for me to meet Governor Faubus without hate. But I have learned to fight for what is right without hatred. I want Moral Re-Armament for the children of the South and of America. We can see on the horizon a new day.' The Columbia Broadcasting System in its review of 1959 described this hand shake as possibly the most significant news event of the year, which could mark the end of a hundred years of civil war in the United States of America.

In the Republics of South America the hurricane is blowing, too. Millions read the news of an answer. Millions more hear it over the radio. In one week alone all the main newspapers of Montevideo carried reports of the world work of MRA, and eighteen leading papers of Argentina, Uruguay and Peru carried 51 articles. A leading editorial in *La Prensa*, the largest newspaper of Peru, said, 'Moral Re-Armament has a unique strength for the ideological battle in the world today. It is an insistent call to all who believe in a supreme Creator to confront those who preach atheism. It is a world effort to defeat materialism. The morally re-armed are not an easy prey to materialist indoctrination.' Eudocio Ravines, one of the greatest revolutionaries of our time who, trained by Mao Tse-tung, introduced Communism to Peru and Chile, met in Moral Re-Armament a superior ideology that changed him. He says, 'The basic problems of Latin America are not under-development, but corruption and Communism. While our countries welcome economic aid, alone it cannot touch the root problem. Without a moral ideology, it may even aggravate the problem. The best export the United States of America or any nation can send to Latin America is Moral Re-Armament.'

In a long lifetime of experience that has taken me to all parts of the world and brought me in touch with every sort of people, I have never seen a greater hunger and a greater hope than we find today. Man must choose the road of common sense or he will inevitably take the path of common suicide. Mr P. J. Little, the well-known statesman and thinker of Ireland, put the challenge clearly in the Dublin *Sunday Press*. His article about Moral Re-Armament occupied two central pages. It was headed, 'World War III—the war of ideas—the Battle we cannot lose.'

He said, 'The Cold War has only to heat up to boiling point for ten seconds, and civilisation will be blasted into eternity. Ideas, not bombs, will determine who wins the battle of ideologies, and on this battle depends the length of time we have left to live and whether our children will ever grow up.' But the far-seers of this century recognise in Moral Re-Armament the certainty of cure. My friend, Robert Schuman, of France, who has twice written the foreword to the French edition of my published speeches, puts it this way, 'Moral Re-Armament is a philosophy of life applied in action that I have seen reaching the millions. It is a world-wide transformation of human society that has already begun.'

It needs a hurricane of common sense to bring men to their senses, restoring the Communist and the non-Communist world to sanity and unity before it is too late. That hurricane is sweeping through every nation today, and in the midst of the hurricane the still small Voice of the living God, an unseen but ever-present Guide, willing and able to speak to the men of the Kremlin, the men of Washington, to the millions everywhere, leaders and led, who have lost their way and seek to find it.

It is so normal. It is so practical. It is a hurricane. And it is common sense.

A MESSAGE TO CYPRUS

On the occasion of the Independence of Cyprus, 16 August, 1960[1]

CYPRUS has a mighty destiny under God to demonstrate unity to the divided nations of the world. Her fighting men and women will pioneer a new way of doing things for mankind. Cyprus will be the herald of a new world order for nations, the island where remaking men and remaking the world takes first place.

If a country is to survive today it must live and give an ideology to everyone within and without its shores. An ideology superior to selfishness in East and West.

As St Paul of old walked across your historic countryside working miracles, so Cyprus today will work miracles of unity in the world by the way she lives as a nation. A hate-free, fear-free, greed-free land peopled by free men and women, a country of God.

---

[1] On 16 August, 1960, the first Cypriot flag to be sent abroad was raised at the MRA World Assembly at Caux in the presence of representatives of forty-one nations. This flag was a gift from Archbishop Makarios, first President of the Republic of Cyprus, who said in a message to Dr Buchman: 'We follow with keen interest your great task for a changed mankind and a better world, in which we mean to play our part.' The Vice-President of Cyprus, Dr Kutchuk, said: 'The ideology of Moral Re-Armament will find roots in the hearts and minds of all. It will save the world from Communism, dictatorship and war.' The first Ambassador to Washington, Zenon Rossides, said at Caux: 'If there is a case where the spirit of Moral Re-Armament has worked successfully, it is certainly the case of Cyprus. Indeed it is that spirit that brought about a settlement, in a case which seemed hopeless of solution, even by force.'

A MESSAGE TO NIGERIA

Dr Buchman sent the following message to the people of Nigeria, 30 September, 1960, in honour of Nigerian Independence.

WITH ALL MY HEART I congratulate Nigeria on her Independence.

Her destiny is to be a nation walking upright—35 million people going not left, not right, but straight.

She will be a pilot nation for the world, setting a course, chartered by God and steered by men who are obedient to Him.

I have come to know and love her leaders and people, whose inspired initiative at the MRA Assemblies in Caux and Mackinac and throughout the world has already helped shape the course of history. Through that breath-taking film *Freedom*, written at Caux and produced in Nigeria, the world is being taught the great truth that it is not colour, but character that counts.

With what is right, not who is right, regnant in affairs of state, Nigeria will produce a pattern of unity and faith for the continent of Africa that will give the answer to Moscow and Peking, Washington and London.

The world is waiting to see what God can do through one nation wholly given to Him. Nigeria can be that nation.

ALL THE MORAL FENCES
ARE DOWN

An Easter Message for the whole world given at the Easter Conference for the Moral Re-Armament of the Nations, at Caux, April 1961.

IN OXFORD a few months ago, my old friend Sir Richard Livingstone, once Vice-Chancellor of the University and a leading educator of the world, said, 'When you and I were young there were moral fences on the road of life. We did not always keep to them. But we always knew when we crossed them. But today all the moral fences are down, and look at the world. Your job is to build these fences anew.'

In country after country it holds true. In one country people shamelessly admit their leaders have their mistresses and are just not honest. They say men in the Cabinet have their price. That country is very close to Communist take-over. Today whenever the moral fences are down, Communism walks in.

Leaders of Japan came to see me. They said the moral fences were down in their country. They admitted they were down in their own lives. Corruption, mistresses, dishonesty in politics, had become a way of life. These men and women decided to build the moral fences again in their lives and in their nation. Then came the rioting in Japan at the time of the American-Japanese mutual security pact. The Government fell. It was a critical moment for Japan and the world. Prime Minister Kishi sent word a short time ago, 'At the crucial hour men trained in Moral Re-Armament in labour, youth and politics stood up and refused to compromise with evil.'

Then we met the leaders of the Zengakuren student organisation which had created the riots of 300,000 before the Diet buildings. They had mobbed the car of James Hagerty, Press Secretary to President Eisenhower and kept the President from visiting the country. The Chairman of the Foreign Relations Committee of the Diet at that time, speaking recently in Washington, said, 'That moment was another Pearl Harbor in the relationships between my country and America.' These youth leaders changed. They saw how Communism through their moral weaknesses had used them in an effort to take over their country. They have put their experience in a play. They call it *The Tiger*. It clearly shows how men without moral standards become the tools of men with an ideology, and how so-called private sins become a public menace, and how through Moral Re-Armament they found a new direction for themselves and for their nation.

The statesmen who understand the real nature of the ideological battle immediately called these young men and women with their play to their aid. They came to Germany. They played in all the major cities and to units of the armed forces.

In France the leadership concerned with rebuilding the moral fences of the nation invited *The Tiger* to Paris. Among them were Robert Schuman, the President of the Senate Monnerville, General Bethouart and Gabriel Marcel. It was national news. A film producer said he had never seen a Paris audience so gripped.

It was Robert Schuman who said to me at the Japanese Peace Treaty Conference in San Francisco, 'You made peace with Japan two years before we signed it.'

As the moral fences are repaired the answer is being brought to the anti-feelings about other nations which are so prevalent today. It was in Paris at Mont Valerien, the World War II shrine to the French Resistance, that Madame Anthonioz, the niece of President de Gaulle, and Madame Ely, welcomed for the first time since the war representatives of the German nation. They were a group of mineworkers who through Moral Re-Armament had found the answer to the ideological infiltration of their nation. They said at that time, 'We do not ask you to forget. We do ask you to forgive and unite with us to remake the world.'

In sharp contrast with the form of pressure being exerted on their neighbours by nations which have deliberately rejected moral standards, is the work of another Frenchman. For forty-five years he was a Marxist, a seaman, Victor Laure, one of the favourite pupils of Marcel Cachin. He and his wife, Irène Laure, who was a member of the Central Committee of the Socialist Party and a leader of the three million socialist women of France, decided to change and rebuild the moral fences in the family life, in France's relationships with Germany and North Africa. Chancellor Adenauer was one of the first to write a letter of condolence to Madame Laure just a few weeks ago on the death of her husband.

German and French leaders say of Victor and Irène Laure, 'These two have done more than any other living couple to bring about understanding between our two countries.' These two had found the element of unity at Caux. They were restored to the Church and married there. Said their son, who pioneered this work in Brazil, 'It is unusual for an adult son to be present at his parents' wedding.'

It was Victor and Madame Laure whom Mohammed Masmoudi, Minister of Information for Tunisia, first met when he came to Caux. He said at that time, 'I was as full of hate as a bomb is full of explosion. I had a letter from my mother saying, "God bless you, my son, and God curse the French." But after meeting the Laures, I replied, "God bless me. I need it. But do not curse the French. I have met French people with whom we can work to build a solid bridge between North Africa and Europe." '

This way of restoring broken fences has been forgotten. Victor Laure is an example of what God intends men to be and to do for their nations. Victor also made friends with the first Prime Minister of independent Morocco who found a new approach to the French-Moroccan division. He wrote me, 'I am determined to make absolute standards the basis of our Government.' And his late King, Mohammed V, sent me this word, 'You will find Morocco is ready soil for Moral Re-Armament. We need this ideology to maintain the freedom we have won.'

The Japanese leaders with their play, *The Tiger*, are now in America. They have received standing ovations from packed-out houses in the Carnegie Hall in New York, in Washington, and in the Henry and Edsel Ford Auditorium in Detroit. In New York they met Mr Hagerty whom they had mobbed at the Tokyo airport. He saw their play. He was so moved he came to the stage afterwards. He said, 'This is more than an apology.' He recognised one young Japanese as one of the men who had been threatening him through the window of his car. The news of this astonishing sequel to the story of last year's riots has swept across America by television. It has been seen by the millions in the Philippines in the same medium, and in Japan.

Police chiefs throughout the world are welcoming this message. In Washington the police arranged a special showing for their men, including the White House security agents. Commissioner James O'Brien, Deputy Mayor of New York, who welcomed the Japanese at Carnegie Hall, was also responsible for showing an MRA film and giving the news of the advance of MRA to police chiefs of the world meeting in their Annual Convention in New York. They admitted this was the one thing which had the fundamental answer for the acute problems they face.

The military men of the world, too, are responding. One of the senior Generals in America received these young Japanese. He said to them, 'Both President Eisenhower and I were puzzled why, after we had done so much economically for Japan, there was such resistance to America and to the visit of the President. Now I understand, You men have a spirit that money cannot buy. It must be built into every nation.'

General Eisenhower, when he received the Japanese Zengakuren student leaders in Palm Springs last week, said, 'I am for you one hundred per cent. I cannot tell you how happy I am to have you come and tell me of the changes that have taken place in your lives. This is the last act in the June riots and it has a happy ending. I hope to go back to Japan in the Fall but I don't expect to see you there. I expect to see you in South America and other places taking this message there. We have got to have an absolute conviction and be ready to sacrifice. Mankind is not going to live in peace until they have a higher moral plane on which to conduct their affairs.'

Now these young men are planning to take their message into South America. They know that Communism gallops across lands where the moral fences have been destroyed. It edges forward through the soft spots in men's characters. They know that a man who can be bought with women, men, drink, position, power, will be used by Communism in its bid for control. Moral breakdown is the problem. Moral Re-Armament is the answer.

The leaders of Hollywood welcomed these Japanese to America. In a message to their opening in the Carnegie Hall they said, 'The ideology of Moral Re-Armament must become the policy of our nations. You are equipping the nations of the world with the ideology to out-match Communism and answer its causes.' Think of the miracle of Hollywood beginning to build moral fences for the millions. Through movies and television, Hollywood producers, actors and technicians are preparing films on Moral Re-Armament for the world.

Stars like Muriel Smith, called the greatest voice on film today, and Ann Buckles of Broadway fame, are devoting all their lives and energy and talent to restore to the nations the moral standards which in the past so much of the product of Hollywood has been tearing down.

It was Muriel Smith's song, *The world walked into my heart*, which she sings in *The Crowning Experience*, now filling theatres with record audiences on every continent, that won the heart of one of Japan's great political personalities, Saburo Chiba. He recently visited me in Europe. He said,

'Moral Re-Armament taught my grand-daughter to recognise right and wrong. It has given me the courage to live and speak the full truth before all men.' It is his conviction that the leaders of the nations must unite to restore the moral fences around the world.

He was received by Chancellor Adenauer in Germany, by leaders in France and Rome. Everywhere the response was the same. Having seen the power of the play in his own Japanese, he understood the work of St Francis, for St Francis built the moral fences in the Church when he produced a play before the door of the Cathedral in Florence that healed the rift between the Mayor and the Church.

From Rome, Mr Chiba went to Rangoon. There on the front page of *The Nation* was headlined his conviction, 'Moral Re-Armament the answer to Communism.' He told of the determination of himself and his colleagues to build an Asian centre for Moral Re-Armament in Japan, an alternative to Peking and Moscow for the leaders of these nations. Prime Minister Kishi and Mr Chiba are building the fences again in Japan with some success.

One of Mr Chiba's colleagues in Burma is U Narada, Secretary of the Presiding Abbots' Association, who has distributed the Moral Re-Armament pictorials with the aid of his eighty thousand monks through the length and breadth of the land. More recently they had *The Crowning Experience* shown officially at the fifth All-Burma Assembly of the Presiding Abbots' Association in Mandalay. He says, 'Our work is to make Moral Re-Armament the policy of our nation.'

U Narada had just returned from meeting with leaders of Kerala in South India. These men are now taking the answer they have worked out in Kerala to Bengal, which threatens to become the Yenan of India. As a result of their change, the *Kerala Janatha* reported recently that of 612 members in six branches within the area covered by one Communist-controlled village council, there are now only 74 left on the rolls. The former Secretary of the Kallara branch of the Communist Party describes the Party as 'struggling for breath,' and is quoted as saying that 'Moral Re-Armament has shattered the Communist Party's centres of exploitation.' This man had been a full-time Communist worker for thirteen years. Through MRA, he says, 'At last I have begun to understand the meaning of right and wrong. God is telling me to put right what is wrong in my past in order to see things clearly in the future.' These men are determined to restore the moral fences in India, for they know that when the moral fences come down the enemies of freedom come in.

Take the Congo. For nearly a year a force of Moral Re-Armament has been building up the fences in that strife-torn land. Among them are former Mau Mau leaders from Kenya working with white settlers; black and white South Africans; and three young Americans who gave up Holly-wood contracts to use their genius in song to bring an answer to nations. Through the months of violence and chaos they sang their songs in Swahili, Chiluba, Lingala and French on the National Radio. Twice a day at the most popular morning and evening hour of broadcasting, their message went out to the millions. They met with thousands of the Congolese and the United Nations forces in the Congo, and the records of their songs are popular everywhere. With their friends they gave training in Moral Re-Armament night after night to the troops and their officers. The

American Ambassador, introducing these Colwell brothers to a diplomat visiting the Congo, told him: 'These men have been a bulwark in the front line of the battle here. They stuck in there with their radio broadcasts even after the Communists had taken over.'

The Moral Re-Armament force were invited by the head of the Sisters of St Augustine to the ceremony when the new Congolese nuns were to take their vows in St Peter's Church, Leopoldville. Dr Close, formerly surgical resident at the Roosevelt Hospital, New York, one of the only two white surgeons to remain on duty when the crisis was at its height in a hospital of 1,200 beds, earned the gratitude of the nation for his services. When he and his MRA friends arrived at the Church they were received and conducted to seats of honour among the parents of the new nuns. They were the only white people there, except for the clergy and the European nuns, among a congregation of 2,000.

The Moral Re-Armament force was invited to Katanga. There the Mwami Mwata-Yamvo, Grand Chief of the Lunda and greatest tribal ruler in Katanga, received them. The King's drummers sounded a beat heard for fifteen kilometres around to summon the Elders and people to the palace. The King, wearing his beaded robes and crown, was carried in his ceremonial chair to the Assembly of the People. Seated with the King were the Elders, also in beaded head-dress, and the Royal Princesses.

Traditional spearmen and modern soldiers stood on guard. The King said, 'I am grateful for what you have brought us. You have taught us many new things. Stay with us a long time.'

The Moral Re-Armament force went to President Tshombe with the conviction, 'A president who sets a new standard of discipline and a new pattern of living will build an incorruptible nation.' The Colwells sang him a song written in his own language. President Tshombe told them, 'Everywhere you go people will accept this ideology. We will all be brothers.' When told of the reception given by the Grand Chief Mwami Mwata-Yamvo, his face lit up and he said, 'He is my father-in-law. I was born there.' Leaders of Katanga said, 'When some people come to us we fire off guns and make a lot of noise, but they leave nothing behind. Your coming has created a peaceful revolution.'

An official of the Swiss Red Cross unit in the Congo said on his return to his country, 'Moral Re-Armament are doing the only thing that is really effective in the Congo.'

In Lucerne, in the Catholic heart of Switzerland, the showings of *The Crowning Experience* have broken all records. 'The Hollywood Reporter' carried the headline: 'Half of population attends MRA film.' The story says, 'In Lucerne, Switzerland, this city of 70,000 inhabitants and during a period of low cinema business due to continually fine weather, the Moral Re-Armament feature, *The Crowning Experience*, starring Muriel Smith and Ann Buckles, has chalked up its 35,000th customer within a 32-day run. This is an all time attendance record for a film of non-Swiss origin.'

The news of the response in Catholic Switzerland has been translated into the Latin American tongues. Translated into Spanish, printed on miniature sized pages, it was dropped from the air on Cuba by the largest Cuban newspaper now published in Miami.

The Japanese students are planning to take their play *The Tiger* to the South American republics with its answer to subversion and Communism. There is the need for an intelligent and unified thrust forward in these countries, where economic aid is necessary but cannot succeed unless it is backed with a moral ideology that changes men. Miami, Florida, is the throttle that affects the speed of the movement between the South American republics and the rest of the world today. At Miami from April 14th to April 24th will be held an Assembly for the Americas.

In the invitation they say, 'We need political and economic measures, but above all we must create a new type of man.'

The dockers of Brazil wrote and produced a film describing how they had ended gang warfare, the pilfering and the inter-union rivalry to make their port once again prosperous and peaceful. When Mr Kishi, as Prime Minister of Japan, arrived at the port of Rio, he was met by waterfront workers changed through Moral Re-Armament. One of them who had worked for thirty years as a militant dockers' leader, took off his trade union pin and gave it to Mr Kishi in thanks for the help given by the Japanese dockers whom they had met at Moral Re-Armament assemblies. Mr Kishi proudly wore that trade union pin when he returned to Japan.

A French Ambassador to Brazil says, 'I have met these men. Every word is true. When I arrived in Brazil, gang warfare was rife in the docks. Black and white were settling their differences with knives. The police did not dare enter some sections of the dockers' quarters. One day, I heard that a veritable revolution was under way among the dockers and was changing the spirit of the port. This story is not fiction. It is a human tapestry woven in the lives of men who have found a new wisdom. They are convinced that their experience has a message for all nations.'

These films of MRA are going from Catholic centre to Catholic centre in Latin America at the invitation of Catholic priests. They are welcomed for the new life they bring and the radiant hope that things can be different.

Admiral Sir Edward Cochrane will be at the Miami Assembly. He was one of the great Commodores of convoys in World War II and was decorated for his courage. He knows the leaders of South America and has been travelling for years in those countries. His ancestor, Admiral Lord Cochrane, known as 'Cochrane the liberator,' is a household word throughout Latin America.

Men will be coming to Miami from Peru, Argentina, Uruguay, Paraguay, Chile and Brazil. The Brazilian dockers' leaders will be at Miami. Former Communist leaders, who through Moral Re-Armament have changed and are giving an answer to their countries, political, industrial and labour leaders from America will be there. Rajmohan Gandhi, grandson of Mahatma Gandhi, will be coming, and Peter Howard, the journalist and playwright from Europe.

These men, with delegates from many parts of the world, are going to study and train in Miami.

An American Admiral, who went three times to similar assemblies for training in MRA and whose wife went for a fourth time, was asked by his strategy board in Washington to tell them what was going on at these assemblies. He replied, 'I learned what an ideology means—to start doing what we should have been doing all along and to do it all day, every day, for the rest of our lives.'

SOLID ROCK OR SINKING SAND

A message from Caux, May, 1961

A MONTH AGO I sent an Easter message to the world, *All the moral fences are down.* There was an instant response. From the statesmen and the ordinary man, in country after country, came the word, 'That is the problem. Help us to rebuild those moral fences for our nations and the world.'

General Bethlem of Brazil is a man who is doing just that. In Miami, Florida, he dropped down on a group of leaders from all the Hemisphere. There was the General commanding the army of Peru. There was the President of the Parliament from Uruguay. There was the representative of the Minister of War from Argentina, the wife of the Minister of Reconstruction of Chile, dockers' leaders and industrialists from Brazil. There was the man who founded the Communist Party in Peru and brought in the first Popular Front Government in Chile.

There General Bethlem also met General Inoue from Japan, and with him the force of Japanese youth with *The Tiger*, their play about the answer to the Tokyo riots. He met Chief Walking Buffalo from Canada with his Braves and Counsellors. He met businessmen from Switzerland, labour leaders from France and Germany. He met Philip Vundla, elected spokesman for 600,000 Africans, whom the police once described as the most dangerous man in South

Africa; and Vaitheswaran, six years a dedicated Communist in South India, whose change has helped give Kerala the solid rock of an answer to Communism. He met William Pawley, son of a former United States Ambassador to Peru and Brazil. From Britain he met Peter Howard, the author, and Rear-Admiral Sir Edward Cochrane, great-nephew of the famous Lord Cochrane who helped liberate Chile, Peru and Brazil. He met a Jamaican leader who said, 'You men have the only hope for the Caribbean. We must mobilise now for this answer, otherwise we shall quickly go the way of Cuba.'

General Bethlem had held two diplomatic posts as Ambassador of Brazil to Bolivia and Pakistan, but now he was on a trip with his wife for a holiday in New York. As he listened to these men speak, he was gripped by their unity that was like a rock because God was in command. This was the answer for the hemisphere. Within a week he had turned around and was leading an advance force of these very men to Brazil, which was followed a few days later by a planeload of 129 from twenty-four countries, to initiate what the newspaper *El Pais* of Montevideo called, 'The greatest ideological offensive undertaken on the Latin American continent.' The General eagerly went back to give Brazil the solid foundation for world leadership that he had longed for for his nation. As his advance-guard he took with him Rajmohan Gandhi, grandson of Mahatma Gandhi, Admiral Cochrane, Vaitheswaran, and Takasumi Mitsui of the great Japanese industrial family. They prepared the way.

When the main international force arrived they were met by radio, press and television. In fact, one enthusiastic television cameraman got on the plane before the visitors could get off. It was national news.

Immediately they spoke at a lunch to four hundred leading industrialists and businessmen, including the representatives of Ford, General Electric, Goodyear Rubber and Swifts. General Bethlem said, 'Both North and South America are at the most critical points of our history. Against the background of Cuba, Venezuela and Bolivia where I have been Ambassador, and the new Russian offensive starting in Mexico on May Day, the inescapable choice for Latin America is Moral Re-Armament or Communism. I know you businessmen, because I was like you. We ask our wives to live purity, but we are not pure. We ask our workers to be honest, but we are dishonest. I have changed and committed my whole life to this fight.'

To General Bethlem's surprise and astonishment these businessmen three times halted his presentation at that lunch with standing ovations. Some people may say this is an incredible response, but here is the fact. Immediately General Bethlem and his force were invited to speak to a meeting of six hundred leaders of the industrial and business life of Brazil and to take an hour-and-a-half's television programme.

Chief Walking Buffalo of the Stoney Indians and his party created such a stir coming to this luncheon that hundreds of school children crowded into the lobby to meet him. For half an hour he told them how, in the previous year, one hundred million people had seen and heard him on the warpath in his ninetieth year in a 62,000 mile tour for Moral Re-Armament. He spoke of the time he made me a blood-brother twenty-eight years ago, when he gave me the name of 'A Wo Zan Zan Tonga—Great

Light in Darkness'. While the Chief was speaking, there came a message from across the street from the Mother Superior of Sao Paulo's most famous convent school for seven hundred children from leading families, asking him to come with his friends to speak to a quickly convened school assembly. The response was electric. Said the Mother Superior, 'This will be a marking day in the annals of this college.' Said another Sister, 'This is the work of the Holy Spirit.' After a television programme that reached a four million audience on the number-one programme of the week, a Mother Superior said, 'This is a very profound message. We must work together. You must go to all the Catholic schools. They will respond.'

This can be the normal life of these countries, for which people have been saying there is not much hope. Otherwise these businessmen and their families with all their money and social life will lead to an absence of God, spelling the breakdown of the moral fences of democracy and, eventually, to Communism.

On May Day the Japanese launched their ideological weapon *The Tiger* in Latin America. Crowds outside the Municipal Theatre in Sao Paulo were so great that the traffic was stopped. General Bethlem introduced on the stage a force of 150 people from twenty-four countries, and read cables from Italian and French Socialist leaders, from seventeen mineworkers of Britain, from the dockers of Holland, India, the United States and Brazil, and from Hollywood stars. Former Prime Minister Kishi of Japan cabled, 'Tonight is being followed by millions of Japanese who are joining this fight to root out Communism, exploitation and slavery all around the world. Your fire and passion for a way which is not Left nor Right but straight, will give the South American Republics their true destiny.'

Mrs Dorothea Buck, former President of the General Federation of Women's Clubs with membership of eleven million women, received a rousing ovation when she challenged the women of North and South America to 'lay down their comforts and complacency and to unite to take up this ideology without which our children and grandchildren will live behind the Iron Curtain.' Dr Raul Migone, former Minister of Labour in Argentina, summed up his convictions when he said, 'Moral Re-Armament is the chosen weapon for humanity not only to overcome Communism, which I am absolutely convinced it will do, but also to show the way for mankind as a whole.'

These men of action and responsibility like General Bethlem get this message on the move. It is like a current in the air. Take the story of that remarkable man, Prime Minister U Nu of Burma. He visited Moscow, and being attracted by their concern for Asia said they should be invited to the next Afro-Asian conference. But then he came to Finland. There he found the ideological plays of Moral Re-Armament. He knew the effect they had had in his own country. He came at nine o'clock in the morning with the Prime Minister and Foreign Minister of Finland. What he saw in that theatre changed his policy. On his next stop in Stockholm he called in the press and apologised for the hasty statement which had suggested the inclusion of the Soviet in the conference.

U Nu knew that Burma was a nation deeply influenced by MRA. U Tin Tut, former Foreign Minister who had been to Caux, spoke of it as 'the one unfailing light'; and Aung San, the first Prime Minister, whose widow as Ambassador in India closely follows this work, said, 'This is what I want for the whole country.' U Narada, the Abbot who is the Secretary to the Presiding Abbots' Association responsible for 75,840 Buddhist monks, has mobilised these monks throughout the country who believe in the validity of this message for Burma. He says, 'My colleagues in the all-Burma Presiding Abbots' Association and myself have accepted the responsibility of rebuilding the moral fences in our country. Then we will have new men, new nations and a new world.'

These monks are enthusiastically at work, and have shown the MRA film, *The Crowning Experience*, in the presence of the Prime Minister at the national celebration at the Peace Pagoda in the open air to crowds so large that they had to sit on both sides of the screen. The Speaker of the Chamber of Deputies said, 'This film is tailor-made for Burma. It exactly fits the need of the country.'

The last time U Nu came to America he told reporters in New York that he was coming especially to Arizona to see me because of the urgent need for this message to his country. He had already sent his daughter to be with us at our assemblies. His word on leaving me was simply, 'Come soon, come soon to Burma.'

Meanwhile, U Narada and five Abbots are coming to Europe for the Assembly in Caux, Switzerland, and will celebrate with me my eighty-third birthday in June. These worthies are welcome here and the highest in the land also, who long to come and find in the quiet of these mountains the key to their country's destiny.

289

In Japan it is the former Prime Minister Kishi and his chief adviser, Mr Saburo Chiba, who are planning the delegation for this Assembly, with Senator Ohtani, a director of the World Buddhist Federation and adviser to a five million strong Buddhist group in Japan. Senator Ohtani says, 'What Asian Buddhism now needs is Moral Re-Armament. We in Japan have been given the light of MRA. Now we must sweep the whole world with this light.'

It is just a year now since a force of Moral Re-Armament left from Caux to work in the Congo. What is the battle they are fighting? It is a difficult task. But they are meeting with such a response that the Minister for Information and National Defence in Leopoldville says that 'Moral Re-Armament has saved the Congo from a far greater catastrophe.'

The other day they were invited to the controlled area of the Lower Congo, in which are the Ports of Matadi, Boma and Banana. *En route* they encountered several Congo Army road blocks. At one the sergeant said, 'Moral Re-Armament! We listen all the time to your radio broadcasts,' and he began to sing one of the songs. He was overjoyed to meet the Colwell brothers from Hollywood, who had put those songs twice a day on the radio in the languages of his people. At every road block, as the soldiers realised the MRA men were in the car, they crowded enthusiastically around, and at the last block before entering Matadi, the soldiers cheered them for bringing the answer to Communism.

At the end of the road in Boma the square was a sea of faces as ten thousand people crammed into the Civic Centre to see the MRA films and hear these men speak. That crowd stood for four hours and when asked if they wanted more, roared their approval and said, 'We will stay all night for more of this.' Said one, 'We want the MRA force to stay for a month right here to spread this idea.'

The Auxiliary Bishop of Matadi said after the film, 'You say what is straight and right. This is the good and only way, the way of MRA which we all need. I congratulate and thank you. I will give you my fullest support so that the masses will follow this idea.'

Africa can be lost in the sinking sands of the materialism of East and West. Leaders of Africa welcome Moral Re-Armament because it is the solid ground on which a hate-free, fear-free, greed-free continent can be built. Marking the independence of their country the Government of Sierra Leone invited the representatives of fifty-six nations to see *The Crowning Experience*. The Deputy Prime Minister presenting the film said, 'I have decided to throw my whole weight into this work of Moral Re-Armament.' Humphrey Wood, officially representing Moral Re-Armament at the Independence Celebrations, presented my message: 'Sierra Leone's destiny is to be a nation guided, not by the will of others but by the will of God to follow what is right. Strong as a lion she will be among the nations. The whole world is anxiously waiting to see what God can do through one nation wholly given to Him. Sierra Leone can be that nation. My heartiest congratulations.'

Introducing *The Crowning Experience*, which was repeatedly interrupted by applause, Manasseh Moerane, Vice-President of the thousands of African teachers of South Africa, said, 'Political independence is important; economic stability is important, but above all a new nation needs an ideology. We in Africa cannot afford neutralism. We have got to stand for what is right.'

Bremer Hofmeyr, whose family have held six Cabinet posts in South Africa, said, 'Moral Re-Armament is the ideology that sets men and nations free, that keeps men and nations free, and unites free men to win the world.'

President Tubman of Liberia has also asked for the men of Moral Re-Armament to present *The Crowning Experience* to the Pan-African Conference which opens this week in Monrovia. He says, 'I invite the leaders and people of Africa to join in this supreme task and to give priority to the moral re-armament of our nations.'

This African statesman echoes the convictions of Eudocio Ravines of Peru, former Latin American delegate to the Comintern, who spoke at the Moral Re-Armament Hemisphere Assembly in Miami. He said, 'The fundamental answer to Communism in Latin America is moral and spiritual. Events in Cuba are happening because the Americas have not lived an ideology superior to Communism. That is where we Latin Americans are responsible. But neither has the United States exported moral values to Cuba. It has exported dollars and tourists and those things which made Latin Americans cynically call Havana the cabaret of North America. Moral decadence opens the door to Communist penetration. Many people say that Communism is the product of poverty, hunger and underdevelopment. However, I say with the authority of having successfully conducted one of the greatest Communist movements in creating the Popular Front in Chile, the cause of the penetration of Communism is corruption and moral decadence. Now the Government of the United States is offering millions of dollars to solve the economic problems of Latin America. But military aid and dollars alone are not enough. This is the moment for America to export a moral ideology to Latin America. Therefore, the mission of Moral Re-Armament is of fundamental and particular importance.'

From this Assembly in Miami returned two Swiss businessmen who had given evidence of the striking response to this answer from industry, politics and press in Catholic central Switzerland. One said, 'I came back from America with the deep conviction that my job was to be ready to pack my bags and travel to bring this answer. In a world crisis like today the old style businessman simply doesn't make sense. Businessmen without a superior ideology only help Communism. I think of the industrialists who gave Castro thirty million dollars and have lost it all. And of the corruption that has become a way of life for businessmen in many Western lands and brought us to the edge of the abyss. We need men and women who will pay the full price of change, honesty and fearless leadership in our nations if the world is to be saved.'

The Moral Re-Armament Assembly at Caux in June will be the focus for leaders from every continent who are seeking solid ground for statesmanship. His Excellency Bernard Hardion, a senior diplomatic adviser to the French Foreign Office and former Ambassador in Brazil, said, 'Moral Re-Armament is a modern chivalry. Chivalry was inspired by faith and belief in God. It was not a substitute for religion. We must once and for all end this defence of a past forever dead. We must take the offensive in the battle for the future and for the submission of men to the Divine Voice.'

Dr Azikiwe, the first African Governor-General of

Nigeria, who architected his country's freedom, told how he discovered in Caux the idea of 'not who is right, but what is right,' which 'proved to be a pearl of great price at a time when we were on the threshold of a great political awakening.'

The Catholic philosopher Gabriel Marcel spoke to the foreign press in Geneva. He said that in Caux he had seen a power that brought 'a radical and lasting transformation in people. It is magnificent, and cannot be gainsaid.'

Robert Schuman said of his experience at Caux, 'I am accustomed to conferences, but they are very different from this. Normally they end with great disappointment. Here we find nothing but satisfaction and hope.'

General Marcel Carpentier, who commanded the ground forces of NATO for Central Europe, sounded a challenge at the most recent Assembly in Caux: 'We need a floodtide of Moral Re-Armament to sweep across the world. Then men in government will be forced to make the right decisions that spring not just from the intellect, but from our hearts and faith.'

Like a mighty army moves this force across the world. Men and women of all races and nations united with a common commitment. The world is on the knife-edge of decision. We must go all out to save our nations. When men change and are gripped by the fire and passion, the purity and honesty of a moral ideology, miracles happen. The foundation is laid of a new world, not on the shifting sand of corruption and compromise, but on the rock-like character of God-directed men and nations.

BRAVE MEN CHOOSE

Given on the occasion of Dr Buchman's eighty-third birthday and the opening of the World Assembly at Caux, 4 June, 1961.

FORTY YEARS AGO this month there came to Oxford a man who had some knowledge of life, some insight into the ways of East and West, who had spent days with Gandhi in India and Sun Yat-Sen in China. In what is now Kerala he met an English bishop who said: 'You must go to Oxford. They need the experience you have found.'

During those forty years, the conviction he brought to Oxford has been a live issue, rousing men and nations through those who have chosen or rejected his challenge.

It was an Oxford man, a Member of Parliament for twenty-five years, a man who played a part in the Cyprus settlement, who this week spoke up for this conviction in public debate. A week before, the head of a College spoke boldly of it in introducing that great African film, *Freedom*, to an Oxford audience. These men, and many others, are in the line of those who in Britain's history have brought integrity into national life by their decision. The title of this speech, *Brave Men Choose*, is taken from a book by an Oxford man on this very theme, that brave men turn the course of history.

One such man in Oxford was Professor Streeter. The message rang a clarion call to this great scholar. It challenged him. It touched him. In Oxford Town Hall, before many members of the University, he said: 'I have been watching this work with what diplomatists call "benevolent neutrality." Tonight I have decided. . . . During these last years I have felt the world situation becoming more full of depression, more full of despair. There is a great deal of goodwill, but there is not enough of it to solve our tremendous problems—war, class-war and economic breakdown.' Later he said: 'Modern civilisation can only be saved by a moral awakening. It can happen in Britain. It will happen if those who lead Britain learn to find in God their inspiration and direction. And Britain thus led would save the world.'

'I have decided.' There is the key.

Eleven distinguished members of senior Oxford paved the way for Dr Streeter's decision, among them the Master of Balliol, the Master of University College, and others who later became heads of colleges. They stood for justice and fair play for this message. It captured a wave of men in Oxford. Oxford became a voice to the world of a revolutionary faith.

It was another great Oxford man, the late Marquess of Salisbury, who speaking in the House of Lords said: 'The cause of the world's state is not economic. The cause is moral.' He echoed Dr Streeter's conviction when he said: 'If I may use a phrase which is common in a great movement taking place at this moment in this country and elsewhere, what you want are God-guided personalities, which make God-guided nationalities, to make a new world. All other ideas of economic adjustment are too small really to touch the centre of the evil.'

He, too, decided, and to his home invited this man to meet with the leaders of British life to see how they could unitedly give a moral and spiritual leadership to a world on the brink of collapse. Under the Hatfield trees he walked with friends old and new, among them Lord Lytton, who was later to say that that walk had left an indelible mark on his life.

In East London, in the cradle of the British Labour movement, where Moral Re-Armament was launched, there were also brave men who chose. There was Tod Sloan, Keir Hardie's fellow fighter from the docks. He wrote: 'Chaos cannot obtain if we work, live and practice Moral Re-Armament. It is a real laughing, living, loving obedient willingness to restore God to leadership. This to me is the only revolution that matters—the change of human nature—and it does happen.'

There was Ben Tillett, pioneer of the dockers' unions across the world. From his death bed he sent this word, 'Tell Frank Buchman to go on fighting. You have a great international movement. Use it. It is the hope of tomorrow. It will bring sanity back to the world.'

The Earl of Athlone, who first met this message in 1929 when he was Governor-General of South Africa, speaking in a radio broadcast to the British Commonwealth in the early days of the war, said: 'The call for Moral Re-Armament has encircled the world, and become a source of fresh hope to millions of men and women. Heads of States, national, civic and industrial leaders of all classes, creeds and parties have welcomed it as the cure for that deep disease of the spirit from which civilisation is suffering.

'Moral Re-Armament stands for a change of heart, for that new spirit which must animate all human relationships. It calls on us to make the will of God the guiding force, as for individuals, so for homes and nations.'

As the ideological struggle intensified across the world, a growing multitude caught the fire of these pioneers. For only men ablaze for the right can ever hope today to win men who burn for the wrong. 'Fire from heaven', that is how Don Sturzo, patriot-priest of Italy, described Moral Re-Armament in a message sent to the World Assembly on Mackinac Island. His thinking inspired the Christian Democrat parties of Italy, France and Germany, which have given three great Europeans to the world—Prime Minister de Gasperi, Prime Minister Schuman and Chancellor Adenauer.

Prime Minister de Gasperi expressed his conviction that Moral Re-Armament by going 'to the root of the world's evils will bring about the understanding between men and nations for which all people long.'

Prime Minister Schuman wrote: 'What Moral Re-Armament brings us is a philosophy of life applied in action. It is not a question of a change of policy. It is a question of changing men. Democracy and her freedom can be saved only by the quality of the men who speak in her name.'

Chancellor Adenauer knows the value of Moral Re-Armament. He says it has played 'an invisible but effective part in bridging differences of opinion between negotiating parties in important international agreements.'

These brave men chose. Now a world-wide army is surging forward on every continent.

Four weeks ago there arrived in Brazil, a focal target of the Kremlin in Latin-America, a force of 150 from twenty-four countries. Thousands flocked to see the Japanese play, *The Tiger*, showing the answer to the Tokyo riots. Thousands more who could not get in saw films giving the answer to conflict of race, class and ideology.

The President summoned this force to the capital, Brasilia. Led by General Bethlem, former Ambassador of Brazil in Pakistan and Bolivia, the man whose decision had brought them to his continent, there came to meet the President a modern group of men and women ablaze with conviction. The President heard from the grandson of Mahatma Gandhi, a former Mau Mau fighter from Kenya, a former top Communist student leader from Kerala, an American educator whose experience of Moral Re-Armament had led him to give his life to Negro education in America, the son of an American ambassador to Brazil and Peru, an Indian chieftain from Western Canada, a Nigerian nationalist, a member of the great Mitsui industrial family of Japan, a Frenchwoman who was a member of the central committee of the Socialist Party and a leader of the three million socialist women of France, and a British admiral, descendant of the Lord Cochrane who helped liberate Chile, Brazil and Peru.

The *Corriere della Sera*, carrying this news to Italy, wrote: 'President Janio Quadros received today a delegation of Moral Re-Armament at his residence. He gave them a cordial welcome and said: "I have followed the activities of Moral Re-Armament now for several years. I am convinced that the world as it is today cannot survive unless men stand for the ideals for which you are fighting. The disorder in the world today—economic, social and political—is due to the fact that men have stopped being concerned about spiritual and moral forces. I have listened with deep emotion to your convictions. I want to let you know that as far as I can I will do all that is possible so that we in Brazil will understand better the moral values of our civilisation." '

Responding to the invitation to come to the Conference for Moral Re-Armament which opens in Caux, Switzerland, on June 1st, Quadros said, 'I will send a personal representative.'

When he learned that the Japanese play, *The Tiger*, was available, he telephoned to the General in charge of his military household and said, 'Provide all that is needed to bring *The Tiger* to Brasilia. Instruct the Mayor to obtain the theatre, provide transport in the city and, further, have the Air Force put at their disposal so that this work can be known in city after city through all the centres of Brazil'.

General Bethlem, describing in the Press the impact of this force, writes: 'For the first time on this continent Communism has been confronted with a positive alternative and for the first time it is being made to retreat. I have found a real revolution in MRA. We Brazilians are being challenged to give this to Communists, non-Communists and anti-Communists alike. Many of us have been confused through our moral compromise. I have found clarity through change. We need to wake up. The ideological war is already here. Which way Brazil goes, so goes Latin America. The situation is deadly serious. A former Minister of Foreign Affairs told me, "Cuba has brought us to the brink of war. MRA may be the last hope. If Brazil gets in the world will get it". The Minister of War said, "We will do everything we can to make Brazil the capital of the answer. You have the winning idea in MRA".

'In the Catholic University of Sao Paulo where, it was stated, eighty per cent of the students were pro-Castro, one professor-priest said, "Since you have given your films and plays and held an Assembly in our University, there have been no political demonstrations. Moral Re-Armament is being talked about everywhere."

'A missionary monk, who had come down from North Brazil where the Communists are training small armies and guerilla bands in the hills, said, "Brazil is just like Spain was before the civil war. Can you fill my truck full of your literature so I can distribute it through all the cities up and down the Amazon?"

'The owner of a national newspaper said to me, "Many of us have lost faith. We have regained it again through MRA." The president of the largest newspaper of Latin America said, "MRA is not only an idea on the march. It is a force on the march. Our newspaper is at your disposal. Everyone must be reached with this idea."

'The inescapable choice for Latin America,' concludes General Bethlem, 'is Moral Re-Armament or Communism. We will never succeed in this fight unless we change men. We are out to clean up the nation and the world. I have committed my whole life to this fight.'

General Carpentier of France, servant of his country in many campaigns and former Commander-in-Chief of the Central European ground forces of NATO, who flew to Brazil to join this force, spoke to a vast audience in Rio de Janeiro. 'From the heart of the best men,' he said, 'must come this tremendous wave of Moral Re-Armament which will win over Communism. In this ideological war we must confront Communism with another ideology. That ideology is MRA. It is because I am convinced of that that I am here to conduct a war.

'We need tactics, strategy and means. Some people think that strategy can come from a meeting of men who are responsible in the political field, but I do not believe it. I have read in the newspapers for the last ten years accounts of men who meet in Washington, Paris and other great countries. But it is from all free men who fight for Moral Re-Armament that the answer will come.'

Workers and military find unity in this ideology. Damasio Cardoso, militant dockers' leader of Rio, told all his fellow-workers and their families, 'I pray to God that what happened in my family will happen to every family in the docks. We are either for God or against God. The choice for all of us is MRA or Communism.'

The Catholic priest in the docks, who before Cardoso's change could not enter the quarter where 600 docker sand their families lived, added, 'By their fruits ye shall know them. MRA is a tree. You can see its fruit. Moral Re-Armament has become a much more powerful weapon than any military weapons of Russia or North America. The most powerful weapon is absolute honesty, purity, unselfishness and love. I want to declare here that in me MRA has a friend, admirer and fellow worker.'

That gifted artist, Louis Byles, from Jamaica, ninety miles from Cuba, speaks for many in Latin America and the Caribbean when he says, 'We have very little time left.' He starred in that film *The Crowning Experience* as the man who plays the part of a convinced Communist captured by the fire of a superior ideology. He has just shown this film to the leadership of his island. Said one of the Government officials, 'This is not a film. It is God. We must get this out immediately to Jamaica. It is exactly what we need.'

It will take brave men to free, unite and save the continent of Africa. Philip Vundla, who was the elected spokesman for

600,000 Africans of Johannesburg and was a founder of the African mineworkers' organisation, says, 'There is great bitterness in our country. South Africa is being used to divide East from West on the basis of colour, but the real issue is not colour but character. It is not only the white men who have to change in South Africa. We have to change too. We need it, and I wish everybody to know that.'

Vundla chose the ideology that brought unity and rejected division. His choice almost cost him his life at the hands of extremists, but his steadfastness has won him the respect of friend and foe alike.

In Kenya, threatened again by bloodshed and chaos, the branch secretary of one African party faced the choice between two ideologies. He said, 'I had an airplane ticket to the Communist conference of African leaders. Instead I came to the Moral Re-Armament assembly. I did not know there were such people committed to eradicate hate, fear and selfishness. Our leaders went to the other conference with a calabash filled with the waters of freedom, the Communists punctured it, and our freedom is pouring out. MRA will seal the holes so true freedom can be maintained. I must bring the light of this answer to our country in darkness.'

A woman former Mau Mau leader, detained for eight years, said, 'Here my hatred of the white man has ended. We women played a big part in leading our nation in the wrong direction. Now we must play the fullest part in rebuilding the country.' Calling her children to stand beside her, she said to each in turn, 'Forgive me. I have been full of hate and have led you into hatred.'

Another former Mau Mau district secretary said, 'Bitterness has been the disease in our land. From my heart and

303

home it spread like fire until there was bloodshed and chaos everywhere. God give us all new hearts to put right what is wrong in time.'

At the recent Conference for Heads of African States in Monrovia, great applause greeted the special showing of *The Crowning Experience*. 'We are your debtors,' said President Tubman. 'Everyone in the country must see this film'. He added, 'I will make every possible effort to meet Dr Buchman in Caux this summer.' Two out of the six pages in the Conference edition of the *Liberian Age* printed the news of Moral Re-Armament underlining the statement that 'Africa can be lost in the sinking sands of the materialism of East and West. Leaders of Africa welcome Moral Re-Armament because it is the solid ground on which a hate-free, fear-free, greed-free continent can be built.'

President Tubman shares the view of the Maharajah of Mysore, who said at a showing of *The Crowning Experience*, 'The only hope for mankind is to give no quarter to the powers of evil, internal or external. Human nature is so constituted that it cannot be taken for granted that good will automatically prevail over evil in an indolent or uninterested world. It is of the utmost importance that we carry on this task of Moral Re-Armament with ceaseless vigilance. The armament of morality is invisible, but it is of matchless power. And its army includes, or should include, the whole of mankind. Let us all, both individuals and nations, enroll ourselves in this army.'

From Geneva, where the fate of great portions of the Asian and African continents is being discussed at the Conferences on Laos and Algeria, a Swiss editor spoke over one of Europe's most powerful radio stations, reaching millions on both sides of the Iron Curtain. He said, 'Through all the confusion caused by many different meeting places, press rooms, delegation headquarters and police bodyguards, move the men and women of Moral Re-Armament who have come down from Caux, high above the Lake of Geneva, and with a very compelling sense of dedication are making available to friend and foe alike their Whitsun message. This, too, speaks of overcoming difficulties in the meetings of politicians from East and West and quotes Robert Schuman's word that it was only in Caux that he found encouragement and hope.'

The future of Asia may well be decided by which idea wins the Buddhist nations. Leaders from Japan, Laos, Cambodia, South Viet-nam, Thailand, Burma, Ceylon and India are convinced that Moral Re-Armament is the ideology with the answer. Buddhism is expected to be made the state religion of Burma. Five senior Abbots from that country have come to plan at Caux for the mobilisation of the Buddhist world in the ideological struggle. These revered leaders were seen off at the Rangoon Airport by a hundred monks and senior officials. They have just been received in Oxford by the heads of two colleges, by the Mayor of the City, and the President of the Union. They were shown the rooms in Christ Church, where this work had its beginnings forty years ago.

This is the word of a man on his eighty-third birthday who has spent a long life up and down the world meeting and knowing men, who in 1915 paid the first of eight visits to Japan and was there the guest of those who laid the foundation of modern Japanese finance and industry, Baron Sakatani and Viscount Shibusawa, whose grandson, a

Minister of Finance, his great-grandson, and even his great-great-grandson, are working with this force today. They come with former Prime Minister Kishi and other leading Japanese to Caux this summer to forge a unity of statesmanship among the free nations. They carry forward the work of which General Ho Ying-chin, former Prime Minister of China, says, 'More unity has been created between the nations of Asia at one Moral Re-Armament assembly in the Philippines than in ten years of post-war diplomatic activity.'

It is the word of a man who has known the personal friendship of viceroys and governors of India and of the men who opposed them, and brought them together: who knows the problems of Africa at first hand since 1929, and these statesmen of Europe and the Americas for more than fifty years. He has seen the development of two materialist ideologies and the devastation of two world wars, the retreat of freedom, and now the advance of a mighty answer.

We are facing world revolution. There are only three possibilities open to us. We can give in, and some are ready to do just that. Or we can fight it out, and that means the risk of global suicide. Or we can find a superior ideology that shows the next step ahead for the Communist and the non-Communist world alike. What we shall never do effectively is to patch things up by pretending that basic differences do not exist or do not matter, nor by supposing that an ideological challenge can be met by economic, political or military means alone. Absolute moral standards are not just questions of individual conduct today. They are the conditions of national survival. We need to scour out the dirt in our national life, our political life, our economic life, our school life and our home life through a change in men. Wherever men give man the place in their lives that God alone should have, slavery has begun. 'Men must choose to be governed by God, or they condemn themselves to be ruled by tyrants'.

There is no neutrality in the battle between good and evil. No nation can be saved on the cheap. It will take the best of our lives and the flower of our nations to save humanity. If we go all-out for God we will win.

> 'Then it is the brave man chooses,
> While the coward stands aside,
> Till the multitude make virtue
> Of the faith they had denied.'

SUPPLEMENT

CONTEMPORARY PORTRAITS OF FRANK BUCHMAN

I

EARLY DAYS

From Life Changers *by Harold Begbie, 1923*

QUIETLY AND UNOBTRUSIVELY, an interesting work has been going on for the last four or five years among the undergraduates of many Universities, not only here in England but all over the world. This work, by its own development, has attracted the attention of the religious authorities of many countries, and largely originated from the activity of a single person.

Some years ago I made the acquaintance of this man . . . We became friends; we corresponded with each other; at intervals we met and discussed the progress of his work. Then, in the summer of the year 1922, I accepted an invitation to meet a number of University men from both sides of the Atlantic who were to gather in a house party . . .

The character of these men, some of them so brilliant in scholarship, others so splendid in athletics, and all of them, without one exception, so modest and so disturbingly honest, was responsible for my reawakened interest. They were men of the first class, men whom one may fairly call not only the fine flower of our English-speaking civilisation, but representatives of the best hope we possess of weathering the storms of materialism which so palpably threaten to overwhelm the ship which carries the spiritual fortunes of humanity. It was impossible in their company to doubt any longer that the man who had changed their lives, and had made them also changers of other men's lives, was a person of very considerable importance. One regarded him with a new interest, a fresh reverence . . .

In this work he is engaged at the present moment, and he believes that a new knowledge of religion is spreading among men who may exercise a strong influence on English-speaking civilisation during the next fifty years.

2

HOW THE OXFORD GROUP BEGAN

From For Sinners Only *by A. J. Russell, 1932*[1]

THE STORY of how Frank's own life was changed, as told by Harold Begbie in *Life Changers*, is an absorbing and inspiring narrative. Frank is a character who grows on you—in a book, in life. After the first chapter you want to meet him. When you meet him you may have reason to wish you hadn't. But if you remove the reason you will find Frank still there and that you have obtained release from spiritual defeat . . .

'His carriage and his gestures,' said Begbie, 'are distinguished by an invariable alertness. He never droops, he never slouches. You find him in the small hours of the morning with the same quickness of eye and the same athletic erectness of body which seem to bring a breeze into a breakfast-room. Few men so quiet and restrained exhale a spirit of such contagious well-being.

'A crisp accent marks his speech, and is richly noticeable only when he makes use of colloquialisms. The voice is low but vigorous, with a sincere ring of friendliness and good humour— the same friendliness and good humour which are characteristic of his manners. He strikes one on meeting as a warm-hearted and very happy man, who can never know what it is to be either physically tired or mentally bored.'

Then the writer strikes the happiest of all descriptions of Frank.

[1] By permission of the Author and Messrs Hodder and Stoughton.

'I am tempted to think,' says he, 'that if Mr Pickwick had given birth to a son and that son had emigrated to America in boyhood he would have been not unlike this amiable and friendly surgeon of souls. Fuller acquaintance of "F.B." brings to one's mind the knowledge that in spite of his boyish cheerfulness he is of the house and lineage of all true mystics from Plotinus to Tolstoy.'

The first serious crisis came in Frank's life when a fellow-student at Mount Airy Seminary, Philadelphia, accused him of ambition. This accusation smote him severely, and he chose the most difficult quarter of Philadelphia for his initial labours. The invitation to his first church was not without humour. It said, *The question of salary must for the time be left unstated.'* Meaning there could be no stated salary, because all the money collected for the non-existent church was seventeen dollars, mostly in pennies. But someone gave a new corner shop, and this, under Frank's vigorous direction, grew speedily into the Church of the Good Shepherd . . .

There grew out from it a hospice for young men which developed into a community of hospices spreading through other cities . . .

Experience with the younger generation at the hospice taught Frank how to handle the grown-ups; especially never to lose his temper, as no one was likely to pick it up. From a child he learned later never to laugh at other people's faults ('You are just as funny yourself'). Frank's secret of getting boys up early on Sunday mornings was not to scold but to announce there would be pancakes on the table at nine sharp. After that all were down on time, some before time . . .

And now Frank had trouble. Both hospice and settlement were under the same control—a committee of clergy and laity. After five years there came a clash, bringing about the second big crisis in Frank's life, and leading presently to the establishment of the Oxford Group movement. The business committee were strong on balancing the budget, as business committees always are. Sometimes the budget would not balance—when the young folk were numerous and hungry. So the Committee requested Frank to reduce the rations. The spirit of Oliver Twist stirred within Frank, who resented the order, and nursed ill-will against the six persons who were dominating him in this respect.

'Here,' he frankly admits, 'I failed. I said the Committee were behaving badly. Yet my work had become my idol. All I should have done was to resign and let it go at that. Right in my conviction, I was wrong in harbouring ill-will. I left and came abroad, my health badly affected by overwork. *En route* I had the vision of "Care" in Horace's Ode, following me on a charger, always just behind. I could almost hear the horses' hoofs and feel their breath on the back of my neck.

'Travelling through Italy, and other parts of the Continent, I found my way back to England, and so up to Keswick, where a convention was in progress. And there something happened! Something for which I shall always be grateful.'

A tiny village church. A tiny congregation. A special afternoon meeting. The speaker—a woman! No thunder, no lightning, no cloud, no supernatural voice, but a simple, straightforward, conversational talk to a gathering of about seventeen persons, including Frank. The woman speaker spoke about the Cross of Christ, of the sinner and the One who had made full satisfaction for the sins of the world.

'A doctrine which I knew as a boy,' says Frank, 'which my Church believed, which I had always taught and which that day became a great reality for me. I had entered the little church with a divided will, nursing pride, selfishness, ill-will, which prevented me from functioning as a Christian minister should. The woman's simple talk personalised the Cross for me that day, and suddenly I had a poignant vision of the Crucified.

'With this deeper experience of how the love of God in Christ had bridged the chasm dividing me from Him, and the new sense of buoyant life that had come, I returned to the house feeling a powerful urge to share my experience. Thereupon I wrote to the six committeemen in America against whom I had nursed the ill-will and told them my experience, and how at the foot of the Cross I could only think of my own sin. At the top of each letter I wrote this verse:

When I survey the wondrous Cross
On which the Prince of Glory died,
My richest gain I count but loss
And pour contempt on all my pride.

Then I said,

My dear Friend,

I have nursed ill-will against you. I am sorry. Forgive me?

Yours sincerely,

FRANK

'A further test of this new experience came to me later on when I returned home. Attending church on Christmas morning, whom should I see in front of me but the person whom I considered to have wronged me most of all. He had a bald spot on his head, and at one time, whenever I sat facing it in committee meetings, I used to think the letter "I" was written all over that spot. That morning I forgot even the bald spot itself, as the true Christmas spirit of peace on earth, goodwill to all, reigned in my heart. I naturally wished this former opponent on the Committee a Merry Christmas, and meant it, though as I did so he was looking on the floor as if seeking a lost pin. But he, too, wished me a Merry Christmas, and appreciated the fact that at the Cross I had learnt the great truth never to be resentful against anybody, including committees.'

The foregoing story of the change in his life was told me by Frank himself . . .

And now let Loudon Hamilton, one of Frank's friends, formerly a master at Eton, tell you, as he told me, the story of how Frank arrived in Oxford, guided to put his challenging convictions into operation in the intellectual centre of England. Especially do I recall the way in which Loudon expressed his feeling of boredom, with a tinge of vague curiosity, at being asked to meet 'an American professor from Cambridge'. (Frank had spent a short time in Cambridge before coming to Oxford.) The rest of this chapter is in Loudon Hamilton's words:

'Care to meet a man from Cambridge?'

This somewhat mystifying request from a Rugger-playing Rhodes scholar floated across the quad one summer evening in 1921. We do have manners, so we said, 'Yes.' Our Rhodes athlete brought forward a man of middle size with manners and clothes that gave no clue to his job, but his eyes were large and alert. Thus entered Frank to Oxford. There were no announcements, no advertisements. Yet there began then in Oxford an influence admittedly more far-reaching than most of the organised, patronised, and authorised movements in religion.

One man had entered Oxford carrying a vital message, himself in tune and touch with God.

We invited him to attend our Philosophic fortnightly meeting. At first, it was a serious evening—in the wrong sense. The occasion was a philosophic debate—we became very profound. Who was it who wittily said that in Oxford we don't always stop talking when we have finished what we have to say?

Eleven o'clock came—so far Frank had said nothing. Coming from Cambridge, this was unexpected—so he had to be asked. Picture the crowd: ninety per cent ex-officer undergraduates from majors downwards; men with reputations from the Intelligence Service, from the Navy, veterans of twenty-one or twenty-two with rows of medals never seen or referred to.

There were the men of influence in college. Most of them played games or rowed, some really well. On Sunday a few—very few—would go to chapel. Now we were deep in armchairs and the air was delicious with Dunhills. The moment Frank began, the atmosphere changed. He picked up some thread in the discussion and used that to weave his pattern. He began to tell of changed lives. He described the changes in men so like ourselves that interest was riveted at once.

How else could it have been done? By sermons? By uplifting appeals? By philosophic subtleties? All these were familiar, but here was something new. Or was it new? At least fresh, and therefore interesting. Somehow our debate had been forgotten. We went out saying to one another, 'What do you think of this fellow?' A thing of rare courage had been done among men accustomed to courage of another sort.

A week or two later Frank returned to Oxford with three Cambridge men to spend the week-end. They came to tell us what their contact with Frank had meant to them. Yet they were not speaking about a man. These men were not the type that one generally associates with religious enthusiasm; one of them was a leading Cambridge Rugger Blue, the other two were ex-officers of the cultured, attractive type. More than that, they seemed to have a radiance, subtle yet distinct, and a good fellowship among themselves that were as attractive as they were unforced.

That evening in our rooms these men spoke easily, yet convincingly, of a new power that had come into their lives to help them with their problems. They immediately captured the attention of the Oxford men. Granted that it was doing what was not done—i.e., talking about personal religion—yet it was done in a way that could offend no one, but only gain their confidence.

Their words were the words of honest men out to share something good with anyone who had the sense to receive it . . .

Following their visit, groups of men would drift together in the quad and discuss this apparently new thing. Discussion rapidly changed to deeper interest, even to astonishment, when it became known that some of the atheists and agnostics were different. There was abroad in the College an air of expectancy—what was this all about?

The new quality of honesty became infectious. It continued to operate the following term at Oxford. Old friends began asking the reasons for new changes. A group of six met one night. A few nights later another six men were invited. Forty-four men actually turned up, and we adjourned to the Junior Common Room. Four of the men had fortified themselves before coming and were slightly tipsy.

The vitriol of their attacks somehow failed to penetrate the charm and reality of the atmosphere. We were definitely on the side of the angels. The message had established itself among us, and to oppose it was not primarily a sin against God, but a breach of good form. Prayer was offered publicly from a University pulpit thanking God for the illumination that had come to Oxford.

3

FRANK BUCHMAN'S SECRET

From For Sinners Only by A. J. Russell

WHAT IS THE SECRET of Frank's power? He revealed it to me on the afternoon of Easter Day, during one of his gay chats over tea at Oxford.

'I was very busy (Frank began) working eighteen to twenty hours every day. So busy that I had two telephones in my bed-room. Still I was dissatisfied with the results. There was a constant coming and going, but the changes in the lives of my visitors were inadequate, and not revolutionary enough to become permanent. So I decided on a radical procedure—to give that hour of the day from five to six in the morning when the phones were unlikely to ring to listen for the Still Small Voice to inspire and direct . . .'

It is impossible to understand Frank at all unless he is thought of as always in God's presence, listening for direction and accepting power, which he says is the normal way for a sane human being to live. Frank is an example of the psychologically mature man, thoroughly integrated round the highest relationship possible to man. He does not wander voluntarily in his spiritual life: he goes direct to the Source all the time, and expects the Source to come direct to him. This discipline at the heart of the movement means complete freedom. The paradox of Christianity.

Frank is a child listening to God and obeying Him implicitly, and getting all those around him to do the same. And no one will ever understand this movement who does not accept this as a working hypothesis, whether he believes it or not at the start. After a time he begins to see it is true.

4

SON OF PENNSYLVANIA

On Dr Buchman's sixtieth birthday, 4 June, 1938, the Allentown Morning Call, his home-town newspaper, devoted a page to the story of his career. A few paragraphs are quoted below. The Editor wrote: 'Now on his sixtieth birthday anniversary, from his many friends of his boyhood and youthful days in this city, will go forth the sincerest wish and hope that the burning zeal that has propelled his idea with singleness of purpose during all the years may continue strong for the consummation of all the lofty purposes which that idea embraces.'

FRANK BUCHMAN has his roots in the soil of Pennsylvania. If you visit Pennsburg with him—a rare experience—he will show you the old swimming hole where he would swim, permission or no, and old Jonathan's cherry tree whose fruit was so tempting on a warm day. He will yarn with deep affection about those old places, surrounding them with the magic of his childhood, and you know that here is a man who, after travelling the world over, loves no place as well as the Pennsylvania town where he was born.

Buchman today is the same quiet, forceful American. He is six feet tall, strongly-built, clean-shaven. He is disciplined, alert, full of vitality. His eyes have the depth of a man who knows the world. They sparkle with friendliness and humour and yet look down the vistas of history. But you carry away an impression not of the bold features but of the life which animates them.

His freedom-loving ancestors came from Switzerland in 1740 aboard the sailing ship *Phoenix*. One of them fought with Washington at Valley Forge. A branch of the family pioneered in Minnesota. The others settled in the town of Pennsburg. In this community of sturdy Americans of revolutionary war ancestry, Buchman speant his boyhood.

'His father,' says the *Call*, 'is still remembered as one of this community's ethical businessmen, a Christian gentleman.' His mother was a 'quiet, cultured woman of deep insight.' From her he gained the iron self-discipline tempered with an irresistible sense of humour, which are today his familiar characteristics. From his father he learned his understanding of human nature, the genius of making friends which has endeared him to thousands around the world . . .

He never forgets old friends. One of his earliest companions died this winter at the age of eighty—Mary Hemphill, whom he took from a tenement to be the cook at his boys' hospice in Philadelphia. He found her broken and destitute after the death of her husband, but she soon became the life of the household with her grand Irish humour. Whenever he came to America, he would squeeze out the hours to slip down to see Mary, taking his friends with him. The last time was two years ago. The present was dim in her ageing mind, but the years of service in the hospice stood out vividly. 'He's a great friend,' she said, pointing to Frank Buchman; then smiling, 'but he makes you walk a chalk line.' We laughed and understood. There was a titled lady present and others of worldly position, but Mary was queen of the evening. Frank Buchman treats all people alike. They are all regal souls to him.

As he loves men, so he loves nations. He carries the world in his heart. The greatest tragedy to him is the spectacle of nations losing their way; the greatest need in the world is the need for emboldened leadership; the greatest sin, the sin of an inadequate plan. 'Some nation,' he says, 'must find God's will as her destiny and God-guided men as her representatives at home and abroad. Some nation must produce a new leadership, free from the bondage of fear, rising above ambition and flexible to the direction of God's Holy Spirit. Such a nation will be at peace within herself, a pace-maker and a peacemaker in the world.

'Will it be America?'

5

FRANK BUCHMAN'S LEADERSHIP

By the Hon. C. J. Hambro, formerly President of the Norwegian Parliament, in his Foreword to a war-time edition of Dr Buchman's speeches, 1944

DR BUCHMAN'S LEADERSHIP is not explained by his words alone. His strength, the strength given to him, is to create an atmosphere, to make a small group of men and women or a tremendous gathering eager to listen to God, and willing, at least for the moment, to yield their own selves, and open their hearts to God's plans for them.

This atmosphere is not created by any kind of mystic rites, by ceremonies, incense or music. No stage is set; there are no paraphernalia. Frank's approach is realistic; it is factual; it is business-like. He is more like a scientist or a physician than a priest or a mystic. He has as deep a distrust of sentimentalism and emotionalism as he has of authoritative pompousness and clerical unction. He has a stronger belief in silence than in words; and the secret of his power lies in the 'quiet time', in the disciplined effort to sweep the mind clean of all things trivial and temporal and make the soul ready to listen to the voice of God. He knows that God is not in the wind and not in the earthquake and not in the fire, but in the still small voice.

And the miracle happens that by appealing, not to emotion, but to reason, to common horse-sense—and by the compelling strength of his spiritual conviction—he communicates this knowledge to nearly all those who are present at his meetings. The sceptic, the cynic, the infidel, the atheist—even the journalist —who has attended one of those gatherings, sometimes unwillingly, reluctantly, shamefacedly has to admit that he has felt, at least for a fleeting moment, what, for want of a better explanation, he agrees to call the presence of God.

It is quite simple, and at the same time it is not easy to explain. The Oxford Group did not bring any new message; for it was all there. But they made aggressively alive what had been dormant; they ploughed and harrowed and disseminated the good seed over a soil that had lain fallow for so long a time that people had forgotten that it should bear fruit.

Frank Buchman and his team did not pretend to re-create people. They tried to change them. And wherever the Group went there was this same stirring of the deep waters.

As we were looking on this modern Christian brotherhood, there came to many of us some words written by G. K. Chesterton in his beautiful little book on St Francis of Assisi:

'The servants of God who had been a besieged garrison became a marching army; the ways of the world were filled as with thunder with the trampling of their feet, and far ahead of that ever-swelling host went a man singing.'

Now, between Frank from Assisi and Frank from Allentown there is as much difference as between daily life in Italy in the twelfth century and daily life in the U.S.A. in the twentieth century. And still there is this deep spiritual kinship, a connecting dream, a vision, an action.

For under Frank Buchman's very serious consciousness of

responsibility, behind his often quite stern efficiency, behind his keen and sometimes ironic sense of humour, there is the lovable little boy who more than anything else would like to go singing far ahead of an ever-swelling crowd. And as a matter of fact, that is what Frank has been doing for a number of years, followed by men and women, who through him have been liberated and are no longer besieged by the forces of egotism and selfishness, people who are living in a new spirit of fellowship and in a complete freedom from fear, because they have nothing to hide.

'By their fruits ye shall know them.' And the fruits of the Oxford Group were very sweet. Those who saw with an open mind and an open soul how Frank Buchman's team worked, felt about them something that might have been articulated in the words Chesterton used about the Crusaders:

'They were renounced by their children and refuted by their biographers; they were exposed, they were exploded, they were ridiculed, and they were right.'

These men and women came, and no matter how critical we were, no matter how easy it was to be sarcastic at their expense, there were some things that could not be laughed away. They had a quality of life which we were lacking; they had succeeded in forgetting their own egos; they were always eager to help and to serve; they could talk quite openly and naturally about things that we stored away in the secret places of the heart until we could not find them when we wanted them, because we had lost the key to our own treasury. They could gladly admit their mistakes and apologise for them; they could openly make restitution if they had wronged anybody. And, the most obvious thing of all—they were happy; there were no secret burdens weighing on their minds.

As I am trying to do what my friends have asked me and write some introductory words to this book, my thoughts go back to that first house party in Norway, in 1934, to my wife whose great-hearted conception of hospitality, whose tremendous sense of humour, indomitable energy and sovereign disregard of and disbelief in difficulties and obstacles made those first house parties in Norway possible. My thoughts go to Frank Buchman, the catalyst who made possible the united church front in Norway in this war, my thoughts go to Frank, the untiring, open-hearted, smiling friend, in gratitude for all that he has been and done. We know that whenever we have been true to him we have been true to ourselves.

My thoughts go to all those who came—in curiosity, in disbelief, in suspicious longing. I see Freddie Ramm, whose life in the prisons of Germany burst through the walls of Nazism as a hymn of triumph. I see Ronald Fangen who came out a victor after two years of solitary confinement in dungeons and dark cells; Bishop Berggrav, who was confined to a log cabin in the woods with his Gestapo bodyguard. I see men and women who were in concentration camps, some who have died and some who have lived a dangerous life to the tune of 'A Mighty Fortress is our God'—which some of them had never sung until they came to that house party at Hösbjör. To all of them Frank Buchman meant something important. Not all of them who came were changed—and we all need constant change—but all of them were in some way altered; life was never again exactly what it had been before that experience.

The Germans decreed in Norway that the Oxford Group was a part of the British Intelligence Service and should be harshly suppressed—a most flattering and slightly ridiculous compliment to the British Intelligence Service. The Gestapo feared and hated the Oxford Group as they could never fear and hate the British Intelligence Service. They hated them as men hate and fear the ideals they have lost and prostituted, the faith they have betrayed. They feared them because instinctively they knew the Oxford Group was part of God's Intelligence Service preparing the way for an ultimate defeat of the principles of evil.

6

THE GROWTH OF A WORLD FORCE

From The World Rebuilt, *by Peter Howard, 1951*

FRANK BUCHMAN is an American of distinguished Swiss descent. One of his ancestors was the successor to Zwingli in Zürich and translator of the Koran into German. After his family came to America in 1740 they settled in Pennsylvania. One ancestor fought with Washington at Valley Forge. Another was the first man to enlist in Abraham Lincoln's army during the war between the States.

In the year 1921 Frank Buchman was invited by a British military adviser to join him at Washington during the Disarmament Conference. It was a significant occasion for two reasons. First, because on the train to Washington the impelling thought filled Buchman's mind, 'Resign, resign, resign!' He faced the moral challenge to be willing to abandon the financial security and comfort of a salaried position for an unknown road. Second, because the Conference sessions confirmed his conviction that plans for world peace were inadequate unless they reckoned with the necessity of a change in human nature.

Soon he was enlisting and training people of every stratum of society to bring to their nations a basic change in economic, social, national and international relationships, all stemming from personal change. Within a few years, through the impact of a returning group of Rhodes Scholars who had met him in Oxford University, Buchman's work was to acquire nationwide significance in South Africa. The Press of that country first bestowed on his friends the title of 'The Oxford Group'.

The work spread rapidly. By the 'thirties it had become worldwide. Norway's delegate at Geneva, later to become President of the League of Nations, said: 'Where we have failed in changing politics, you have succeeded in changing lives, and given men and women a new way of living.'

In 1938, realistically facing the fact that armed conflict could not finally decide the ideological issue in the world, Buchman launched the programme of Moral Re-Armament which stated the need of moral force to win a war and to build a just peace.

Frank Buchman's insight and action began to stir the nations to prepare for the ideological conflict. This was precisely what the Fascists and Communists feared most, that to the industrial and armed might of the democracies should be added the super-force of an inspired ideology. His action roused the best patriotic forces in the democracies and inevitably the opposition of the subversive forces. As early as 1917 his experiences in the Far East had taught him the godless basis of Communism. Likewise he clearly understood the basic materialism of Fascism. He said: 'We have Communism and Fascism, two world forces. And where do they come from? From Materialism which is the mother of all the "isms". It is the spirit of anti-Christ which breeds corruption, anarchy and revolution. It undermines our homes, it sets class against class, it divides the nation.'

From the beginning he was heavily attacked by all who did not wish to see a moral ideology take root in the world. The Communist attacks were based on the usual technique of calling anyone they feared a Fascist. The Nazis said that his work 'supplies the Christian garment for world democratic aims . . . It is clearly opposed to National Socialism.'

Yet some of the very people who told Buchman 'leave us alone' or 'go and change Hitler', and whose own complacency almost sold out the democratic cause a few years after, were the people who later hinted that MRA's efforts in Germany proved that Buchman was pro-Nazi. The fact is that Buchman never met Hitler, and Hitler was too cautious to get into Buchman's orbit. Nor was Buchman an intimate of Himmler or of any other member of the Nazi hierarchy.

The influence of Buchman's work did stretch into Nazi Germany, just as today it is penetrating behind the Iron Curtain. Indeed, Ludendorff's magazine at one point warned solemnly that 'the sweet poison of Moral Re-Armament is seeping over our borders'. Small wonder that even before the war, the Nazis banned MRA literature. Their invading armies had instructions to suppress MRA wherever they went.

Were these facts not in themselves a tribute to Buchman's effectiveness? And might not history have taken a different turning, if the democracies had themselves been armed with an ideology of change and known how to bring it to Germany and to every nation in the years between the wars?

Today when events have been successively proving the rightness of Buchman's ideological insight, while continuing to stress the danger of Communism he has increasingly emphasised that anti-Communism is not a cure. The answer, he says, lies in a moral and spiritual ideology adequate to cure the moral weaknesses of our civilisation and creative enough to win the allegiance of masses of people in every land who justifiably look for change.

Although statesmen have sought his aid, sometimes publicly and more often privately, although he is humanly speaking the leader of a major world force, yet Buchman has never lost his humour, and his unique caring for individuals and their needs has grown through the years.

In this task of remaking the world to which he has dedicated himself he has shown another great quality rare in our time, of developing and training others to take responsibility. He often says, 'You have never succeeded unless you have trained ten men to do your work better than you can do it yourself.' The continuance of his life work is secured for the future by the principle of revolutionary teamwork.

His love for people, his sensitiveness to their needs and failures, his gift for creating in them the will to live their best, is an art. It is the secret of the growth of his work. It is an art which he says can be normal for every man. A Scottish miner, Peter O'Connor, said of an interview with Frank Buchman: 'In my half-hour with you I was helped more than by any other living soul.' To which Buchman commented, 'It was not my art. It is God's art.'

Since engaging on this work thirty years ago Buchman has never had a permanent home. His force of fully trained personnel is in the hundreds. They work without salary, yet they never go hungry. Says Frank Buchman of this fact, 'Where God guides, He provides.'

Thousands of people, convinced of the basic necessity of this answer, sacrifice to advance this revolutionary force. There have rarely been large gifts. There have been thousands of small gifts not from surplus, but from sacrifice. His work is financed and maintained in the spirit of the American Declaration of Independence: 'With a firm reliance on the protection of Divine Providence we mutually pledge to each other our lives, our fortunes and our sacred honour.' From the early days Frank Buchman's work has advanced through the sacrifices of those who believe in it. Men offer for the faith they hold most dear the things they count most precious. People have given of their wages, their capital, their houses, their savings.

In Britain, for example, dockers, miners and shop stewards in many parts of the country have formed fighting funds. This enables their delegations to come to Caux and contribute to the running of the Assembly there.

A former European Communist, asked whether industrialists contributed to the funds of Moral Re-Armament, replied: 'Some do. I wish more did. Every worker should rejoice when businessmen begin to invest in a force that is fighting effectively for social justice and a new world order.'

The accounts of MRA are audited yearly and deposited with the authorities according to regulation.[1]

Under the Income Tax Act of 1918 the incorporated body of the Oxford Group in Great Britain is now recognised as a charity, and is entitled to the accompanying privileges, including the right to reclaim tax on gifts received under covenant.

Every pound in MRA goes far further than in any commercial concern or government department. The advance of the work has been out of all proportion to the size of its budget. For when workers, however highly qualified or experienced, give service without salary, administrative costs are cut to a fraction.

Every activity of MRA is planned to combine the greatest advance of the work with the most economic use of funds and services so sacrificially provided.

Frank Buchman is a man with a host of friends across the world.

Typical is this letter from a changed veteran Communist leader in the Ruhr, twenty-five years a member of the Party until he met Frank Buchman:

'The fight is tough but it is a fine thing, and I am grateful to be able to be in it with my family. The Good must conquer. All my spare time I spend in talking with people about this ideology and also, as well as I can, I try to live as an example of it. I have many human mistakes and weaknesses to overcome, and my family also. God has to help us time and time again. But of one thing I am certain, I have never been so happy and so contented as I am today. That I owe to you.

'Now I must stop this pen-work and give you warmest greetings from all my family, which consists of myself, my wife, my daughter and my son-in-law. At the same time I wish you the best of health.

'But above all I wish success to this wonderful ideology in all lands, so that mankind can once again become happy.'

[1] In Britain the auditors are Messrs Price, Waterhouse and Company.

II

THE MAKING OF A MIRACLE

*An informal talk by Dr Frank Buchman at the World Assembly for
Moral Re-Armament, Riverside, California, June, 1948*

THIS AFTERNOON I want to take you back forty years to the
time when the then Chairman of the Democratic National
Committee asked me to come to State College, Pennsylvania,
and see whether I could do anything to settle the differences
between the faculty and the students who did not seem to understand each other. He was on the Board of Trustees and he was
worried. And he ought to have been worried. There was a
strike on, a students' strike. The atmosphere was antagonistic
and he had an idea that I could find the solution. I had no such
idea at all. I frankly told him I didn't think it was my job. But
he kept after me and finally I consented to go.

It was there that I found the laboratory that made what is
happening here possible. The life of the students reflected the
godlessness of the place. The first night I got there, there were
nineteen liquor parties. Someone said it was so wet you could
float a battleship.

Nowadays students' strikes are nothing unusual. I went to
Lima, in Peru, and the first thing the British Minister told me was,
'There is a students' strike on.' The same thing in Santiago, or
Cairo. Wherever you go now you find them, but in those days
they were a rarity. One effect they had on the students was that
they could never win at football. And their studies were anything
but A's, and there was a sense of a fog surrounding that whole
place. It was a beautiful spot, in the very centre of Pennsylvania,
and the College Alma Mater goes:

> Where the vale of old Mount Nittany
> Meets the Eastern sky,

Proudly stands our Alma Mater
On a hilltop high.

It's high and it's glorious—but there was defeat everywhere. That's the product of some of our modern education. That's one of America's problems.

Now where do you begin? My job was to turn this university Godwards. This was the problem. The solution would have to be a miracle.

There were three men who were the focal points of the life of that university. The first of these was a fellow with the name of Bill Pickle. Now remember what our friend Calosso[1] said today. I am going to tell how this message reaches the ordinary man, the poor man, just the man Calosso talked about. Bill Pickle was an important factor in the life of that university. He was the illegitimate son of a colonel. He had a wife and twelve children, and everybody called them the Pickles. His job in the day-time was to be hostler for the local physician. At night he worked for the students to whom he peddled liquor. I used to see his stealthy figure sneaking about the spiral staircases leading to the students' rooms at all hours of dark nights. He was a friend not only of all the undergraduates, but of all the recent graduates and the old Alumni. At football games and college festivals Bill was a busy man. There was a State law against saloons and he had to supply liquor for the whole place.

Bill soon knew of my arrival and he used to say he would like to stick a knife into me. He was strong, stockily built, with a furious walrus moustache and the looks of a roaring pirate. But he had all the charm of a wonderful sinner who could become a compelling saint. I'll let you into the end of the story. He came to England with me and was at the Oxford house party. He went to the League of Nations with me. And I'll never forget when we

---

[1] A previous speaker was Signor Umberto Calosso, Member of the Italian Parliament, and editor of *Umanita*. Signor Calosso had described Moral Re-Armament as 'the Gospel pronounced to the poor'.

went out to Croydon airport and before we flew to Geneva together, he prayed that the plane would get there safely.

Let's see how this story develops because this is the sort of thing you are going to do. It will mean a lot to you and it will develop you just the way it developed me. I learned many lessons in Penn State that are the foundation of what we are doing now.

Now the second character of the story was a graduate student who possessed every physical grace and charm. He was one of the most attractive personalities I ever met. He was the son of a Supreme Court judge and the grandson of the Governor of a State. His name was B. At the moment he is in England, has spent the winter in London where he has recently been in my home. He came to Caux last year.

We became friends. He was a Southerner, and every Southerner likes fried chicken and beaten biscuits for breakfast. I had a wonderful cook, Mary. She was a marvellous soul. I wish I had time to tell you her story, how she and her two sons were won. That's another miracle.

Now B. loved to ride, and we rode together a great deal. I knew he was a type of person with whom you used intelligent restraint and nonchalant reserve. I didn't ever talk to him about the things that meant most to me. Never. We talked about everything else under the sun; and that is an art you need to learn. But B. was getting more interested and intrigued with the atmosphere around me.

One day he said, 'Let's ride to the Club.' I'll never forget it. It was a sleety day, the sort of day that rain freezes on the telegraph wires. I thought to myself, 'Let's ride to the Club! Has he lost his senses?' I thought of the horses' legs. It was snowy. It was winter.

We walked those horses fifteen miles to the Club. We settled in for a good dinner. I was chilled to the bone and had several cups of coffee. Then we went to bed.

It was one of those nights when coffee does its work. I heard the clock strike ten, eleven, twelve, one. Finally, as the clock struck two, my friend said to me, 'Are you asleep?'

'No. Are you asleep?'

'No. Would you like to talk?'

'Yes. What about?'

'I wish you would tell me what Jesus Christ means to you.'

So I told him. We talked on and on for several hours. Finally he said, 'I'm not going to be a Christian.'

'Who asked you!' I said.

'Not you. I know you are cautious and prudent. I know you respect my reserve.'

So I asked him what he believed in. 'Confucius,' was the surprising reply.

So I asked him to tell me about Confucius. He didn't seem to know a great deal about him. So I told him about my visit to Confucius' grave and how I had been entertained at tea by the seventy-sixth descendant of the sage and seen his seventy-seventh descendant on a day that was so cold that he had to wear four coats.

Then I said to him, 'Try your Confucianism on a chicken thief who is a friend of mine, on his wife and five children, and see how it works.'

B. agreed. And for the next few months he gave money to the chicken thief's wife to keep the home together, and paid for treats for the children. He spoke to the chicken thief himself. Somehow he didn't have much success. The chicken thief was soon in jail for catching chickens by pressing a sponge soaked in chloroform under their beaks, and carrying them off unconscious. One of his sons, who was in the same business, accompanied him to jail. The student worked with the family, did everything for them, and tried to behave as a true Confucianist.

Finally he came to me in utter despair, and said, 'I give up. The more I give them, the more they want.'

B. was learning an important lesson. He was trying to solve the

Y

whole problem of social service without Christ, treating the immediate surface conditions without touching the root cause.

Now B. was willing to try anything. 'What would you do, Frank?' he said. 'Would you pray about it?'

So I suggested that since he hadn't got far with the chicken thief now in prison, we might pray for Bill Pickle. B. agreed readily.

'You pray,' said I. It is always better to get other people to do the praying when possible.

So B. prayed. 'O God, if there be a God, help us to change Bill Pickle, Mrs Pickle and all the Pickles. Amen.'

Some of you would say it wasn't an orthodox prayer, but it soon brought an answer.

Next day Bill was playing baseball with a team of which he was the manager. In the evening B. and I were on our way to visit some friends who had a lovely country place. They were a charming French family from Haute Savoie, just across from Caux, and the Chinese Minister from Washington was coming to stay with them in the country. They had invited us to see some cows and lassoing of steers—which they thought would interest the Chinese Minister. As we went through town, suddenly B. said to me, 'There's Bill.' He'd been celebrating the victory of his team and was now challenging everybody to a fight.

Frankly I wasn't too keen to meet Bill, but B. said, 'We've been praying for him, now's the time to do something.'

Bill came in sight. Now, I have a good-sized nose. You've noticed that! I thought to myself, 'What if Bill hauls off . . .!' I once asked a Chinese friend what he would do under these circumstances. 'Approach him from his blind side,' he told me.

So I walked up to Bill and put my hand on his biceps so that if he did haul off he wouldn't haul so hard! But what to do next. The thought flashed into my mind, 'Give him the deepest message you have.'

'Bill,' I said, 'we've been praying for you.'

To my surprise all the fight went out of Bill. Tears came into his eyes. He pointed to the church tower. 'See that church over there? I was there when the cornerstone was laid. There is a penny of mine under it.'

I said, 'Bill, your mother must have been a good woman.'

He said, 'She was a great woman.'

Then I introduced B. 'My friend's been praying for you too.'

'That's decent of him,' said Bill. 'He's a gentleman.' Bill went on, 'Why don't you come and see me some time?'

I said, 'Fine, but any time is no time. Make it some time.'

Bill said, 'Come next Thursday night at seven.'

No duties in life ever conflict. You've got time for Bill when you are on the way to the Chinese Minister. You've time for B. And you make a date to see Bill next Thursday night at seven.

So next Thursday we went to see Bill in his unpainted house on Pickle Hill which some wag had christened 'Heinz Heights.' It was very interesting. You felt that every knot-hole had an ear or an eye, but there wasn't a soul in sight. Bill had told the neighbours that we were coming, and Bill imagined we were coming to change him. That's just what we were out to do, but we didn't do it the way he thought we would. And Bill had shaved for the important occasion, though generally he shaved only once a week.

We talked about baseball. We talked about football. Of course he went to every game. Bill knew all about horses. We talked all the jargon of college life. Then the time came to go. Bill said, 'I've enjoyed your visit.' You see he could tell all his friends that we hadn't changed him. But it's amazing what that sort of an interview will do if it's backed by prayer. Bill began to hang about us. He enjoyed our company. He wanted fellowship.

A few days later there was a horse show and he went with B. to see the horses. They spent the whole afternoon talking horses. Bill voted it the best afternoon ever.

Of course the effect on B. was that he began to drop the words 'If there be a God . . .' He said, 'There is no question that there is a God, because He is answering our prayer.' So B. felt himself more and more one of us.

Now this was a State institution and it was a place where you would be very careful about talking publicly about Christianity and the things that meant most to you, but the following Sunday a Bishop arrived to speak to the students. I was on the platform and just before his address the Bishop said to me, 'Do you mind if I put up decision for Christ to these men today?' I thought to myself, 'What does this man dream he is doing? Doesn't he realise he is in a State college?' You see, my idea of the Holy Spirit was a sort of five-by-eight picture, and I didn't think much would happen. But the Bishop went ahead and the first man to stand up was my friend B. He committed himself, and some eighty fellows followed his example, for B. was one of the most popular men in the University. It was new to me. I had never seen it before. I had never been reared in that tradition. It is amazing how we are reared in our different traditions, and mine was very conservative and very cautious.

Now many people would feel that it had been a successful meeting and leave it at that. But B. wanted to go further.

He said, 'There are a lot of things I don't understand, and I don't know anything about my Bible or prayer, and I don't know much about winning people.'

So I said, 'Let's spend the summer together.'

We set off for the West. That was the first time I ever went to Mackinac, just forty years ago. What a wonderful place Mackinac Island is! Then we went on to Montana, where B.'s grandfather used to be Governor. We learned the truths of the Bible every day, prayer and the fullest openness between us, sharing everything most naturally. That is how we spent the summer. Then it was just with one man; now it happens with five thousand, ten thousand people.

Supposing that was the basis of the training of the Cabinet in your country. Supposing that they were guided by God and could give to the people who came to them a satisfying experience of Christ, wouldn't that be the answer? You give it to labour and management. Think of Caux last summer where the only thing that bridged all the gaps of party and nationality was that we had this knowledge. Well, this was the laboratory in which I learned it.

I learned another thing at State College. When Bill peddled liquor to these students I often saw them carried down at night. I have seen real catastrophe in the lives of students, and I say, very sincerely and very bluntly, it's a hell of a life if you don't have the Gospel of Jesus Christ. There is only one thing which is adequate and it is someone who can change you, someone who loves you. If you have this power, men and women will come to you night and day for an answer. All sorts of people.

That French family who lived in the country had a Catholic chapel on their estate and a wonderful Irish priest, who also served the student congregation. He saw what was happening. We got people in the masses and then sent them back to Mass. Some had been pretty thoughtless about going to Mass, but when we got among the masses and prepared them, they went back to Mass with a real experience. We never had any trouble in that University between Catholic and Protestant. And the priest was all for it. He would come and want to know how to change people himself.

This is an art that everyone wants to learn, and heaven help us if we don't learn it. We need to learn it for the sake of our own children. Your own children must come and tell you about themselves and you will share with them because you know what a rascal you were yourself. That is the way to win your children, and that is the reason why this crowd of youth flocks around. They will go to a man who understands them, who doesn't talk too good or appear too wise, a man who shares.

And then I learned another thing. I was so busy with people coming to make appointments with me that I had to have two telephones in my room. But I had another telephone, one that brought me messages from the Living God. He told me what to do and I wrote it down. There is no virtue about writing it down, but I have a treacherous memory. It is just like a sieve. Everything goes through and I forget; so I write it down. If you have a memory that keeps things in a photographic way, you are to be complimented, but I am a stupid man and I have to write them down. Isaiah had this experience, 'The Lord God hath given me the tongue of the learned, that I should know how to speak a word in season to him that is weary; He wakeneth morning by morning, He wakeneth mine ear to hear as the learned.' I believe there was a Church Father a long time ago who did just exactly what I do, who wrote down what the Lord said to him. And the Chinese tell us that the strongest memory is weaker than the palest ink.

I came home from my trip with B. via New York. One of the things I did there was to buy a new beaver hat as part of my winter's outfit. I paid more for it than I should have. I wore it the first night we got back to State College. We were walking down the street and who should we meet but Bill. Bill was an actor. He looked at my hat and then walked silently and admiringly around me. He didn't shake hands or even say he was glad to see me.

He said, 'You know, I would do almost anything for you if you would give me that hat.'

I said, 'Bill, that hat is yours on one condition—if you will go with me to the Student Convention in Toronto.'

He said, 'I don't mind if I do: I'll be up to see you in the morning.' And off he went with the beaver hat on his head.

Morning came, and there was Bill in the doorway.

'I can't go,' he snorted through his moustache. 'I've nothing to put my clothes in.'

Bill was like a lot of people who say 'No' and mean 'Yes'.

'Don't worry about that,' I said, 'I'll get you something.'

'No,' said Bill, 'I'll get it. They'll give me something up on the hill.'

Now I must mention the third of the men in the University, besides Bill and B., who was a focal figure for its change. He was the agnostic Dean. Everybody loved him, popular, easy of access, charming, hospitable. A man's man; but an agnostic. But he had a praying wife. He's the sort of husband that some of you women here have. You find them darned difficult, don't you? You are patient but they are difficult. They have their own ideas, about money, about the use of capital, about taxes. It's amazing how they've worked things out for their own satisfaction and comfort, but from the woman's standpoint they are not entirely satisfactory. The Dean heard about my invitation to Bill. You see, Bill's daughter was a maid in the Dean's house. She told Mrs Dean and Mrs Dean told the Dean, and so the Dean came to see me.

'I hear you are going to take Bill Pickle to Toronto.'

I said, 'Yes', not knowing what his reaction would be. I thought I would be regarded not as a fool for Christ's sake, but merely foolish.

But the Dean went on, 'I think this thing is going to be a miracle. I wondered all along who would do something for Bill and I believe you're the fellow.'

I said, 'No. That's not my job. I think that's the job of the Living God.'

'But I would like to have a part in it,' said the Dean, 'and pay for Bill's journey.'

So we started out for Toronto with seventeen students, Bill Pickle and myself. I can still see that morning on that little station. Bill wore the beaver hat, leggings and a stock which made me think of a poodle's legs crossed. In his hand was a scuffed little imitation alligator-skin bag.

Now what were the reasons why Bill went on that trip? There

were five: (*a*) he wanted the trip; (*b*) he heard the liquor was good in Toronto; (*c*) he wanted the fellowship; (*d*) he wanted to see what Toronto was like; and the fifth, which I didn't find out until we reached Toronto—he thought I would buy him a fur overcoat to match the hat.

On the train I suggested we might have something to eat. For some reason Bill was against food. He was planning how to get a drink when we got to the first junction. Among the party of seventeen he recognised one of the students to whom he used to sell liquor. His nickname was Bonehead. He was one of those fellows who used to be a big drinker and now was president of the Christian Association and really stood for something in the University. At the junction Bonehead, closely followed by Bill, made for the swinging doors. Then he saw there was no dining-room but only a bar.

'Say, Bill,' said Bonehead, 'this is no place for us.'

Bill argued with him, but Bonehead resisted, and by being firm, as Bill later said, he laid the foundation stone of Bill's Christian life. Together they went to the dining-room. When I arrived there I found Bill sitting quietly having a full meal.

At the next junction point Bill knew the places where there was liquor, but by now he felt everybody had their eye on him. Have you ever had that feeling? Everybody looking at you, but nobody is. Well, that's your conscience.

The next meal was on the train. Bill and I had one of those seats just for two. One of the men who used to be an agnostic gave thanks for the food. When agnostics change, they do wonderful things. I would never have done it.

Then Bill said suddenly, 'That fellow spoiled my meal.' At first I thought he meant the coloured waiter who had served him, but Bill said, 'That fellow thanked the Lord for his food. My mother used to do it, but I didn't know people did it any more. We never thank the Lord for ours.'

We reached Niagara Falls and there the blow fell. He found we were going to spend the night in a Temperance hotel. I hadn't arranged it. Bill dug his heels in and said he would not stay at any Temperance hotel. He didn't see how any man could make it pay without a bar. And what would Bill's friends say if they heard he had slept in a Temperance hotel?

'Don't worry about a little thing like that,' I said, 'let's go upstairs and turn in.'

I suggested a bath.

Bill said, 'A bath!' and glared at me over his walrus moustache. 'Do you want me to catch my death of cold?'

'No, Bill.'

'Don't you know,' he went on, 'down our way we sew up in November and don't unsew again until March.'

I didn't press the point. He put on his nightgown over his red flannel underwear. Unfortunately he had to sleep in a folding bed. He was a little suspicious of it, but finally got in.

I came back into the room again and said, 'Bill, we've forgotten something. We've forgotten to pray.'

'I can't do them things,' said Bill.

'I'll help you,' I said.

Bill got slowly out of bed and on to his knees.

'You begin,' said Bill.

'Our Father,' I began.

'Our Father,' said Bill.

'Who art in Heaven,' I said.

'Who art in Heaven,' continued Bill.

All of a sudden Bill said, 'I used to know that.'

'Of course you did,' I said. 'It's a prayer a great many people pray.'

Bill said, 'You lead along and I'll follow.'

So that's the way we managed the Lord's Prayer. And we went to bed.

Next morning to my intense surprise on the railroad platform what did I see but B.'s luggage plastered all over with 'Niagara

Falls Temperance Hotel' stickers. There were even five on the handle. B. accused me. I said, 'No.' Bill played possum. Later he owned up. Bill was feeling at ease with the students so much that he could play with them. The wall which separated Bill socially from them was already breaking down. And Bill used to say that was the only money he spent on the trip. 'I gave the porter twenty-five cents to put those stickers on.'

We got settled in our hotel in Toronto. I proposed we go to the meeting in the afternoon. The Governor-General was presiding and six thousand people were going.

'No,' said Bill.

'What are you going to do?' I said.

'I hear that fur is cheaper in Canada than in America,' said Bill, 'and I think I want to go out and look at fur overcoats.'

'That's a good idea, Bill, but I think we ought to go to this meeting first.'

'I'll go on one condition,' he said. 'I'll sit in the back seat if you'll sit with me.'

How many people are there who sit in church or go to anything in which they are not overly interested and sit in the back row. But of course, this doesn't apply to anybody here!

Bill wasn't a bit interested in the first speaker. He spent his time counting up the number of people present to see if I'd told the truth about six thousand people being there. Quite a lot of people sit in church figuring up the week's profits while waiting for the service to end. So Bill wasn't so different. But he didn't count long. He soon found there was a goodly number there.

The second speaker was a coloured man. That interested him.

Bill said, 'Why, that man was so black that charcoal would have made a white mark on him.'

He told a story of foster-parents and a foster-child and a foster-grandchild, and how the grandchild disowned the parents. Bill was nodding or vigorously shaking his head all the time. Every

342

word was hitting him between the eyes because that, too, was the story of his family. Bill left the meeting with me.

'Frank,' he said, 'did you tell that speaker about me?'

I said, 'No, Bill.'

We went back to our little sitting-room and the nineteen of us had a little gathering, and Bill said to me, 'I want to say something.'

'Go ahead, Bill,' I said.

He got up as if he had been shot out of a cannon. 'I'm an old man of sixty-two, and I've decided to change my life. I have grandchildren, and I can't bear to think of them turning on their grandfather like that foster-child, because all my life I've been disobedient to my Heavenly Father. Old Bill will be a different man.' Then he went out, beckoning me to follow him.

'Frank, I want you to sit down and I want you to write to the old woman,' he said.

The old woman was Mrs Pickle and she was a wonderful soul, a heart of gold and what a cook!

Soon after we set out for home. We got back to the station where Bonehead went to the right door. It's amazing how fast news travels. We were just getting off the train, Bill was still on the steps and I was just back of him, and there was a liquor missionary. Bill's old friends had heard what had happened and had brought along two bottles of the best. Whatever else happened, they wanted to take Bill home drunk. They handed Bill the first bottle. Bill took it and let it slip through his fingers on to the brick floor. The next attempt was more subtle. They pulled the cork of the second bottle and held it under Bill's nose so that he could smell it. Bill gave a quick tap to the tempter's wrist, and again the bottle crashed.

Now I've been reared in circumstances where I could have liquor all my life and whenever I wanted it. But there's one reason why I don't touch a drop. It is because of fellows like Bill Pickle. You don't win them if you touch a drop, just that cocktail. I don't tell anybody else not to drink. Anybody can do anything he wants. Everybody has the liberty of the Spirit, but for my part, I think of fellows like Bill.

It's exactly the same with smoking. I don't smoke, but I don't say it's wrong for you. But I couldn't do it, because Bill in the old days was a regular chain smoker. When he changed, everything just dropped off. No smoking, no drinking. Although I never said anything to him about it. It is amazing how these— I won't call them sins, I just call them nice little vices—can sometimes be the key to a man's whole life.

Calosso spoke of a movement among the poor. Well, that's what we had as a result of Bill. It was the talk of the town. But not everyone was enthusiastic. One clergyman told me he did not want Bill in his church.

'Don't worry,' I said. 'He likes a church where he can take part and talk back if necessary.'

The next Monday Bill came in.

'Have you heard about it?' he said. 'They don't want me in church.'

I felt as if I'd been stabbed. I thought this would be too much for Bill.

'Don't worry, Bill,' I said. 'We'll have a church of our own.'

Bill said, 'That's the funniest thing. I had the same idea.'

We didn't have a church but we had nineteen of the local janitors who knew Bill well and we used to meet every Saturday night.

Bill said, 'We want you to come and talk to us.'

I said, 'Well, it's your show, what would you like me to talk about?'

Bill shook his walrus moustache. 'Tell us about the Apostles' Creed.'

I said to myself, 'The Apostles' Creed!' But I agreed.

Saturday night after Saturday night we met. They were always there. We never had to coax those fellows to come. We reached the passage, 'And Jesus Christ went down into Hades or Hell,' and Bill said, 'Now, now, that's one thing I don't believe. That was no place for Jesus Christ.' So we cogitated on a way out.

At last Bill said, 'I've got it straight. I guess He went down there to "redd things up". (That is a colloquialism in Pennsylvania meaning to clean things up.) Let's go to the next point.'

From that time Bill's influence in the University was a modern miracle. When the graduates came back at Commencement, they didn't get tight. Bill was their favourite guest and he refused to grace their parties if there was liquor. They preferred an interesting character, so they had their parties without liquor, and Bill was the life of the party telling his old-time tales with new zest and on a new plane. In the University we had twelve hundred men in Bible class out of sixteen hundred in the University. That was a big institution in those days, and of course it is tremendous in size now. After three years' work it was no longer good form to hold drinking parties. The College began to win their games, and scholarship improved. Dr John R. Mott came and people from all corners of the earth to see the wonders God had wrought.

As for the Dean, he became such a great soul. Bill gave him the thing he said he always wanted but was never quite sure existed, the certainty that these things worked out as a living reality in the lives of people. He saw it work out in Bill's life and in the maid in his home. He saw that whole family change and become a veritable dynamo in the life of the University.

B. was led as a result of this experience along with one of his friends to give some years to teaching in one of the leading colleges for Negroes in America. The whole college became interested in the problems of the Negroes of the South. It was the foundation of much of the rural coloured work in America.

I hadn't any part in all this other than that I let God use me. Bill we buried ten years ago. It was just after the great meeting in the Constitution Hall in Washington where the world took part in the launching of Moral Re-Armament in America, when statesmen and leaders everywhere hailed MRA as the one hope of humanity. Bill's funeral was worthy of his life.

> O God, to us may grace be given
> To follow in their train.

In Bill's train and Mrs Pickles' train—who is lovingly and affectionately called by her own name, Mrs Gilliland—and in the train of those children.

I have come to the conclusion, Calosso, that there are only two classes in the world: the changed and the unchanged. It is the changed who will give us the ideology of an inspired democracy. 'Behold how these brothers love one another.' So, in closing, I want to leave with you the lines of a poem:

> Father, forgive the cold love of the years,
>   While here in the silence we bow;
> Perish our cowardice, perish our fears,
>   Kindle us, kindle us now.
>
> Lord, we believe, we accept, we adore,
>   Less than the least though we be;
> Fire of love, burn in us, burn evermore,
>   Till we burn out for thee.
>
> O for a passionate passion for souls,
>   O for a pity that yearns,
> O for a love that loves unto death,
>   O for the fire that burns;
>
> O for the pure prayer power that prevails,
>   That pours itself out for the lost,
> Victorious prayer in the Conqueror's name:
>   The Lord of Pentecost.

III

FOREWORD TO THE FRENCH EDITION OF
REMAKING THE WORLD[1]

ROBERT SCHUMAN

Foreign Minister of France

THE EDITORS of these speeches have decided to entrust the writing of the preface to a man in political life, a Cabinet Minister in office. We have to admit, however, that thus far statesmen have been only moderately successful in 'remaking the world'. The fact remains that it is their duty, more than anyone else's, to apply themselves to this task; and it is to their advantage to welcome every assistance offered to them.

If we were being presented with some new scheme for the public welfare or another theory to be added to the many already put forward, I should remain sceptical. But what Moral Re-Armament brings us is a philosophy of life applied in action.

It does not claim to have invented a new system of morals. For the Christian, the moral teaching of Christianity is enough, and he draws from it all the principles which must guide his life as a man and as a citizen.

What we do need, and what is quite new, is a school where, by a process of mutual teaching, we can work out our practical behaviour towards others; a school where Christian principles are not only applied and proven in the relationships of man to man, but succeed in overcoming the prejudices and enmities which separate classes, races and nations.

---

[1] Published in Paris, 26 May, 1950. New and revised edition, *Editions de Caux*, 1958.

To begin by creating a moral climate in which true brotherly unity can flourish, over-arching all that today tears the world apart—that is the immediate goal.

The acquisition of wisdom about men and their affairs by bringing people together in public assemblies and personal encounters—that is the means employed.

To provide teams of trained men, ready for the service of the state, apostles of reconciliation and builders of a new world, that is the beginning of a far-reaching transformation of society in which, during fifteen war-ravaged years, the first steps have already been made.

It is not a question of a change of policy; it is a question of changing men. Democracy and her freedoms can be saved only by the quality of the men who speak in her name.

That is what Dr Buchman expresses in simple and moving words. He has declared war on materialism and individualism, twin generators of our selfish divisions and social injustices.

May he be heard and followed more and more, in all nations of the world, by those who today still clash in fratricidal hatred.

IV

DOCUMENTS RELATING TO THE
SPEECHES

I

DR B. H. STREETER AND THE OXFORD GROUP

Dr B. H. Streeter, Provost of The Queen's College, Oxford, one of Europe's outstanding scholars with a wide knowledge of world affairs, especially in India, China and Japan, was one of the Senior members of the University who attended the 1934 Assembly in Oxford. Speaking before many of his colleagues at a meeting of the Assembly in Oxford Town Hall in July, 1934, he said:

I HAVE BEEN watching this movement more particularly during the last two and a half years. Hitherto my attitude towards it has been what diplomatists call 'a benevolent neutrality'. In speaking to some of my friends I have compared this attitude to that taken up towards the early Church by Gamaliel—that most amiable of the Pharisees.

The reason I have come here tonight is to say publicly that I have decided that I ought now to cease from an attitude of benevolent neutrality towards what I have come to believe is the most important religious movement of today.

During these same last two and a half years I have been also watching the world situation, and have felt it becoming more and more one full of depression, full of despair. There is a great deal of goodwill; but there is not enough of it to solve our tremendous problems—war, class war, economic breakdown.

This movement seems to be able, not merely to change some bad people into good, but also to give new heart and a new courage and a new sense of direction to those who are already men of goodwill. That is why I have come to the conclusion that in an age of growing world despair it is my duty to associate myself with this movement.

May I add that I come to the Group, not as a person with perhaps some little reputation in his own sphere of study, or as the head of an Oxford College; I come as one who has already learned something from the Group, and hopes to learn more; and who hopes that by so doing he may be of a little more use than might otherwise have been the case.

Dr Streeter prepared the following statement a few weeks before his death in an aeroplane accident in Switzerland in September, 1937

I WAS DRAWN to the Oxford Group not primarily by failure to meet personal or family problems (though, since coming into it I have got much help in regard to such problems), but by my despair of the world situation. The more I have seen of the trend of things, the less grounds I have found for hope.

I was one of those who expected much from the League of Nations, and from the various projects started since the war for dealing with economic conflict and social reform. These things are failing humanity, not from any imperfection in the machinery, but from the lack of sufficient goodwill in the mass of mankind and in their leaders, to make such machinery work.

I saw how largely the moral energies of Christianity were demobilised, partly through differences of opinion on points of doctrine or church organisation, but still more by failure to realise in actual life the religious and moral ideals which Christians are unanimous in professing.

The Oxford Group is recalling the churches to their proper task of saving the souls of nations as well as individuals; it competes with no Christian denomination, though it aspires to revivify all. By 1934 I had seen enough of the Group to realise that it was making bad men good and good men better more rapidly and on a more international scale than any other movement. And I decided that it was my duty to step into the boat and handle an oar instead of continuing to shout from the tow-path a judicious mixture of criticism and encouragement.

I went with the Group to Denmark three times, and what I saw there convinced me that the movement was not merely an instrument of moral rebirth and psychological liberation for individuals, but was capable of moving nations as such by initiating a new mental attitude in economic and political conflicts.

Evidence accumulated of the effect on the conduct of everyday life. We heard, for example, of a rise in the standard of commercial honesty in certain circles in the capital, of a readiness in leading politicians to approach the discussion of burning economic problems in a spirit of friendly and constructive conference rather than in one of party bitterness and intrigue. Customs officers reported an unfamiliar influx of conscience money, and there has been a marked diminution in the statistics of divorce. Thus in one country, in the space of one year, there has been born a new spirit in facing the conflicts which threatened the collapse of civilisation.

History shows that in case of wars, revolutions, strikes and other major conflicts, a relatively small weight of public opinion on the one side or the other, or the presence or absence of moral insight and courage in a few individuals in positions of influence, has often turned the balance between a reasonable settlement and a fight to the finish. Modern civilisation can only be saved by a moral revival. But for this it would suffice if every tenth or hundredth person were changed. For each such person raises the level of those whom he touches in the home, in business, and in public affairs.

What I saw happening in Denmark can happen in Britain. It will happen if those who lead Britain learn to find in God their inspiration and direction. And Britain, thus led, would save the world. But the opportunity must be seized during the period of uneasy respite from major calamity which at the moment appears to lie ahead.

2

HISTORY WAS WRITTEN AT KRONBORG

An article by Carl Henrik Clemmensen in Dagens Nyheder, *Copenhagen, 10 June, 1935*

I AM SITTING late into the night and thinking of everything that happened. I can see the whole review passing again before my eyes. I can see the endless stream of people pouring in over the small bridges across the moats and ramparts. I can hear again the swelling wave of song from the thousands of voices rising and falling like a sea between the bright courtyard walls, with their lofty green copper roofs, like a fine delicate pastel high up against the blue summer sky . . .

Twenty years ago there was an unknown man who determined, in God's name, to change the world by changing the lives of the people who composed it. The beginnings were small . . . Today, Whit Sunday, the same man stood in Kronborg Castle and spoke through Denmark to the whole of Europe. With him on the platform sat a loyal host of his whole-hearted fellow workers who travel up and down the world with him, men and women of many different nations. Here, too, on the platform were the Danish Cabinet Minister for Church Affairs with his family, a declared supporter of the movement, and the Bishop of Copenhagen, who ended the meeting, deeply moved, by expressing to Frank Buchman the grateful thanks of the Danish Church.

Here was the whole castle courtyard packed as it had never been at any meeting hitherto, although only a small proportion could get seats. All ages were represented here, every party, every class, every stratum of society. There must have been more than ten thousand people in the courtyard itself and thousands more on the bastions—a real mass demonstration on an impressive scale . . .

Frank Buchman can point to the lives of thousands in every corner of the globe who have definitely been changed through him; people who now in their turn have been mobilised as life-changers. I have heard of nothing else like it in our age. Other contemporary movements have conquered nations. This man had the determined vision of the conquest of the world . . .

Think of the other remarkable things that happened at this meeting: the distinguished actor-manager who stepped up on the platform and in his clear ringing voice read the story of the first Whit Sunday from the Acts of the Apostles; the butcher from Nyborg, and the saddle-maker from Copenhagen, who stood side by side with the young Count and the Dean and witnessed to the new life they had found through the Oxford Group; a young concert singer from Finland in her beautiful gay national dress, who told us that she understood now for the first time what the real purpose of her singing could be, and then sang Bach's triumphant 'Hallelujah' which rang out like the song of a bird over the great courtyard; and last of all the moment just after the Bishop of Copenhagen had pronounced the bene-diction, when the huge crowd stood there for an instant in hopes of getting still something more. Movement, like a wave swelling through the crowd, the confused sound of many voices, a woman's voice calling to a friend . . . Then suddenly a few people begin to sing Ingemann's 'Pilgrim Song', and everyone stands still, bare-headed, joining in the singing.

What stands out in one's memory afterwards? The vision of Frank Buchman's opening challenge to Denmark to listen, as a nation, to the voice of the living God, and his glowing appeal to Denmark to become the peacemaker in the international family . . .

During Professor Runestam's weighty contribution I sat and reminded myself that this was the son-in-law of Archbishop Nathan Soderblom, who on his very deathbed gave his blessing to the Oxford Group. And last of all came the Dean of Copenhagen, Dr Paul Brodersen, tall and strong, burning with zeal to proclaim in as personally stimulating and challenging a way as possible the message of the spiritual revolution which this movement means to the whole Danish people.

'Live out your faith in your life!' he cried. 'Live it out so that it can show others the way, and march in step to bring this new illumination to our people!'

3

STATEMENT BY THE PRIMATE OF DENMARK

During the visit of the Oxford Group to Jutland in August, 1935, the Copenhagen daily newspaper Berlingske Tidende *published an interview with the Primate, Bishop Fuglsang-Damgaard.*

THE BISHOP OF COPENHAGEN is in Aarhus, just at this time when the Oxford Group is daily gathering thousands to its meetings there. Sitting in the shadow of the beautiful old vicarage behind the cathedral, he told me what these months have meant to him personally and to the Danish Church. Every word he spoke is alive with his experience:

'It is a fact that intellectuals and workers have in great measure been estranged from the Church. Inside the Church we have often discussed this problem. The Oxford Group has shown us the answer.

'For many years it has been a serious problem how we should combat the growing number of divorces. Now we hear married couples tell one after another how they have found a new life.

'The Oxford Group seeks to be living Christianity. That does not mean that it has no doctrine. It builds on the accomplished work of Jesus Christ as set forth in the New Testament. Its aim is to bring to life and make real for each person the articles of faith with which his own Church provides him.'

4

LAUNCHING MORAL RE-ARMAMENT IN AMERICA

Extract from the Congressional Record, 8 *June*, 1939

NATIONAL MEETING FOR MORAL RE-ARMAMENT
SPEECH OF
HON. HARRY S. TRUMAN
OF MISSOURI
IN THE SENATE OF THE UNITED STATES

MR TRUMAN. Mr President, on Sunday, 4 June, there was held in Constitution Hall, Washington, the National Meeting for Moral Re-Armament. I had the honour at that time to present the following message from the President of the United States, which opened that great assembly:

The underlying strength of the world must consist in the moral fibre of her citizens. A programme of moral re-armament for the world cannot fail, therefore, to lessen the danger of armed conflict. Such moral re-armament, to be most highly effective, must receive support on a world-wide basis.   FRANKLIN D. ROOSEVELT

That meeting was sponsored by members of the Cabinet and Members of the Senate and House of Representatives, and the invitation to the meeting contained messages from the Secretary of State, the Secretary of War, the Attorney-General, the Speaker of the House, the leader of the Senate majority, former President Hoover, the Senator from Kansas (Mr Capper), the Senator from New York (Mr Wagner), Hon. Joseph W. Martin, Jnr, the minority leader in the House of Representatives. There was also one from John J. Pershing, General of the Armies of the United States in the last war.

The principal address of the evening was delivered by Dr Frank N. D. Buchman, founder of the Oxford Group. There were messages from the House of Lords of Great Britain signed by twenty-five members of that body, and a message from the House of Commons signed by two hundred and forty members of that body.

I think it is particularly appropriate, Mr President, to record these messages from Great Britain in the proceedings of the Senate today because of the presence here of the King and Queen of Great Britain, and because of the fact that included among the signatories are men who both personally and officially are associated with Their Majesties.

This document then quotes the address of Dr Buchman in Washington (see page 91), and a number of the messages,[1] *including the following:*

FROM MEMBERS OF THE HOUSE OF LORDS:

'We, being members of the House of Lords in Great Britain, wish to congratulate you at the great meeting to promote moral and spiritual re-armament, which is about to take place in Washington. Unity and peace, whether national or international, can grow only amongst men and nations who become spiritually equipped with faith and love. The responsibility before God rests upon every individual man and woman, with us and with you, that they answer to this call.' Signed by twenty-five members of the House of Lords.

FROM MEMBERS OF THE HOUSE OF COMMONS:

'We, the undersigned members of the British House of Commons, send greetings on the occasion of the national meeting for moral re-armament in Washington. We join you in affirming our loyalty to those moral and spiritual principles

---

[1] Given in full with signatures in the *Congressional Record*.

which are more fundamental than any political or economic issue and which are the common heritage of our peoples.

'There is urgent need to acknowledge the sovereign authority of God in home and nation, to establish that liberty which rests upon the Christian responsibility to all one's fellow men, and to build a national life based on unselfishness, unity and faith.

'Only if founded on moral and spiritual re-armament can democracy fulfil its promise to mankind and perform its part in creating a mutual understanding between nations and restoring peace to the world.'

Signed by 240 Members of both Government and Opposition parties.

Other messages came from representatives of British Labour, industry and commerce. The document concludes this section with these words:

May I say again, Mr President, how fitting it is to record these messages from Great Britain in view of the great welcome which the Nation's capital has just given to the King and Queen, and of the fact that moral re-armament is strengthening those spiritual qualities which are the common heritage of our peoples, and the strongest bond between us.

Then follow messages from members of the Netherlands Cabinet; from representatives of the Swiss, Danish, Finnish, Norwegian and Swedish Parliaments; and from leaders in France, Turkey and the Balkans. Finally, Senator Truman summed up the occasion with these words:

It is rare in these days, Mr President, to find something which will unite men and nations on a plane above conflict of party, class, or political philosophy. I am sure that I voice the sentiment of all of us here today in expressing gratification at a response so remarkable to a need so urgent, and confidence that America will play her full part in this cause on whose fortunes the future of civilisation must largely depend.

MORAL RE-ARMAMENT:
THE FOUNDATION OF NATIONAL LIFE,
THE HOPE OF WORLD SETTLEMENT

BY THE RT. HON. THE EARL OF ATHLONE, K.G.

A broadcast arranged by the BBC, 1 *December,* 1939

SINCE ITS BEGINNING here in Britain just over a year ago, the call for Moral Re-Armament has encircled the world, and become a source of fresh hope to millions of men and women.

Heads of States, national, civic and industrial leaders of all classes, creeds and parties have welcomed it as the cure for that deep disease of the spirit from which civilisation is suffering.

In all parts of our Empire there has been the readiest response. In the United States President Roosevelt has urged that Moral Re-Armament should receive support on a world-wide basis.

A year ago on Armistice Day I was one of those who used these words: 'Moral Re-Armament must be the foundation of national life, as it must be of any world settlement. The miracle of God's Living Spirit can break the power of pride and selfishness, of lust and fear and hatred; for spiritual power is the greatest force in the world.'

This is true as never before today.

Moral Re-Armament stands for a change of heart, for that new spirit which must animate all human relationships. Its purpose is the practical application by everyone everywhere of the standards of honesty, purity and love. It calls on us to make the Will of God the guiding force, as for individuals, so for homes and nations.

Surely these living principles have ever been the true strength and security of our nation and Empire! In fresh and whole-hearted acceptance of them now lies our moral strength for these dark days—the answer to our fears and to our griefs, our one sure hope for a new world.

In all of us there is that deep longing, however humbly, to be builders of the new world—a world where man can cultivate the arts of peace and achieve that moral and spiritual progress which will alone insure that industry and science can be used for the enrichment and not the destruction of mankind.

This is the same conviction which is so clearly expressed in a message I have just received from the recent chairman of the Trades Union Congress, Mr Joseph Hallsworth:

'Everywhere we see the failure of human wisdom to find that super-national plan which could unite the nations in a common purpose for the establishment of universal brotherhood. Moral Re-Armament is now calling men and women everywhere to listen to God for His plan.'

As I speak to you tonight I think of the millions in Britain, throughout the Empire and in other countries who are striving to listen to the Voice of God. From our common obedience to His direction there can yet be born a world which is free, united and at peace.

In our own country civic leaders have today issued a call to our citizens which I should like to read to you. It bears the signatures of Lord Mayors, Lord Provosts, Mayors, Provosts, Chairmen of Councils and other civic leaders from all parts of Britain. These signatures include those of the Lord Mayors and Lord Provosts of Aberdeen, Belfast, Bristol, Cardiff, Dundee, Edinburgh, Elgin, Glasgow, Hull, Leeds, Leicester, Liverpool, Newcastle-upon-Tyne, Nottingham, Perth, Portsmouth, Sheffield, York.

The Call runs:

'TODAY, when our whole world is threatened with ruin, we feel more urgently than ever before the need for that new force of Moral Re-Armament which can create a new world, a world of sanity and order, a world of plenty and of peace.

'We cannot live for ever from one crisis to another, from

one war to the next. We seek a hate-free, fear-free, greed-free world, where every nation can enrich the common life of all, where every man has his work to do. This, not recurring crisis and destruction, is the God-given destiny of mankind.

'Amid the failure of human wisdom, there is still one Supreme Source from Whom all can draw new power, new hope, new illumination. God speaks directly to the heart of every man and woman who is prepared to listen and obey.

'We deeply need the leadership of God-led men and women who base their lives on the Christian principles of honesty, unselfishness and faith. Such men and women will not only make the morale of the country impregnable; they will today create and spread that spirit which will ensure a just and lasting peace.

'This new spirit must come. We owe it to ourselves, our children and our children's children. One hundred million listening to God across the world can realise the words of the prophet of old: "All thy children shall be taught of the Lord, and great shall be the peace of thy children."

'We call on you to play your full part in this highest form of national service. May our own community be in the vanguard of this advance, to lead the world on to sanity and peace.'

May I add one further word? Our thoughts go out tonight to all who are facing special sacrifice and danger. We are grateful for their courage and devotion. We pray their labour may not be in vain and that their victory will open the way towards the new world we are endeavouring to build. For all of us alike the guiding Voice of God is ever available, strengthening and directing.

There is today a deeper struggle which faces mankind everywhere—the struggle against the menace of human selfishness in ourselves, in our nation and throughout the world. On the issue of this struggle the future depends. Victory in it will surely bring that enduring peace and prosperity, and that hate-free, greed-free, fear-free world for which everyone of us longs.

THE BATTLE LINE IN AMERICAN INDUSTRY

Senator Harry S. Truman made the following statement on the occasion of a special presentation of the Moral Re-Armament industrial drama, The Forgotten Factor, *in Philadelphia, 19 November, 1943.*

IT HAS BEEN the job of the Senate War Investigating Committee, of which I am Chairman, to look into the home front situation and make recommendations. We have listened to many hundreds of witnesses, taken five million words of testimony, obtained the considered view of responsible Americans ranging from the highest government and business officials to tank welders and airplane mechanics. I have personally travelled over 100,000 miles.

Seeing America from the inside in this way has given me both great pride and deep concern. Pride as an American at the magnitude of the effort put forth by both Management and Labour. Concern over the spirit of division which exists on the home front—class against class, farm against city, party against party, race against race. The forces of disunity in our national life appear to be stronger today than perhaps at any time in our history. And they are growing stronger.

Men in industry know of the battle for control which is going on in many of our major war plants. Most Management and Labour in the country want to co-operate to win the war and build a lasting peace. But there are extremists in both camps who don't make the job any too easy. They represent an alien philosophy of conflict and so play into the hands of foreign ideologies.

There is only one answer to this sort of thing. We must start now to draw the true battle-line in American industry—between the responsible and constructive forces in both Management and Labour against the small but active minority who believe in a finish fight.

If we can succeed nationally in bringing mutual understanding and teamwork between the right-thinking leadership on both sides of the industrial picture, then we will not only increase production. We will save American industry for America and pave the way for the greatest era of peace and plenty we have ever known. If America can win the battle for industrial teamwork, then we will be on the road towards winning the greater battle for national unity. And we can bring victory in this battle as our contribution to the peace table.

The time is ripe for an appeal not to self-interest, but to the hunger for great living that lies deep in every man. What Americans really want is not a promise of getting something for nothing, but a chance to give everything for something great. We want something we can fight for with equal intensity in war or peace—something not confined to combat areas or election campaigns. We want to feel that what we are doing for the war effort is at the same time laying sound foundations for the future.

I have known this group since 4 June, 1939, when I read a message from the President to the national meeting for Moral Re-Armament in Constitution Hall, Washington. I was struck at that time by the clarity with which they saw the dangers threatening America, and the zeal and intelligence with which they set about rousing the country. I wish *The Forgotton Factor* and the war revue *You Can Defend America* could be seen by workers and executives alike in every war plant in the country. There is not a single industrial bottleneck I can think of which could not be broken in a matter of weeks if this crowd were given the green light to go full steam ahead.

We need this spirit in industry. We need it in the nation. For if America doesn't catch this spirit, we will be lucky to win the war, and certain to lose the peace. With it there is no limit to what we can do for America, and America for the world.

THE WAR-TIME PROGRAMME OF MORAL RE-ARMAMENT

An article in The Army and Navy Journal, *Washington,* 6 *May,* 1944

'NAPOLEON'S axiom, "Morale is to material as three is to one" has been upset. The ratio now stands at six to one.' This statement of General Marshall's takes on new importance as we make preparations to strike with an invasion force. Our leaders know that to the excellence of arms and training must be added the decisive weapons of heart, mind and will to absorb the shock of battle and carry through to victory.

An important factor in building this fighting spirit on both battle front and home front has been the programme of Moral Re-Armament. In a report recently published here, a group of British leaders, political, industrial and military, write: 'National strength springs from the spirit of the people. In time of war that spirit is decisive, and it will be no less needed in the years after victory. For this reason we, with large numbers of representative citizens in this country recognise the vital importance of the work for Moral Re-Armament and believe that they should be given every encouragement in their essential national service. Their work has proved its success in bringing to life for men and women of all classes the great spiritual values which are the fabric of our nation and for which we battle.'

The MRA programme was outlined for America eight months before Pearl Harbor in terms of sound homes, teamwork in industry and national unity, in a widely-read handbook entitled *You Can Defend America,* with a foreword by General Pershing. This was dramatised in a war revue of the same name which in the next year and a half was shown before a quarter of a million people in over twenty States, and which was the spearhead of campaigns to build a war-winning spirit throughout the nation.

Since Pearl Harbor Moral Re-Armament has been credited by competent observers such as Senator Truman and Congressman Wadsworth with increasing war production in many key aircraft plants and shipyards. Senator Truman said of MRA: 'They have rendered great assistance to the all-out war programme by creating the spirit of co-operation between management and labour, reducing absenteeism, heightening all-round efficiency and increasing production. There is not a single industrial bottleneck I can think of which could not be broken in a matter of weeks if this crowd were given the green light to go full steam ahead.'

Maj.-Gen. Francis B. Wilby, Superintendent of the U.S. Military Academy, after inspecting the results of their work on the home front, said: 'This is the arm behind the army.' Admiral Richard E. Byrd described it as 'the fight for a new America, strong, clean and united.'

In Britain, which has faced invasion and blitz, MRA has played a distinctive part in toughening the spirit of the people.

During the four and a half years of war, soldiers, sailors and airmen of the United Nations have thronged MRA's training centres in America, England, Canada and Australia. A soldier visiting the London MRA headquarters the other day said, 'MRA added a plus to my training. I knew what I was fighting against. Now I know what I am fighting for.'

In Norway and other occupied countries Moral Re-Armament has stood up as an unshakable centre of resistance to the Nazi oppression. Though some of its leaders have undergone imprisonment and death, MRA remains a bulwark for a liberated Europe.

We are fighting a war not alone of arms but of ideas. The victor must be strong in both. Cutting through the selfish, soft materialism and moral confusion of the last two decades, MRA has taken the soldierly virtues of discipline, sacrifice and team-work, of patriotism essential both in war and peace, and applied them fearlessly to home life, industrial and national life. In this battle MRA has cut across and drawn the fire of self-seeking subversive elements and rallied the constructive and patriotic forces in the defence of the nation.

8

THE WORLD FOR WHICH WE FIGHT

On 4 June, 1945, in San Francisco, Rear-Admiral Sir Edward Cochrane, presented Frank Buchman with a book from Service men of the Allied nations. The inscription reads:

To
DR FRANK N. D. BUCHMAN

A THOUSAND SERVICE
MEN AND WOMEN SEND
THIS MESSAGE FROM THE
WAR FRONTS OF THE WORLD

GREETINGS, love and gratitude on your birthday, from the world's battle fronts—from Britain and the Atlantic, from Western Europe, Italy and the Mediterranean, from Africa and the Middle East, from India, South-East Asia and the Pacific.

Through these years of endurance your inspiration has armed us to fight on. As we march into the years of victory, your conquering philosophy is our hope—the fighting faith that will bring resurrection to nations and team-work to a divided world.

In our great democracies, you have taught us how to triumph over the tyranny of alien creeds and the false ideologies of materialism. We stand with you on that world battle-line in the war of ideas. When victory in arms is finally ours we, with you, will battle on to build a sound world, morally re-armed and God-controlled—the world for which we fight.

GESTAPO REPORT ON THE OXFORD GROUP

The Gestapo report, Die Oxfordgruppenbewegung, was compiled in 1942 by the Head Office of the Reich Security Department. The discovery of this 126-page document during the German retreat from France was first disclosed in an Associated Press despatch by the distinguished American columnist, DeWitt Mackenzie. On 29 December, 1945, the following letter appeared in The Times.

CHRISTIANITY IN GERMANY

A NAZI DOCUMENT

SIR,

Nazi Germany's determination to destroy Christianity has been apparent for many years, but nowhere has it been more categorically stated than in a secret *Gestapo* report which has now been discovered. As this document has received less attention than it deserves, we trust that you will allow us to set some brief extracts before your readers.

The document, which, as its title page states, was prepared by the head office of the Reich Security Department, concerns Dr Buchman and the Oxford Group. It denounces them for 'uncompromisingly taking up a frontal position against National Socialism' in that 'they encourage their members to place themselves fully beneath the Christian Cross and to oppose the cross of the swastika with the Cross of Christ, as the former seeks to destroy the Cross of Christ.' 'Frankly, the importance of the Group lies here,' the document continues. 'At the very moment when we (the Nazi Party) are making efforts to suppress Christian conviction of sin, which appears to us the first step towards the enslavement of the German, a movement is emanating from the Anglo-Saxons, who are racially related to us, which regards just this consciousness of sin as a basis for change in national relationships.'

The document further states that the secret police regarded the movement as 'the pacemaker of Anglo-American diplomacy' and as a force working 'to bring about new political and ideological conditions in the Reich.' 'The Group as a whole,' it says, 'constitutes an attack upon the nationalism of the State and demands the utmost watchfulness on the part of the State. It preaches revolution against the National State, and has quite evidently become its Christian opponent.'

Speaking of the influence of the campaign for moral rearmament, the report continues:

'If one considers the names of the chief propagandists for Buchman's call to moral re-armament in England and elsewhere, the political counterpart of the movement becomes plain: the Jewish Western democracies. Nor is there any room for doubting against whom this whole campaign was directed, bearing in mind the year in which it took place, 1938, the year when—as it was said—Germany attacked little Austria, with brutal force . . . The Group breathes the spirit of Western democracy. It supplies the Christian garment for world democratic aims. The Group and the democracies supplement each other and render each other's work fruitful.'

The whole report throws an interesting light on the Nazi mind, as well as finally dispelling the widespread misrepresentations which have been circulated about this Christian movement. We hope that a full translation will be made available to the British public. For it is vital that we should understand the spiritual foundations of democracy as clearly as did our enemies, and that we should sustain with all our strength what they feared and hoped to destroy.

Yours, etc.

AMMON	LYNDEN MACASSEY
HAROLD E. CLAY	CYRIL NORWOOD
COURTHOPE	W. D. ROSS
EDWARD LICHFIELD	

INVITATIONS TO ASIA

IN OCTOBER, 1952, Dr Buchman left Europe for Asia with a task force of two hundred, on the invitation of leaders of several Far Eastern countries.

The invitation to Pakistan was initiated by Mr Jinnah on his last visit to London, and was issued again by the late Prime Minister, Mr Liaquat Ali Khan. It was repeated by Pakistan Cabinet Ministers at the Caux Assembly in 1952.

The invitation to India was issued by a national committee of eighteen political and industrial leaders.

The invitation to Thailand was issued by the Prime Minister, Field-Marshal Pibulsonggram. The Prime Minister said in a message to Dr Buchman: 'No country can survive for long in these days of ideological upheaval without the practice of Moral Re-Armament principles, which belong to the East and West alike and to which people of all races and creeds can subscribe.'

The invitation to Burma had the support of the Prime Minister, U Nu. A resolution, below, was passed at a meeting in the precincts of the Shwedagone Pagoda, which the Rangoon press described as 'the greatest single spiritual event of recent times.'

Dr Buchman's visit began with an Asian Assembly in Ceylon, on the invitation of the Prime Minister and other leaders.

INVITATION TO CEYLON

The nations of Asia, many of which have within a few years entered upon a new phase of independence, require unlimited opportunity to develop a sound democratic way of life. They need technical aid, they need almost every material resource.

Their most urgent requirement is peace. But everywhere nations, whose spiritual and cultural traditions compel them to seek the peaceful solution of problems, fear and prepare for war.

Our great spiritual leaders have taught that men will turn from pride, hate and violence—creators of division and destroyers of peace, only if moral force, channelled in every avenue of life, quickens right thought and action individually and nationally. All who pursue this path must welcome the evidence of reconciliation in families and industries, between class and class, between nation and nation, that attends the work of Moral Re-Armament.

Democracy, when absolute moral standards are enshrined at its heart, makes a stronger appeal than materialism, and has the answer to exploitation and want. This inspired democracy is the common need of East and West. It can over-arch our differences and create the spirit that will make peace permanent.

We therefore warmly invite you and your workers to visit Ceylon so that our people may know at first hand the great movement that you have initiated.

THE HON. DUDLEY SENANAYAKE
    Prime Minister
THE HON. A. E. GOONESINHA
    Minister of State
SIR OLIVER GOONETILLEKE
    Minister of Home Affairs
THE HON. H. H. BASNAYAKE, Q.C.
MR LEO FERNANDO, M.P.
MR A. H. T. SOYSA
MR S. PARARAJASINGAM
    Past President, Rotary Club
MR AND MRS JOHN WEIR
DR G. WIGNARAJA
DR K. J. RUSTOMJEE
MR AND MRS SURYA SENA

SENATOR SIR FRANK GUNASEKERA
MR S. W. R. D. BANDARANAIKE, M.P.
    Former Minister of Health
DR M. C. M. KALEEL, M.P.
    Minister of Labour
SIR WILFRED DE SOYSA
SENATOR MISS CISSY COORAY,
MAJOR T. F. JAYAWARDENE, M.P.
MRS T. GUNAWARDHANA
MRS Z. DICKSON
MR AND MRS A. D. MCLEOD
MR B. R. DE SILVA,
    Chairman, Ceylon Labour Party
DR AND MRS C. C. DE SILVA
MISS I. GUTTRIDGE

INVITATION TO INDIA

We are convinced that the true hope for bringing lasting change in social and economic conditions and for bringing peace to the world lies in multiplying such practical results as we believe to have been achieved by Moral Re-Armament—the giving of a new incentive to industry, the change of heart of capitalist and communist alike, the replacing of mistrust, bitterness and hate between individuals and groups with understanding and co-operation.

We consider, therefore, that such moral re-armament of the nations is the need of the hour and the hope of the future.

We agree with you that no one group, no one class, no one nation or race is adequate to solve the problems we are facing today or to change the course of the world away from unemployment, poverty and war towards an age of security and prosperity and that this will take the combined efforts of all, plus wisdom greater than that of the most brilliant individuals.

The Father of our country, Mahatma Gandhi, has bequeathed us an unquenchable inspiration to live by the highest ideals, and we are eager for India to play her full part in this noble task.

We would like you to know how glad we would all be to see you in India this winter along with an international team so that we may profit by your experience. Together we must succeed in turning the world from crisis to cure in demonstrating an over-arching ideology for Management and Labour, for Left and Right, for East and West.

DR S. N. AGARWAL
  Secretary, Foreign Department Sarvodaya Samaj, Wardha

SIR SULTAN AHMED
  Former Member of the Viceroy's Executive Council

SIR GURUNATH BEWOOR
  Managing Director, Air India Ltd.

SHRI GULZARILAL NANDA
  Deputy Chairman, National Planning Commission

SHRI R. K. PATIL
  Member, National Planning Commission

THE HON. K. M. PATNAIK
  Speaker, Legislative Assembly, Orissa

SHRI RAMNATH PODAR
  Industrialist

THE HON. SHRI CHANDRABHAL
  Chairman, Legislative Council, United Provinces

SHRI KHANDUBHAI DESAI
  President of the Indian National Trade Union Congress

SIR V. T. KRISHNAMACHARI
  Member, National Planning Commission; Chairman, Fiscal Commission, 1950

SHRI G. L. MEHTA
  Member, National Planning Commission

SIR LAKHSHMANASWAMI MUDALIAR
  Vice-Chancellor, Madras University

SHRI KRISHNA PRASADA
  Director-General, Posts and Telegraphs

SIR SHRI RAM
  Former Chairman of the Indian Chamber of Commerce

THE HON. DR B. C. ROY
  Chief Minister, West Bengal

THE HON. DR SAMPURANAND
  Minister of Education, United Provinces

THE HON. A. N. SINHA
  Minister of Labour, Bihar

SHRI J. R. D. TATA
  Chairman, Tata Industries

INVITATION TO BURMA

At a meeting of 1,000 people in the precincts of the Shwedagone Pagoda at Rangoon, presided over by the Ven. Sayadaw U Narada, on 31 December, 1951, the following invitation was proposed by the Chairman and passed unanimously:

'Burma is grateful to Dr Frank Buchman, the pioneer of Moral Re-Armament, for his message from Caux of 8 October, 1951, and for the cordial treatment accorded to the delegates from Burma at the World Assembly of Moral Re-Armament at Caux year after year.

'Burma is confident that she will be able, as predicted by Dr Buchman, to reflect the brightness of MRA to the whole world, especially as the MRA ideology is in complete accord with the excellent teachings of Buddhism.

'Burma feels that the ideology of MRA, embracing the warm love of the Sun and the tranquil purity of the Moon will dispel the dark clouds of hate and bitterness.

'The MRA sapling has taken firm root here and will, when watered with the blessings of 80,000 monks, surely grow from strength to strength.

'MRA has bridged the gulf between the East and the West at Caux. We hope that Dr Frank Buchman will be able to visit

Burma on his tour to the East before long, as his visit is bound to be greatly beneficial in finding a solution to the many problems facing us today.'

II

THE CHANGING SCENE IN KERALA

BY MANNATH PADMANABHAN

From an article in the Amrita Bazar Patrika, 26 *March*, 1961, *by the leader of the liberation struggle in the state of Kerala.*

KERALA is the smallest state in India situated in the southern tip of the continent. It is the first state in the whole world which has voted a Communist Government to power. Again, it is the first state that has swept them off from the seats of power by a mass upsurge.

Thus, when the Chinese army was crossing the Indian border, we in Kerala were engaged in a bitter struggle for the survival of democracy. Meanwhile some of us had returned refreshed from Switzerland after drinking full from the fountain of the MRA at their Summit Strategy Conference in Caux. There we had seen a new world emerge, a world rebuilt for the Will of God to prevail. We discovered how men of the different nations, without any distinction of class, creed or colour, stand united to resist the way of the tyrant and usher in the Kingdom of Heaven. We were captured by the new ideology and returned re-armed for the struggle. We tried hard to forge the bonds of unity between the discordant democratic parties and give the Communists a good fight. We fought them at the elections and won. But the battle was not finally won when the world welcomed the results of the election. As I cabled Dr Buchman, the results indicated that the Communist fortress had not been pierced through. We need an ideological clarity to root out the canker.

Eight days before the poll I introduced the MRA manifesto *Ideology and Co-Existence* to the people of Kerala in their own mother-tongue. It was distributed on a state-wide basis and had an additional coverage of three million through the medium of the press. Most of the Malayalam daily papers—there are thirty of them—brought it out in bold headlines. The *Malayala Manorama*, Kerala's largest daily, wrote an editorial entitled 'True Patriotism' based on Dr Buchman's definition, 'A true patriot gives his life to bring his country under God's control.'

We needed the same miracle in Kerala that we had seen at work in the Ruhr. We therefore decided to cable Chancellor Adenauer requesting that the Ruhr miners with the MRA ideological drama *Hoffnung* come to Kerala. The Chief Minister along with leaders of all the main political parties and communities joined in a Committee to welcome this force. At the reception given by the Governor of the state for the MRA force to meet two hundred of Kerala's leadership, the Governor declared: 'All our problems, economic, political, social and individual, must be solved in the spirit of MRA.' The Chief Minister addressing the international force said, 'I highly value your work. It is important not only for our country but for the whole of humanity.'

Fifteen thousand from every section of life came to see the German miners' play during the week. Students of the University thronged college halls to hear the international force of MRA present an ideology that is remaking the world.

The fifteen million people of Kerala—Hindu, Christian and Muslim—stand together with MRA to turn the tide of Communism in Asia and the world. MRA has taken root in Kerala and we have decided to invite a permanent international force to help carry forward this battle.

V

MORAL RE-ARMAMENT AND CHRISTIANITY IN THE WEST

PROFESSOR KARL ADAM

These extracts from Professor Adam's article[1] are reprinted in full from Vaterland, *organ of the Catholic party, Lucerne, Switzerland.*

SO LONG AS the national forces of the West do not consciously co-operate, but act in rivalry or even in direct opposition to each other, they will be dissipated into a thousand splinters by the gigantic power of Russia, long before America can intervene decisively. So we must stand upon our own feet. The frightening menace of Communism forces us to construct a community, a super-national bloc which will include all the nations as yet free from Russian materialism and which is in itself strong enough to stand up against the Eastern forces of tyranny, ignorance and disbelief. Over against the strictly disciplined might of Communism in the East, fed by a powerful ideology, no Western union based solely on political and economic interests can possibly succeed.

The man who opened the eyes of the whole civilised world to the fact that purely political and economic means were inadequate to meet the situation was the founder of Moral Re-Armament, Dr Frank Buchman. He did so with the most sensitive insight into the needs of human nature and with

---

[1] This article, on 12 August, 1952, was introduced by an Editorial note: 'In Caux-sur-Montreux the Moral Re-Armament Assembly has once again begun . . . the well-known Professor of Dogmatic Theology, Karl Adam, has published in the Tübingen *Theological Quarterly* an exposition which gives direction for Catholics, entitled "Moral Re-Armament and Christianity in the West". The most important passages from this long article are here reproduced in extract form.'

exceptional power and thoroughness. He further revealed the necessity for a *new, better and superior* ideology to be put in the field against the Communist ideology which held the masses in its power. This better ideology would grip and direct not only the social instincts of man, but the full depth and breadth of his whole nature. Buchman says emphatically: 'The real problem is human nature. The world is deafened through its sins and blinded through its selfishness. That is why we need a complete change of the individual, a radical, revolutionary change. Awaken the individual and you awaken the nations.'

The way to rebirth is by the four standards (absolute honesty, absolute purity, absolute unselfishness and absolute love) and from the individual to the family and thence to the changing of whole nations. 'To change the thinking of men we need a superhuman power. This power comes from God alone. It is the Cross of Christ through which God works in us. The message of the Cross of Christ will destroy all selfishness and in the power of the Cross we shall usher in the greatest revolution of all time. All that is needed is to look to the Cross and listen to Christ. Every man can begin to listen to God.' That is why Buchman introduced the 'quiet time', a time of turning to oneself, of meditation upon what God wants of us. It is a conscious placing of oneself in the way of God's guidance.

Moral Re-Armament is not, as its name might imply, merely an ethical movement, but a religious, indeed in the deepest sense, a Christian movement. But it is in no way a confession or a church community. Its aim is to bring back to the consciousness of men the principles and bases upon which each confession must then build with its own methods. Its only aim is to proclaim to the world the old truths with a new emphasis. Buchman recalls the words of St Ignatius Loyola, 'Give me twelve men fully dedicated to God and I will convert the world.'

Since Buchman is not aiming to build another Christian church, but to re-create personal experience of the moral and religious *a priori* from which all living religions begin, it is understandable that numerous non-Christians from India, China, Japan and so on are among the convinced followers of the movement.

Buchman points his Christian and non-Christian followers seriously and emphatically down the road of self-examination and personal experience and he urges the mutual exchange of personal experiences. Not mere dreamers have followed the movement which within thirty years has grown into a great world offensive, but prominent intellectuals, world-famous statesmen and politicians, big industrialists and workers' leaders, trade unionists, dockers and miners, men of all conditions from cabinet ministers to cooks. They all have one aim, to solve the toughest political, economic, social and cultural questions in the light of the Gospel. And it is amazing, it is wonderful, how, time after time, it is always the simple, clear concepts of the Sermon on the Mount which throw light on the most involved political and economic problems. The four absolutes, the challenge to complete surrender to God, faith in the power of the Cross of Christ, and the 'quiet time' which Buchman urges, are basic elements of the Christian life, they are Christianity lived out. That is why Buchman's message is in its very core a Christian message.

One can understand why the Catholic finds no new truths in Caux. But shaken to his roots, he has to admit that in Caux Christianity has been more deeply understood and lived, than in many Catholic communities. In answer to the question, 'What has Caux to give Catholics?' Monsignor E. Fischer, Dean of the Cathedral of Strasburg, replied, 'The first thing that strikes us in Caux is the nagging of our conscience. I believe that outside of the religious orders, there is no place on the face of the earth where so much prayer goes up.'

Behind the religious subjectivism of Caux there is a colossal objectivity, the most objective thing that exists on earth—the Christian revelation, the Christian doctrine, the Christian church.

What gives Moral Re-Armament its great impact and its fighting force is, in the last resort, the Christian ideology, and so, in the last resort, it will be the Christian ideology which overcomes the materialism of the East. It will increasingly be so as it is organised in the Catholic church into a community, far more inclusive than Russian collectivism, a community which encircles the world.

We Catholics, accordingly, are at a moment of decision and of most serious reflection. For we must realise that the materialism of the East would never have found its way into the arteries of men and of whole nations if we Catholics had been sufficiently aware of our responsibilities. We, too, were infected by the worldliness which distinguishes the secularism of the last centuries.

If the hour of decision is to bring about a rebirth of Christianity in the West, then the first thing is a *rebirth of the laity* in the church. The primitive Christian ideal of the priesthood of the laity must shine forth again with new radiance and warm our hearts. The pre-eminence of the priest over the layman should no longer be proclaimed in the church so loudly that the other great word of our Lord which throws light on the whole Christian position should be overlooked, 'You have but one Master, and you are all brethren alike' (MATTHEW XXIII, 8).

Only in this way and in this spirit and in no other way will the Christian West experience a rebirth. Beyond all moral preachment and clericalism, in the name of Christ and in the might of our freedom, and in the face of the cruellest tyranny and the most senseless system ever known, we will create a *una sancta*, a community of love which no devil and no demon will destroy.

The hour strikes in which all Christian communities in the face of the Russian danger stretch out the hand to each other and unite, if not in a union of faith yet in a union of love, for courageous defence against the barbarism of the East. Christianity will protect the West from the powers of darkness. Christianity is Christ. Christ will not die. Christ lives for all eternity.

VI

MORAL RE-ARMAMENT AWAKENS THE MODERN MAN

BY PROFESSOR DR WERNER SCHÖLLGEN

Professor of Catholic Theology in the University of Bonn. From a chapter in his book Aktuelle Moralprobleme[1] (*Moral Problems of Today*).

THE MOVEMENT for Moral Re-Armament has already attracted attention in Catholic circles; pro and con is being sharply formulated. Yet, it seems to me, no really clear and straightforward picture exists of it. There is plenty of literature of all sorts about it. This, however, is still quite inadequate since Moral Re-Armament does not set out to be either a philosophical or a dogmatic system, but to be a religio-ethical way of life of a purely practical nature. Of course such a way of life leads beyond itself to intellectual conclusions and unquestionably contains within itself a very definite concept of the world.

One of the characteristics of Moral Re-Armament is that it refuses to formulate this intellectual side of its work. At this point it refers each person to his own religious convictions. All that it says—and it says it with uncompromising clarity—is that nobody can be part of Moral Re-Armament who denies the moral freedom of the individual and with it the capacity for moral change and for moral and religious commitment. Moral Re-Armament sees its special task in re-awakening in this respect souls who are completely dead, and opening their eyes again

[1] Published by Patmos Verlag, Düsseldorf, September, 1955.

to see the 'forgotten factor,' God, Who demands through every man's conscience that he live out His good will.

Not long ago the well-known journalist, Friedrich Sieburg, wrote an article against Moral Re-Armament in a very derisive and ironical tone. It has an illuminating title, 'It is All so Simple.' The title was a reproach. Now it seems to me this reproach, which was meant to be so annihilating, puts Moral Re-Armament in good company. Do we not find in the Gospels, 'Amen, I say to you, unless you be converted and become as little children, you shall not enter the kingdom of heaven' (MATTHEW 18:3).

The message of Moral Re-Armament is, of course, extremely simple for the intellect that has been overfed with problems. As a result it is perhaps uninteresting for the intellectual. But like all truly simple and, at the same time, fundamental facts, this *basic rule of goodwill* is that much more difficult in practice. Possibly the author of that article would be satisfied if he received a telegram to say that Frank Buchman, the initiator and leader of the movement, had resigned and turned over its leadership to Thomas Mann or some other intellectual of our time. But at that moment the movement would certainly also be dead. It would be as if in the thirteenth century the leadership of the Franciscan Movement had been removed from the simple Saint of Assisi and given to an intellectual of that age, some personality like the great dialectician Abelard.

How then does Moral Re-Armament work, and how does it achieve its undeniable successes? It renounces intellectual efforts. Instead it surrounds each man with the reality of a way of life, founded upon goodwill, the spirit of sacrifice and the moral code of the four great truths—absolute honesty, purity, unselfishness and love.

The great strength of Moral Re-Armament seems to me to lie in the fact that it is restoring tangible sociological effectiveness to the Christian moral code. It brings about this *metanoia* (change) and this must be frankly conceded to the critic Friedrich Sieburg

—not by toning down Biblical moral standards with clever and ingenious compromises but by taking them absolutely, as a child would do. To the horror of experienced, hard-boiled, practical men, Moral Re-Armament dares to call its summary of the Sermon on the Mount into four basic truths quite simply '*The Four Absolutes*.'

This brings us back to our initial question. The success, in fact the great success, of this bold effort, not least among men who have lost all moral ties, is incomprehensible only to the man who believes that St Paul in Romans was speaking merely of a common faculty of Reason. But anyone who wants to take the Apostle to the Gentiles more seriously and feels that he is talking about the living Conscience, about the Voice of God in the heart of man, will find these successes quite natural, as natural as the opening of a lock when the right key is available. Such a man will not comprehend the use, before opening a lock, of an academic thesis on 'the Concept of the Key'. There are, of course, people who need to know about the theoretical side of locks—criminal police experts, safe engineers, and so on. But with all the theories, and even in spite of them, the decisive thing is that a real key does find its way into the appropriate real lock.

Moral Re-Armament expressly teaches its friends to listen to the Voice of God within and to test all manifestations of the conscience before God in the so-called 'quiet time'. All the obvious objections about subjectivism, the possibility of deception, are allowed for in advance. A set of criteria ('tests of guidance') teach how to make careful tests of inner inspirations and decisions. They should be tested by the four basic principles, by the individual's own Christian convictions which he has from his Church, and finally by friendly sharing in the circle of a team, just as in the traditional Catholic teaching on *discretio spirituum acquisita* (The acquired discernment of Spirits) subjective deceptions are to be disposed of by analogous means.

A point which I consider of prime import is that Moral Re-Armament, besides its very strong influence upon modern man, can also, according to my impressions in Caux, claim great effectiveness in reaching the leadership of the coloured peoples. This gives rise to great hopes and indicates one function for Moral Re-Armament, namely, to act as the bridge to a full Christianity . . .

A few points must be briefly mentioned. The decisive one is that Moral Re-Armament rejects any legal or institutional set-up. It is not a church. It is not a sect. No one can join it. No one can resign from it. As a result, therefore, its activity is not directed against the churches with a view to replacing them but concerns itself with the furthest forward areas of the ideological struggle. It aims to build a defensive front of all men of good will, or, as the Caux Assembly programme itself says: 'The purpose of this assembly is to re-arm responsible personalities of Europe and the whole world with an ideology which enables them to create an inwardly sound and living democracy, and to forward teamwork in nations and between peoples.' That is the official formulation of the Caux invitation . . .

On my second day in Caux I had a talk with a French professor. I thought an intellectual from Paris must have special difficulty with Moral Re-Armament's allegedly strong American manner of propagation, so I asked him, 'What do you feel about Moral Re-Armament and why have you come here?' He gave me a friendly smile and said, 'I have no theoretical reasons for coming here, but I have had a decisive experience. Just before the war my wife met the Oxford Group (forerunner of Moral Re-Armament) and she brought my grown-up children under its influence. All I can say is that it is only since that time that I have had a happy home life. You must realise that all who are wholly committed to Moral Re-Armament have had an experience of this sort. Moral Re-Armament has changed their lives at crucial points. It is this great experience—the fact that typical modern men and especially those who are no longer reached by the Churches can thus be won to moral and religious ideals—that has led Frank Buchman, even against the opposition of certain sections, to the great re-alignment and transformation of the former Oxford Group into the Moral Re-Armament of today. This has as its purpose the mobilisation of moral forces for the reform of our economy and politics.'

I was especially impressed by conversations fully bearing this out with a number of Asian intellectuals who with one accord said Asia needs a common moral platform as quickly as possible and immediately available. Otherwise Asia will fall victim to Bolshevism in a very few years without war or overt violence. Such a common platform is certainly not less needed by Europe, which is torn and divided in a thousand different ways . . .

Late one evening I was standing on the empty terrace of the great Caux hotel. Below me, glimmering in the lights, lay Lausanne, at whose University in the first quarter of the century the famous national economist and sociologist, Vilfredo Pareto, had been active. He was the man who gave the world the modern sociological theory of an elite, the idea that the essential factors in history are the small minorities of the so-called leading classes, and that all great changes are actually nothing more than an exchange of elites ('*circulations des élites*'). Lenin and Mussolini used this theory for their own ends, like a recipe from a cook book. Lenin was then living as an exile in Switzerland; Mussolini was a foreign student in Lausanne. Hitler took over their technique.

What a deep impression it left upon me that in the open air of the heights above this very university city of Lausanne where Fascism was intellectually formulated, men are now meeting to create an elite not of force but of goodwill!

VII

WHAT IS MORAL RE-ARMAMENT?

BY GABRIEL MARCEL

From an article in Le Figaro, *Paris, 28 January,* 1956, *by the distinguished Catholic philosopher and Member of the Institute of France.*

WHAT IS MORAL RE-ARMAMENT? It is not a sect; it is a leaven or a seed. Those in whom the seed has been sown are changed from within. That is to say that they have seen evidence of the light of the absolute and, moved by this evidence, they become capable of overthrowing the barriers which separate them from themselves and from each other. At the same time these men and women become radiant and even in a certain sense radioactive. Anyone who has come in direct contact with them is immediately aware of this.

One fact which proves the scope of MRA is that the men of the Kremlin are troubled about it. Especially at Tashkent they make many broadcasts as a warning against a movement which is undermining the very foundations of the Communist ideology.

Indeed, what more direct opposite is there to that ideology than these sudden changes in the direction of peoples' lives which cannot be ascribed to any economic cause? What personally moved me the most was to hear a Muslim teacher from Algeria who was arbitrarily arrested, subjected to serious torture, then expelled from North Africa although he could have had his case cleared. In a voice shaken by emotion this man declared that after meeting the French of MRA who lived their faith and fully recognised their mistakes, he had felt his hatred vanish away and meant to work with the French to build a new Algeria. On hearing this a leading Frenchman from North Africa came to ask his forgiveness in the name of all those who by their blindness are largely responsible for the present tragedy.

It is a hope. Perhaps it is even *the* hope; for without this spirit which brings men together in a complete moral transparency, there is surely no alternative to the vicious circles of deception and mutual revenge. Today from Canada to Norway, from Central Africa to Iran, from India to Japan, by this road human beings have found not only a reason for living, but the amazing happiness of giving and radiating which is the way of true peace —the living peace in the light of a brotherhood which has been regained.[1]

---

[1] See also *Fresh Hope for the World* (*Un changement d'esperance*), edited by Gabriel Marcel (Longman's, London, 1960), in which Marcel writes: 'A revolution is taking place among the nations which is sweeping away the wreckage of a world in ruins. A new hope is seen. A fresh renaissance starts to emerge. All whose stories are told here suddenly found their lives set on a fresh course . . . Change in men opens the door to fresh hope.'

Chancellor Adenauer wrote the introduction to the German edition of this book. He said: 'The book presents the answer to the question of what are the aims of Moral Re-Armament . . . May it make many people think, may it above all pass on to them the truth that the one real hope of nations living together in peace can only be found through a change in the human heart.'

VIII

THE IDEOLOGY
OF MORAL RE-ARMAMENT

BY DR KONRAD ADENAUER

Chancellor of the Federal Republic of Germany

The following exclusive article by Chancellor Adenauer was published in the New York *Journal-American on 31 January, 1960, under the headline: 'Adenauer Calls MRA World's Hope.'*

AT THIS TIME of confusion in Europe we need, and especially in divided Germany, an ideology that brings clarity and moral power into shaping international relations. A nation with an ideology is always on the offensive. A nation without an ideology is self-satisfied and dead.

Communism has gone through many phases—Marxism, Leninism, Stalinism, now Khrushchev. But one thing has remained unaltered—its aim of world domination. We must be prepared to continue the ideological struggle for several decades yet, but I am convinced Khrushchev's grandchildren will not be Communists.

Dr Frank Buchman, founder of Moral Re-Armament, is making a great contribution to international unity and to the establishment of social justice. A lasting memorial to his work is established in the hearts of mankind of this age. The way he has laboured to establish relationships between men and nations on firm foundations of moral values will never be forgotten.

Now is the time to work more strongly than ever for European unity through MRA. A Europe in which freedom and brotherhood should reign can only be created when nations are mutually conscious of their moral responsibility. MRA has given most valuable stimulation to the great work of uniting Europe. Unless this work is carried forward, peace in the world cannot be maintained.

If all nations are to continue to live together, one of the most pressing tasks of our age is to overcome prejudices that exist between people, races and nations. In this field MRA has made an important contribution.

May it above all pass on the truth that the one real hope of nations living together in peace can only be found through a change in the human heart.

We can be grateful to the men and women of Moral Re-Armament that in this world of destruction they have had the courage to raise the banner of moral values. MRA has become a household word in postwar Germany.

The German people gratefully recognise the help which has come so readily to them through MRA. Very soon after the end of the war this ideology reached out a hand to the German people and helped them make contact again with other nations. In Western Germany MRA has worked very forcefully in the creation of good relations between management and labour.

Men and nations cannot outwardly enjoy stable relations until they have been inwardly prepared for them. In this respect MRA has rendered great and lasting services.

We have seen the conclusion after some difficult negotiations of important international agreements. MRA has played an invisible but effective part in bridging differences of opinion between negotiating parties. It has kept before them the objective of peaceful agreement in search for common good which is the true purpose of human life.

Begin with yourself—that, in my opinion, is the basic challenge of MRA. May this challenge ring out far and wide across the whole world and into all nations.

IX

MORAL RE-ARMAMENT CAN BE UNIVERSALLY APPLIED

BY HIS GRACE DR BERNARDUS KAELIN

Abbot Primate of the Benedictine Order, 1947-59
An Address to the World Assembly at Caux, 20 September, 1960

THE IDEOLOGY of Moral Re-Armament can win all men because its standards are universally valid. It is not a religion, nor a substitute for religion. It is not a sect. It has four mighty pillars upon which human living must be based. Every man must accept these ideas if he is honest with himself.

Moral Re-Armament is right in stressing man's need of a definite ideology, a system of ideas which governs men's lives.

An ideology is a compass. A man without a true ideology is like a ship driven here and there by storms of the sea. It is not enough, however, to know an ideology and thus possess the compass. We must use the compass and live the ideology. There are so many people who are very familiar with their religion, but for whom it is unemployed capital. That is why it is such a great satisfaction and source of admiration to me that so many people in Moral Re-Armament live out their ideology seriously and consistently. The word of the Holy Scripture holds good in this respect: 'By their fruits ye shall know them.'

The ideas and ideology of Moral Re-Armament are embodied in the norm which the founder of the Benedictine Order gave to the monks through his rule. He emphasises, as Moral Re-Armament does today, the absolute validity of the four principles and that they must be carried out absolutely and completely. Benedict also wants these four standards of absolute honesty, purity, unselfishness and love to be practised according to his rule. Again and again he attaches the greatest importance to the living of, and not just the knowing about, the ideology.

Just as Moral Re-Armament emphasises that the ideology must not only be known, but put into practice, so Benedict enjoins the abbot and the monk really to shape their lives according to the guidance of God. That is perhaps the secret of Benedict's tremendous success.

During the serious world situation of the 5th and 6th centuries, Benedict taught through his life and his rule what nations must do in order to become and remain sound. So by the 11th century he had become a founder of Western civilisation. I mention this fact to encourage Moral Re-Armament to forestall the danger of world Communism today all over the world.

Whenever I have the chance I will declare that Moral Re-Armament can be universally applied and that it is valid also for us who are priests or in the Orders. It would not be Benedictine to say that we are already perfect. Indeed, the main task for us Benedictines is to strive for greater perfection. It can be said that Moral Re-Armament and the Benedictine Order have the same aim—peace, first of all in your heart so that there exists no division in yourself between what you profess and what you live, and then in the family, in the nation and in the world.

Moral Re-Armament is a new way, designed to forestall a false ideology.

Everyone of us must first of all listen to God and get from Him the strength to carry out the ideology without compromise.

We have every reason to thank God that He has chosen a man, Dr Frank Buchman, to formulate such an ideology and inspire others with it. He is an instrument of God. We of the Catholic Church are grateful that there is such an ideology. It is bringing back to their faith many men who stand aloof or who are going another way—men whom we priests and pastors find it impossible to reach.

May Moral Re-Armament win the whole world. The greatest gratitude we can show to Frank Buchman is to stand up for its ideas.

INDEX